The Politics of Meaning

A new pride my ego taught me, and this I teach
men: no longer to bury one's head in the sand of
heavenly things, but to bear it freely, an earthly
head, which creates a meaning for the earth.

FRIEDRICH NIETZSCHE

Power and Explanation in

THE UNIVERSITY OF ARIZONA PRESS

THE POLITICS
OF MEANING

the Construction of Social Reality

Peter C. Sederberg

TUCSON, ARIZONA

About the Author

PETER C. SEDERBERG is a specialist in comparative politics and political theory. A member of the faculty of the University of South Carolina since 1971, he has served as Graduate Director of the Political Science Program and Professor in the Department of Government and International Studies. He is co-editor (with H. Jon Rosenbaum) of *Vigilante Politics* (1976) and author of *Interpreting Politics* (1977).

THE UNIVERSITY OF ARIZONA PRESS

Copyright © 1984
The Arizona Board of Regents
All Rights Reserved

This book was designed by Linnea Gentry Sheehan
and set in 11/13 V-I-P Electra and Peignot Light.
Manufactured in the U.S.A.

Library of Congress Cataloging in Publication Data

Sederberg, Peter C.
    The politics of meaning.

    Includes bibliographical references and index.
    1. Political science—Addresses, essays, lectures.
2. Meaning (Philosophy)—Addresses, essays, lectures.
3. Reality—Addresses, essays, lectures.   I. Title.
JA74.S43 1984   320   84-2739
ISBN 0-8165-0860-7

TO MORSE PECKHAM
Teacher and Friend

CONTENTS

PREFACE

T HE CONCERNS OF THIS VOLUME resonate off an apparently simple set of related ideas. At the core rests the assumption that meaning is embodied in response. Shared meaning implies mutually expected response. Politics consists of all deliberate efforts to control systems of shared meaning. The seven substantive chapters develop some of the implications of this idea of politics in several significant areas of political analysis: the nature of the scientific study of politics, the problems of conflict and violence, the nature of organizations, the tasks of leadership, the character of certain "primary" political values, and, lastly, the future of politics.

The adopted format allows for a certain flexibility of approach. My purpose is neither to present new empirical findings nor to provide a survey of the vast library written on these subjects. Rather, I attempt to develop a different perspective on familiar terrain in the hope of informing a new recognition of the significance of politics. For if we endow the world with meaning through our responses to it, politics must be seen as the major way for making the world mutually meaningful.

The recognition and acceptance of humanly created meaning and value ultimately suggest our need to accept collective responsibility for our acts, a responsibility which human beings have historically tried to evade. To assume such a responsibility now presents an awesome challenge and one that we can meet only through politics. Politics, however, may also be the means through which another absolutist illusion is temporarily foisted upon the world. Liberation and oppression, responsibility and evasion remain the opposite sides of the coin of politics. The more clearly we recognize this dangerous duality, the better will be our chances of avoiding capture by politics' darker side.

Through these essays, I hope to make a modest contribution to this end.

Unifying the diverse themes of the various chapters is the characterization of shared meaning as involving mutually expected response. Controlling response establishes meaning. Power and explanation, then, may be viewed as interrelated instruments for constructing the meaning of the world. Power is a form of explanation and explanation a kind of power.

Given the interpenetration of power and explanation, what have been conventionally conceived as problems of explanation may also be viewed as an exercise of power. In Chapter 2, for example, scientific method is interpreted as constituting the political instruments of a scientific community of inquiry, that is, the means through which the participants structure each other's response and establish shared meaning. Similarly, in Chapter 4, the problem of defining terms, especially political concepts like coercion, force, and violence, reflects political power relations of a wider community.

Conversely, problems conventionally viewed as power relations may be interpreted as questions of explanation. Conflict, as discussed in Chapter 3, arises out of competing explanations within a culture; conflict resolution, then, establishes a kind of commonly accepted explanation. Organizations are not simply power structures but, as argued in Chapter 5, resemble explanatory structures. Leaders, from the perspective maintained in Chapter 6, perform an explanatory function for their followers.

In the last two chapters we turn to the challenge of developing more adequate responses (better explanations, more effective power). In Chapter 7, freedom and order are seen as dialectically arrayed, addressing the dilemma of the need for predictability versus the need to innovate more adequate responses. The specific issue of constructing more adequate alternatives to the incoherencies of the dominant meanings of modern cultural directives serves as the subject of the concluding chapter.

I borrow shamelessly from many authors to elaborate the central contentions of this book. Two, however, deserve special mention. Morse Peckham, a distinguished scholar of comparative literature and culture, served to catalyze this interpretation of politics. His work on the cultural revolutionaries of the nineteenth century and his more recent investigations into the nature of explanation and its relation to questions of power helped to formulate many of the arguments I develop.

Through Peckham, I also learned to take Friedrich Nietzsche seriously, and he became the second major source of inspiration for my efforts. This book should not be taken for a gloss on Nietzsche's work; rather, Nietzsche often epitomizes the points I wish to make in a fashion I cannot match. Although I cannot claim to be a Nietzsche scholar, I perhaps should state my position on this controversial figure of Western philosophy.

For good or ill, Nietzsche, along with Marx, has exerted considerable influence on the intellectual development of our century. Nietzsche has suffered, if possible, from even more distortions than Marx. I do not see him as a nihilist, although he did understand how the culture crisis of the nineteenth century contributed to nihilism. He denied that meaning or value could be either inherent or absolute, but he did not deny the need for meaning and value. These are created by human beings through their interactions with the world. Only those who crave an absolute ground for meaning find this message nihilistic. The erosion of the sanctions of absolute meaning, as Nietzsche predicted, contributed to the horrors of the last seventy years, but these absolutisms had to decline for they were illusions. Many see Nietzsche as antipolitical. I see him as defining the essential political problem: How do we establish humane systems of shared meaning without the illusory comforts of transcendent absolutes? Although I accept the need to revalue values, I reject Nietzsche's radical individualism as exemplified in the idea of the *übermensch*. Rather, self and society develop through an interdependent dialectic, and revaluation occurs through a process always mutual, always partial, and preferably tentative.

On Counterpoints: All of the chapters, with the exception of the introductory one, conclude with a "counterpoint." These short essays serve to investigate a problem in distinction to, although not necessarily in contradiction with, the major themes of the chapter. They are intended to broaden or deepen our understanding of the general area of concern.

Acknowledgments

This book, like most others, owes its existence to many more people than the one named on the title page. In addition to the inspiration of Morse Peckham and Friedrich Nietzsche, I must thank Steven Hays, William Kreml, Daniel Sabia, and two perceptive, anonymous reviewers for their critical comments and insightful assistance. Given their collective intelligence and discernment, I can only conclude that they bear some responsibility for any errors of fact and reasoning that might remain in the revised volume.

The University of South Carolina has my gratitude for the material support given me, especially the sabbatical and summer research leaves in 1980 that allowed me to begin the initial draft of the manuscript. In addition to the intrinsic rewards associated with encouraging faculty development, University officials can rest assured that I will remember the institution when the royalties pour in.

I also need to acknowledge the intellectual and emotional support given me by Jan Love, who patiently, if somewhat wryly, accepted a man who described himself as a "left-wing Nietzschean."

Finally, I wish to mention the joy given me by my son, Per, who reminds me to pay attention to other sources of meaning and value and who would be miffed if he couldn't see his name in print.

PETER C. SEDERBERG

1

MEANING AND POLITICS

Any meaning is better than none at all....
NIETZSCHE

Meaning

DOES A TREE FALLING UNHEARD in a forest make a sound? This rather weary conundrum of introductory philosophy courses identifies a problem but misses the point. The socially significant issue involves the *meaning* of the sound, not its formal definition. If a tree falls undetected, this event possesses no meaning for human beings. No event has any *meaningful* existence until detected; indeed, we cannot talk about it at all.

The ground of meaning in human communities lies not in the events, whether humanly or naturally produced, but in the responses to them. Further, as Morse Peckham argues, "the meaning of a verbal event [or any perceived configuration] is *any* response to that event (emphasis added)."[1] In some fundamental sense, then, meaning is neither inherent in the event nor simply determined by it. If we wish to identify the meaning(s) of any sign, we should look not to the sign as a thing-in-itself (as the immanentists would have us do), nor to its use (as Wittgenstein suggests), but to the responses to that sign. To argue that a sign has a certain, "true" meaning reflects the judgment that one response is more appropriate than all others. Such judgments are only made by someone for some purpose.

If meaning is not immanent in the event, it becomes a creation, a possession of human beings. The quest for meaning involves the effort to devise *appropriate* responses. To find the world meaningful is to *know* how to respond to it. To belong to a community of shared meaning consists of responding to one another according to mutual expectations. To create a community requires controlling the range of response to situations encountered in common. The existence of shared meaning is a social puzzle to be solved not by a philosophical determination of *the* meaning of an event but by comprehending how human beings establish mutuality in an inherently polysemantic world.[2]

In locating meaning in response, we do not embrace a crude, behaviorist stimulus/response (S → R) model. The same apparent stimulus, even in highly structured psychological experiments, calls forth a range of response (generating the problem of polysemy) while eliciting a certain modal response. Both the range and the concentration of response need to be explained. The conventional explanation for the range involves adding the responding organism to the S → R equation (S → O → R). Presumably, the biography and selective memory of each responding subject contributes to the interpretation of the stimulus and, consequently, to the possibility of different responses. The *precise* stimulus, moreover, can never be located, nor the *exact* response defined. The stimulus remains embedded in a "stimulus field," any aspect of which may impact on the response of the subject.[3] This response, in turn, is delineated within the indeterminant boundaries of a "response package," which is neither fully accessible to an observer nor fully recognized by the subject.

Yet, when subjects are placed in the same stimulus field, essentially similar responses can generally be elicited from a significant percentage. The origins of similar response are simple to state—the behavior is under some form of control—though they remain difficult to elaborate. Behaviorist psychology suggests two strategies for controlling the range of response: Structure the setting so as to simplify and focus the stimulus field as much as possible; and control the prior socialization of the subject in an effort to restrict the range of interpretational variance (while assuming that the undetected aspects of the response have no bearing).

Both strategies are ambitious, indeed impossible to fulfill perfectly, and they may be complicated by yet another difficulty: the nature of the brain itself. This organ, it seems, is not adequately comprehended by a simplistic computer metaphor. The brain is not a binary, programmable, cause/effect system but a stochastic one with the capacity to randomize response.[4] Therefore, control of prior socialization and the current behavioral setting would still prove insufficient to determine response perfectly. To do so, the brain process itself must be controlled, perhaps the ultimate totalitarian objective.

The underdetermination of response, and consequently of meaning, erodes the capacity of human beings to interact smoothly with one another and with their environment. Not that we are threatened with the perfect chaos of a Hobbesian war of each against all; rather, our survival depends upon a high degree of *continuous* predictability, whereas our lives can be ended by an *instant* of surprise.

Enormous energies, including physical coercion, are invested in the effort to narrow the range of response, that is, to establish a particular response (or mutually expected responses) as a common possession of people who must interact with one another. Success in developing mutually expected response (shared meaning) may also lead, unfortunately, to failure, insofar as the established responses are not adequate to meet the demands of the environment. Meanings also need to be modified or abandoned over time if the human species, or a particular member of it, is to survive. Whether a meaning should be maintained or abandoned can only be definitively determined after the fact—a situation that lends a certain tenuousness to human existence, contributing to the ambiguity, anxiety, and tension we all experience.

Simple biological survival, to be sure, need not be posited as the fundamental value or purpose of existence. Rather, whatever purpose we wish to pursue, life itself is a precondition to its realization. The denial of a value may lead a person to prefer death to a continued impoverished existence, but this preference does not deny that life was necessary for the realization of that value. To suggest that a particular pattern of response jeopardizes survival is not to condemn it solely for that reason. Condemnation, if any, will be the product of injury to other values, injury caused by the denial of life.

Shared meaning, embodied in mutually expected responses, results from the outpouring of our energies into the world. Although we are the source of these collective meanings, we are not in complete control of them, either as individuals or as communities. The products of our outpourings, whether physical (e.g., tools and other cultural artifacts) or behavioral (e.g., language, organizations, etc.), attain a reality that confronts us as external to and independent of ourselves. This external "reality" turns back upon us and shapes our responses.[5] In this dialectical fashion we are both the creators and the products of shared meaning. There exists no absolute and transcendent ground for shared meaning. In Richard Rorty's words, "there is nothing deep down inside us except what we have put there ourselves."[6]

As we become conscious of the extent to which shared meanings confront us with a facticity different from our felt interests, we grow alienated. When we recognize the source of these shared meanings in our own responses and try to gain control of them, we engage in politics.

Politics

Our lives take shape under the impact of a web of associations and meanings which are not necessarily of our making or choosing. Such ties cannot be transcended through a simple act of will; the meanings we reject continue to inform our responses, if only because we react against them. Moreover, even if we manage to loosen the grip of a particular meaning, we do so only by embracing another. There is no metasemantic ground on which we may stand; to respond differently is still to respond.

We never become entirely our own "selves," unbeholden to any meaning external to us, except perhaps through insanity. Two pathological alternatives exist: One could respond in the same way to all stimuli (extreme catatonia), or one could respond in a totally random way to essentially the same stimulus.[7] In either case, the person declares independence from any wider community of meaning at the expense of those characteristics we normally associate with being fully human, as well as necessary for survival. The Greeks may well have been correct in believing that our full potential can be realized only within a wider community.

If we move away from these pathological extremes, we must make discriminations as to what constitutes an appropriate response to a particular situation. When we make such judgments, we necessarily enter into association with others, for other people contribute to the environment to which we must respond in a differentiated fashion and are partly responsible for the evaluation of appropriateness. To engage with others implicates us, in a more or less well-integrated fashion, in a wider community of mutual expectations.

The web of shared meanings in which we then become entangled often assumes an almost organic quality, with its own genealogy and dynamism, that encompasses our individual existence. Individual lives seem transitory, but the structures of collective meaning extend indefinitely through time. The form of each of our lives evolves within the associations of established shared meanings. The extent to which each of us can determine these collective meanings is limited. Rather, we respond to the world according to patterns that appear to surround and transcend us. To accept this organic metaphor for society leads us to submit to the objectification of shared meaning. Such submission need not result in alienation, however, if we derive our individual sense of value from our participation in the wider community.

The myth of the organic community, wherein the whole and its parts draw coherence, sustenance, and value from one another in mutual harmony, lies at the core of so many utopian dreams that it must be at least a fleeting part of human experience. Not surprisingly, the conventional vision of a heavenly paradise also reflects this organic conception. When we begin to view ourselves as individuals with interests and values apart from those dominant in the wider community, we lose paradise and find alienation, as Eve and Adam discovered when they ate of the Tree of Knowledge.

Alienation from a wider community contributes to a second metaphorical description of society as an instrument. Our individual identities and needs, from this perspective, are primary, and social structures are supposed to facilitate the purposes we choose. Only through the behavior of individuals over time are these collective "artifacts" maintained. The objectification of shared meanings results when one group imposes its meanings upon the other members of a social arrangement, and it may be ended by active intervention to regain control over one's participation in collective interactions. In this fashion, the structures of mutual interaction may be turned into the servants, not the masters, of human beings. Politics is the means through which control is asserted and alienation overcome.

Neither the organic nor the instrumental metaphor for society is entirely adequate; nor do they together provide the "whole" picture.[8] The communities of shared meaning of which we are a part are never completely stable or coherent, for they are the products of our shifting patterns of response. But neither are our individual selves perfectly coherent or autonomous; rather, they too are artifactual in nature, beset with inconsistencies, and reflect the network of meanings of which we are a part. Organic unity and artifactuality, alienation and political intervention, contribute to almost everyone's experience in some continuously shifting combination. We never perfectly grasp who we are or how we fit into a wider community, because we have no steady high ground on which to stand and take a reading. As Nietzsche pointed out, all seeing is perspective seeing; all truths are perspective truths.[9]

Politics consists of all deliberate efforts to create, maintain, modify, or abandon shared meanings in the attempt to overcome the alienation produced by the loss of a sense of organic unity. To establish shared meaning, mutual response must be structured.[10] Response may be shaped through the application of various forms of power from logical or moral suasion, through bribery, to coercion. The use of coercion, though, indicates the failure of other means to limit response. In turn, if coercion fails, the effort to establish shared meaning necessarily fails, for no other recourse remains. Consequently, the ability to alter or maintain shared meanings short of the recourse to coercion provides one indicator of political success. Insofar as shared meaning is definitively established, politics ceases. The ultimate goal of politics, in one sense, is to end politics. Human individuality and indeterminacy, the "original sin" which threatens paradisiac order, continually frustrate this goal, and the political conquest of politics is always partial and transitory.

This concept of politics is broad, for it implies that all human behavior deliberately directed at controlling mutual response, even that between two people, is political in nature. Most interesting definitions of politics, however, yield similar implications upon close inspection, despite efforts to restrict the concept to activities conventionally associated with governmental operations. Even when developing such restrictions, it is generally conceded that quasi-political activities occur in corporations, churches, and even the family. Whether definitions of politics stress cooperation or coercion, imposed power or implied consent, they all involve efforts to control response and thereby determine meaning. Limiting notions of politics to some "public" arena also ignores the extent to which the distinction between *public* and *private* is itself a political decision subject to continuous reassessment.

Despite its breadth, this definition does not equate politics with all human activities. First, not all human behavior is deliberate. Behavior over which we have deliberated, perhaps conventionally construed as self-conscious, is that taken in response to directions we have given ourselves. In a related fashion, Julian Jaynes suggests that consciousness consists of projecting an analog self moving through an analog world in preparation for taking action in the real world.[11] The projection and the behavior may, of course, be essentially simultaneous. Not all behavior is conscious in this sense, but, as Jaynes observes, we cannot be conscious of when we are *not* conscious. We, therefore, cannot know how much of our behavior is not deliberate, though the indefinite variety of responses we potentially can bring under deliberate control indirectly suggests that it may be quite substantial.

Nondeliberate behavior, although not political, may still have political and semantic significance. Routinized responses may once have been the product of deliberation, although they have ceased to be a subject of conscious direction. As routine, however, they support established communities of meaning. The keen sensitivity of revolutionaries to these political implications explains why questions of ideological purity during a period of revolutionary upheaval penetrate into realms of behavior previously considered nonpolitical or even "natural."*

Politics, moreover, does not comprehend all deliberate behavior, only that deliberate behavior specifically directed at creating, maintaining, or altering systems of shared meaning. An individual engaging in a dialogue with himself is not, simply for that reason, undertaking political action; rather, this deliberation and the actions that ultimately follow must be concerned with shaping shared meaning in some way. A person who consciously engages the natural environment also acts apolitically, unless the purpose is to affect the way others act upon a shared environment. Likewise, a person who considers how to interact or avoid interacting with others may also behave apolitically, although cooperation or evasion may have subsequent implications for a community of shared meaning. A driver merging onto a busy freeway, for example, probably consciously calculates this behavior, and his effort at smooth interaction supports the mutuality of expected response; but this consequence is not the focus of his deliberations. Similarly, a driver who deliberately violates traffic laws does not usually set out to erode shared meaning, although, if enough people behave in this fashion, such erosion may result. The highway patrol officer, in contrast, acts to maintain certain meanings, by force if necessary, and so engages in politics.

The political universe, though significant, is not infinite. Not all behavior is deliberate, and not all deliberate behavior is directed at controlling shared meanings in some way. The arena of politics continually expands and contracts. Revolutionary politics is usually expansionary, whereas a highly tradition-bound community may have a quite limited political sphere. A completely habitualized order would have no politics at all. Such a community is probably only a hypothetical extreme, for it would lack the capacity to adapt to changing circumstances.

Defining politics in terms of the deliberate effort to control shared meaning helps to clarify a confusion about the nature of

---

*What we consider "natural" is often that behavior over which we do not deliberate.

society. The anthropologist George Buelow has remarked that, if ants are social animals, human beings are not.[12] This observation suggests an important difference between animal and human interaction, but I am unconvinced that the "sociability" of one or the other should be questioned. "Society" is one of the convenient, if misleading, hypostatizations of the social sciences. To limit the reifying implications as much as possible, society might be defined as any sustained interaction among two or more organisms. Granted, "sustained" introduces a certain ambiguity, but in practice it should be possible to reach a consensus on what is sustained and what is ephemeral. Predators, for example, do not have a sustained interaction with their individual prey, whereas bees, ants, baboons, and human beings do sustain their interactions with one another.

Nonhuman societies, however, do not appear to have politics. We do not have any definitive evidence that they engage in deliberate efforts to control their systems of shared meaning by giving themselves covert directions to shape patterns of response. If habit is what we have substituted for the incompleteness of our instincts, politics is what we use to create new habits of interaction, maintain existing ones, and modify those we deem to be inadequate. "Verbalization has made men free": free to create, alter, and destroy communities of meaning.[13] Verbalization, the foundation of the capacity to deliberate, makes politics possible.

Verbalization also makes politics necessary, for the ability to categorize the world verbally and to respond to those categories gives human beings a powerful but unstable instrument of control. Categorization enables us to generalize response from familiar to relatively new situations and to establish shared meanings through common categorical response. The verbal categorizations upon which our communities of shared meaning largely depend, however, fail to represent the world perfectly. Consequently, all categories may be undermined by introducing elements of the existential situation that were not adequately subsumed.

As the dominion of instinct and habit weakens, the role of politics in controlling response must expand if communities of shared meaning are to survive. Through political action we overcome the alienation that results from seeing these collective meanings as apart from ourselves. Such is the promise of politics. Through politics one faction may impose the tyranny of their meanings upon the remainder of the community. Such is the threat of politics. Through politics we innovate collective response more appropriate to the demands that confront us. For this reason, politics must be embraced. Through politics we weaken and dissolve patterns of life that have been organically integrated into communities of shared meaning. For this reason, politics must be feared.

2

THE POLITICS OF SCIENTIFIC INQUIRY:
Method and the Control of Shared Meaning

There is *only* a perspective seeing, *only* a perspective "knowing; and the *more* affects we allow to speak about one thing, the *more* eyes, different eyes, we can use to observe one thing, the more complete will our "concept" of this thing, our "objectivity," be. But to eliminate the will altogether, to suspend each and every affect, supposing we were capable of this—what would that mean but to *castrate* the intellect?

Strictly speaking, there is no such thing as science "without any presuppositions";...a philosophy, a "faith," must be there first of all, so that science can acquire from it a direction, a meaning, a limit, a method, a *right* to exist.

NIETZSCHE

Simple Pleasures

I N HUMAN SEXUAL RELATIONS, concern for the feelings and responses of the Other generates a certain degree of tension and ambiguity; consequently, one of the primary attractions of autoeroticism is simplification. Methodological and epistemological debates also seduce us with the promise of simple pleasures. Development of the appropriate grounds of knowledge and the correct standards of validation appears to offer an attractive alternative to coping with the intransigent world outside the scholarly community. As with devotees of other forms of autoeroticism, those obsessed with such issues are frequently indicted for their failure to engage the world directly and bear any fruit.[1]

Yet, as the sociology of science recognizes, scientific inquiry itself is a social activity, in which methodological concerns and substantive issues play a significant part. Indeed, methodology performs a role in a scientific community functionally equivalent to that of politics in the wider communities of the commonsense world. Thomas Kuhn, of course, suggests this comparison when he likens major "paradigm" shifts in the natural sciences to revolutions. (The analogy goes full circle when social scientists draw upon the concept of paradigm shift to illuminate the phenomenon of revolution in the wider political community.)[2] Debates over what should be accepted within a scientific community of inquiry may be likened to a political struggle. These contests concern, at least in part, the development of standards for validating knowledge claims, standards that comprise a methodology and reflect underlying assumptions about the nature of knowledge.

Some who emphasize the political characteristics of a community of inquiry do so in a tendentious manner, often in an effort to undermine what they see to be a dominant and distorting orthodoxy, thereby participating in rather than explicating the character of such politics.[3] Since science seems to stand apart from our other activities in the social world, both in terms of the behavior engaged in and the reliability of the outcomes produced, the presumed distinctiveness of scientific inquiry needs to be taken into account when characterizing its politics. Moreover, critics of neopositivist tendencies in the social sciences challenge the relevance of the assumptions and methods of the natural sciences to the understanding of the social world. Qualitative differences between natural and social scientific inquiry continue to be a locus of political disputes in social scientific communities. The impact of these differences on the stability of social scientific communities of inquiry needs to be clarified.

Explication and clarification of the politics of inquiry require a notion of politics that can be more than metaphorically applied to the conduct of scientific investigation. Conventional considerations of the politics of science, involving the development of research priorities and the manipulation of and by funding organizations, merely reflect the more central problem of how a particular community is created, sustained, or altered. Expanding the concept of politics to encompass all deliberate efforts to control systems of shared meaning provides a richer perspective capable of encompassing the deliberate attempts to structure mutuality in scientific as well as everyday communities.

Scientific inquiry, to be sure, is commonly seen as apolitical, objective, and value free. The powerful appeal of science, and even pseudoscience, however, arises not simply from its presumed ability to reveal the secrets of nature but also from its apparent capacity to resolve disputes over meaning without recourse to either ballots or bullets. Scientific method possesses a reputation for *political* success, even if not fully acknowledged as such, especially in comparison with the perceived failure of other means of conflict resolution. Those who wish to apply scientific method to everyday social activities hope to consolidate a community under the control of particular instruments for structuring response, thereby producing a consensus on meaning.

The scientific enterprise does not transcend politics; rather, it reflects and is a product of the struggle to establish, maintain, or alter communities of shared meaning. Indeed, the belief that human beings can become effective agents of conscious control underlies the rise of both systematic science and politics. We continually draw upon "protoscientific" analysis in our efforts to establish shared meanings in the everyday world. Identifying the similarities and differences of science and protoscience helps to clarify the role of method in the politics of science.

Science and Protoscience

The word *science* comes from the Latin verb *scire*, "to know." The expression "scientific knowledge" is, then, something of a redundancy—knowing knowledge. Redundancies often exist to make a point, and this particular one emphasizes the special status given to knowledge that can be scientifically grounded. Such knowledge presumably possesses a degree of reliability lacking in other forms of knowing (e.g., intuition, revelation, deduction from *a priori* assumptions, etc.). Scientific explanations claim to provide a powerful foundation for replicability, prediction, and control, an efficacy predicated upon the systematic exploitation of the links among explanation (hypothesis, theory), experimentation, and feedback. Experimentation consists of nonverbal behavior guided by explanation, the results of which ("facts" or data) are used to confirm, modify, or abandon the governing explanation.[4] Though the experience of discovery may be essentially apolitical, when scientists seek to have their conclusions accepted by a scientific community, the politics of science begins in earnest.*

---

*I do not wish to imply that scientific inquiry is actually divided into formal stages of discovery and justification. Concern for justification continually affects investigation as it proceeds. I am suggesting that these two concerns may be analytically distinguished in order better to understand the political aspects of scientific inquiry.

One interesting aspect of this encapsulation of the scientific enterprise is that the activity as described appears relatively commonplace. Most elements of the explanatory activity in the sciences do not set it dramatically apart from inquiring behavior in the everyday world. Here, too, we continually conduct experiments under the control of tacit explanations and their consequent expectations, and we frequently use the experienced results to adjust the guiding suppositions. In some general sense, the model is the same whether a person is crossing the street or crossing genes.

What occurs in the everyday world, though, might be best termed *protoscientific* in order to indicate its similarity to, but not identity with, scientific inquiry. The scientific enterprise rests upon the *explicit and systematic* exploitation of the linkages among explanation, experimentation, and feedback. Scientific activities are overdetermined; that is, they are under the control of strict codes for deriving experiments from explanatory hypotheses and relating experimental results back to the explanation. The development and adherence to these codes distinguishes science from protoscientific behavior and makes the product of scientific inquiry more reliable, at least in some areas.

The enhanced ability of a scientific community to resolve disputes over shared meaning lies neither in explanation nor experimentation *per se*. Claims to knowledge based on these explanations and experiments must be validated by the community of inquirers. The emergence of such a consensus is under a form of social control, specifically the dominant criteria used to establish acceptability.* These methodological criteria comprise everything from the conventions governing conceptual clarity and the formulations of hypotheses, through the techniques for structuring experiments, to the rhetoric for reporting results. Methodology also defines the appropriate standards for creating and manipulating explanatory hierarchies. The methods of scientific inquiry function less as techniques for making discoveries

---

*Beyond the general commitment to logic in theory construction and to some type of empirical grounding, there is no detailed recipe of methods common to all scientific disciplines. The general commitment to logic and empiricism does relate them, however, as a common class of knowledge criteria.

than as tools for having conclusions accepted by a particular scientific community. Competent manipulation of the strictures of a methodological consensus contributes to one's success in the normal *politics* of a scientific community. Indeed, as a guide for controlling response, methodology serves as something of an ideology for a community of inquiry.

Method as Ideology

Ideology commonly connotes false knowledge, whereas science implies a drive to "reality" which, if not productive of the Absolute, at least provides a measure of security against delusion. This equation of scientific method with ideology is not intended to denigrate the accomplishments of scientific investigation but simply to emphasize the extent to which any consensus in a scientific community results from a form of successful political action.

Politics, as we define it, aims at the control of shared meaning, that is, patterns of mutually expected response. Ideologies, as they are conventionally defined, and methodologies, however they are structured, share this objective. Common purpose alone, however, does not exhaust the similarities between the two. In addition, scientific method shares four other interrelated characteristics with conventional ideologies that further justify the comparison.

First, like other ideologies, methodology is *explanatory* in nature; specifically, it explains how to go about constructing and supporting explanations. Second, like all ideologies, methodology is, therefore, *prescriptive*. We are admonished to proceed according to its dictates if we wish to produce reliable conclusions and receive recognition for our claims. Such acceptance implies a third ideological function, that of *validation*. Methodological standards validate or invalidate both claims to knowledge and, indirectly, those who make them.

Finally, as in other ideologically based communities, the standards of a methodology are *enforced*. A scientific community may not have the means to impose ultimate sanctions (torture, death) at its disposal, but errant members may find themselves ostracized, mostly through the refusal of learned publications to distribute their work and by the consequent denial of prestige, promotion, or position. Severe transgressions, such as the forging of evidence, can lead to communal disgrace. Interestingly, ostracism and shaming are the typical enforcement devices of communities that lack an effective centralized enforcement apparatus. In an anthropological sense, scientific communities are politically "primitive."

Any conclusion that methodology serves as the ideology of a scientific community must, however, recognize two significant differences from conventional ideologies. First, scientific method constitutes a *procedural* ideology, a set of explanations and prescriptions about how to construct explanations, as opposed to a *substantive* ideology, a set of explanations and prescriptions directly concerned with the world. Admittedly, the distinction between procedural and substantive ideologies may be more a matter of emphasis than of absolute contrast. Every substantive ideology implies certain ontological and methodological presuppositions as to how appropriate explanations within that ideology ought to be structured. Marxism, for example, though primarily concerned with explicating the socioeconomic dynamics of capitalist systems, also possesses a logic and rhetoric to which appropriate Marxist explanations must conform. Alternatively, a procedural ideology restricts the character of the substantive explanations made in conformance with its ontological and methodological assumptions. Explanations developed according to the dictates of scientific method are unlikely to include elements derived from divine revelation.

A second distinctive trait of the procedural ideology of contemporary science is its commitment to innovation. Early stages of scientific inquiry, approximately into the nineteenth century, sought to stabilize explanation. The human mind and the external world were thought to be essentially isomorphic, and only ignorance prevented perfect harmonization. Some members of the various scientific communities undoubtedly still hold this essentially Enlightenment point of view, but the currently dominant perspective accepts the hypothetical nature of scientific knowledge, an acceptance that encourages scientists to exploit the inherent instability of all explanations.[5] This commitment to innovation must be qualified to some extent, for innovative explanations to gain acceptance must conform with procedural prescriptions and may still encounter resistance.[6]

A scientific community, then, resembles other communities in that certain controls are used to engender mutually expected response. In order to participate in a community of inquiry, a person must submit to the dominant procedural ideology. Dominant does not mean unchallenged, for deviant methodologies and the journals that reflect them exist at the fringes of any particular scientific community. As with other political institutions, certain defenders of ideological purity devote considerable effort to demolishing or at least quarantining these "perverted" orientations.[7]

The Politics of Method in the Natural Sciences

Scientists possess two fundamental goals: to discover answers to puzzles and to have their answers accepted or validated by the community of inquirers to which they belong. As Stephen Toulmin observes, "scientific discoveries are typically arrived at not by generalizing from preexisting facts but by providing answers to preexisting questions."[8] Methodology concerns the process of discovery less than how conclusions become established within the scientific community. An explanation, any explanation, can be justified in two basic ways, either by subsuming it under a more general explanation (or theory) that has already gained acceptance or by exemplifying it with more specific statements whose validity will be recognized. The process of subsumption can, but need not, involve a "covering law," while that of exemplification may eventually move from verbal to nonverbal behavior—experimentation—and thereby root itself in some kind of empirical ground. The accepted rules for moving from one statement to another and the recognized criteria for defining relevant evidence are the two general regulators of response contained in scientific method.

These regulators function, as Michael Polanyi states, "as maxims of scientific value and procedure."[9] They cannot, however, serve as recipes for making discoveries; indeed, Polanyi argues that they cannot even demonstrate how to verify or falsify empirical propositions in any definitive fashion.[10] The history of science is filled with instances where scientists have held to established explanations in the face of contrary evidence (usually categorized as anomalies) in the hope, sometimes justified, that these contrary data would be shown to be the result of experimental error or would be accounted for by a yet unspecified emendation to the existing explanation. Contrary evidence must be accounted for in some way before being accepted. To abandon an accepted explanation without having another to put in its place is to abandon meaning, however inadequate, for meaninglessness. As Nietzsche reminds us, "any meaning is better than none at all."*[11]

The rules of evidence and procedure have evolved in response to emerging problems of scientific investigation. For example, as natural phenomena have come to be seen as stochastically rather than determinately linked, rules derived from probability theory and statistics have become increasingly important in evaluating the relations among statements. The accepted rules for linking statements in any field of inquiry form a basis for the procedural validation of a proffered explanation. The more tenuous the link between an explanatory statement and other statements either subsuming it or exemplifying it, the greater the likelihood other members of the scientific community will respond to it in a variety of ways. As in other political

---

*Of course, the recognition of anomalies may serve to stimulate the search for a more adequate explanation.

communities, the weaker the controls on response, the wider the range of behavior will be. Thus, the explanation will fail to structure effectively the shared meaning of the community. The capacity of a group of inquirers to establish and conform with such procedural rules is important, therefore, not only for the construction of explanatory hierarchies but also for the controls that can thereby be invoked upon the responses of other members of the group.

The second general way of limiting the range of response common to the variety of methods in the natural sciences is through exemplification ultimately leading to experiments producing empirical or factual data. But what, exactly, is a fact? Ideally, perhaps, a fact is an observable entity to which only one response is possible. In short, the meaning of an "ideal" fact is indisputable. The actual nature of facts, however, is commonly conceded to be more clouded.

At the fundamental, experiential level, a fact is a perceived sensation. Facts, therefore, are not pure; rather, they have already been selected and organized for a response. To select means to exclude, for we cannot attend to all sensations simultaneously. A perception is a sensation, or a bundle of sensations, organized into a configuration, seen against a background.[12] In addition, since modern science depends upon sophisticated instruments of measurement, what the scientist selects from the instrumentally recorded data as relevant (i.e., something that requires a response) has already been preselected by the design of the measuring instrument. The instrumental extension of human sensation is, therefore, a decidedly mixed benefit, for it adds instrument design flaws and malfunction to the possibility of human misperception (a misperception, that is, from the perspective of another observer who sees something that the first excluded).

After every experiment, whether scientific or protoscientific, a residue of the unperceived, and therefore unexplained, remains. When recognized, these "nondata" become the anomalies that Thomas Kuhn believes to be a source of the "paradigmatic" shifts that he argues periodically punctuate the history of science. Instability of meaning, consequently, lurks at the very core of our empirical knowledge. An experiment produces a "stimulus field" in which an observer may respond to any element, and the elements themselves are not so much discovered as constructed. The purpose of controlled experimentation is to structure the stimulus field as narrowly as possible. The "control" in controlled experiments is, in some sense, directed at the range of response of the experimenter. The success of the controls over any experiment and, therefore, over the responses of the experimenter is never total, and, indeed, the controls themselves may be challenged.

Facts, in the sense of perceived sensations, are not used to exemplify an explanation; *statements* of fact are. Basic statements of fact are those utterances "caused" as immediately as possible by the perception. [13] The movement from the nonverbal to the verbal involves categorizing the perception in some way, however. Even the most referential words are still categories. CAT, for example, identifies no specific cat but an indefinite variety of cats. The only way we can refer to anything with a fair degree of precision is through the use of interlocking categories (e.g., the yellow cat, on the wall, next to the house, third from the corner, etc.). Categorization, since it subsumes perception, is the first stage of explanation.

Statements of fact (that is, categories) add further instability to the generation of feedback. At no point is a category directly tied to the world; on the contrary, "it slips and slides and slithers on top of it." [14] The result, as Roberto Unger notes, is

a spectacle that would be strange if it were not too familiar to be noticeable. Though it is the particulars of perception that are supposed to have concrete reality, it is to the universal [i.e., categories] that thought and action are addressed. The ghosts sing and dance on the stage while the real persons sit dumbly in the pit below. [15]

Once a category has been articulated, it must then suffer interpretation, introducing a further instability (thus, the receiver may misinterpret the cat message and look to the wrong house). Since no category has any inherent meaning that can be discovered, each could elicit an indefinite range of responses. Finally, the world continually changes, "slipping and slithering" away from our categorizations of it (by the time the receiver of the cat message correctly interprets it, the cat may have moved away).

The "facts" fed back to check an explanation, therefore, are not so firm or final as extreme empiricists seem to presume. First, all perceptions are selective, so that something is always excluded. Second, two observers placed in the same stimulus field may have different perceptions—they may "see" the facts differently. Third, since statements of facts are categories, different observers may categorize essentially the same perception differently. Fourth, even if they do categorize the perceptual field in the same way, they may respond to it differently. Finally, even if they share the same response, by the time they make it the world may have changed. Admittedly, the problem of continuity over time is less critical in the natural than the social world. Nonetheless, change does occur, especially in the biological sciences. Pests of various sorts, for instance, continually slip (evolve) away from the explanations of what substances can kill them.

One of the general functions of a commitment to scientific method is to ensure that explanatory statements are systematically checked against the "facts." Yet, the ambiguities afflicting statements of fact can also undermine the stability of explanations. Consequently, scientific consensus is not based upon a vulgar and indiscriminate empiricism. Rather, the emphasis upon accurate measurement and controlled experimentation reflects a kind of principle of "optimal ignorance," that is, an assessment of what is *not* needed to evaluate an explanation.[16] Potential data are structurally excluded in an effort to control the range of possible response; thus, both controlled experimentation and highly refined measurement techniques may be seen as means to preselect facts. Such purification consequently affects the process of hypothesis evaluation. Of course, the simplifying assumptions of controlled experimentation and the techniques and devices of measurement can change at any time, undermining previously validated explanations. Eliminating the assumption of frictionless space, for example, was a necessary basis for fluid mechanics and contributed to the development of explanations of motion that differed from those generated by classical Newtonian assumptions.

The erosion and re-creation of shared meaning go on continually in the natural sciences because no method of limiting the range of response is ever perfect and no methodological consensus is ever complete. Yet the capacity to resolve disputes over meaning in these sciences testifies to the political efficacy of the methodological controls.

The existence of a consensus about the appropriate ways to validate knowledge claims begs the question as to its origins and maintenance. Superficially, the consensus might appear to be sustained by the reliability of the knowledge it validates (and the unreliability of that which it scorns). Such a justification is incomplete, however, for the criteria for determining reliability are themselves part of the consensus. Alternatively, viewing methodology as a kind of procedural ideology suggests that the consensus may be primarily sustained by a social organization. Polanyi remarks:

Indeed, nobody knows more than a tiny fragment of science well enough to judge its validity and value first hand. For the rest he has to rely on views accepted second hand on the authority of a community of people accredited as scientists. But this accrediting depends in its turn on a complex social organization. [17]

As a social organization, a scientific community possesses a variety of mechanisms for accrediting its members and thereby fostering a methodological consensus. [18] Those who are accepted into the community of inquirers have a long period of apprenticeship during which they develop convictions as to the overall purpose and procedures of the enterprise. These convictions are continually reinforced both by a sense of fellowship and group loyalty, as well as by economic rewards. The other side of reward is punishment, and, as we already noted, deviant members face the threat of some form of ostracism.

Nevertheless, as both Kuhn and Polanyi indicate, the history of scientific discovery has been characterized by relatively dramatic alterations of perspective that cannot be adequately accounted for by an image of the scientific enterprise proceeding in accordance with a total consensus on appropriate method, supporting and supported by a coherent social organization. To paraphrase Kuhn, such shifts represent a movement away from normal to revolutionary politics. These intense controversies in the sciences come to resemble those in other political associations in which a "pretender" challenges the established authorities. [19] Polanyi and Kuhn agree that such disputes cannot be resolved through simple appeal to the methodological controls. Kuhn, in fact, metaphorically compares the ultimate resolution of such disputes with conversion.[20]

In such a period of revolutionary politics, the scientific community's commitment to the basic controls of scientific method (logic and empirical validation) remains unchanged, but what these principles entail alters. These disputes usually involve fundamental conceptions of the nature of the problem, conceptions that transcend the sphere of method. A shift in fundamental perspective necessarily affects what are considered to be the relevant facts (observations previously discounted as anomalies or experimental errors may now be taken seriously), the design of experiments, and the logical structure of explanations.[21] If the dispute over structure is sufficiently profound, the social organization of the scientific community will crumble, and controversies over which participants should be accredited will become increasingly severe.

The effectiveness of the methodological controls on the responses of scientists, then, partially depends on the extent to which the members of the community of inquirers construe their field of inquiry in essentially the same fashion. If such fundamental agreement exists, the methodology will function as a standard of "objectivity," insofar as two different members can follow the methodological guidelines to the same conclusion about the validity of a knowledge claim. Yet no transcendental standard of objectivity exists. Extreme positivists (and their opponents) seem to assert that the natural sciences have such a standard in the appeal to brute facts.[22] But there are no brute facts, only construed ones, and the factors affecting the construction of facts are partially rooted in a communal consensus on the nature of the subject under study and the appropriate methods for validating explanations about it. In a sense, objectivity seems to possess a certain irreducible element of circularity, a circle sustained through political control.

The controls on response in the natural sciences are not, however, matters of mere fancy that can be altered at a whim, even though they may not be absolute or immutable. The commitment to empiricism and logical clarity means that statements that cannot produce supporting evidence or be plausibly linked to accepted scientific propositions will tend to be rejected. Although facts are not "brute" and logic is not a reflection of the divine mind, neither are they merely arbitrary. Any system of rules for linking statements must at least be coherent on its own terms (even though it may be challenged by another system), and any statement of purported fact must be linked to an observational field independent of the observer (even though it cannot define all the potential aspects of that field). We could, of course, reject any form of internal (logic) or external (fact) controls on our explanations, but only by leaving the community of inquiry altogether.

Polanyi also notes an extrascientific source of standards of value in the natural sciences—that of intrinsic interest.[23] Insignificant explanations of what are taken to be trivial observations will tend to be ignored by the scientific community, but the definition of significance can be affected by values and powers external to the scientific enterprise. Nonetheless, the recognition that judgments of scientific value are at least partially determined by some notion of significance serves as a useful caution to those social scientists tempted by a "mindless" empiricism. A fact is not significant merely because it is a fact.

The politics of method in the natural sciences, despite reservations about the immutability of logic and the indubitability of facts, demonstrates a record of considerable success in resolving disputes and temporarily establishing shared meaning. The capacity to restrict the range of response through appeals to the codes of a methodological consensus seems associated with three factors. First, the categories manipulated by the natural scientists are human interpretations of phenomena that do not (presumably) assign meaning to their own behavior. Second, on the whole, natural categories are relatively amenable to precise specification and measurement, allowing for both reasonably unambiguous feedback and the use of precise (i.e., mathematical) rules for linking statements. Third, the areas of natural scientific interest (as distinguished from those of technological concern) have remained relatively remote from the core interests of other social institutions. Consequently, "irrelevant" feedback is limited and can be fairly easily contained. When the interests of these other institutions are affected, however, feedback reflecting their concerns and not susceptible to conventional methodological controls may develop. Recent examples of such feedback include political and religious reactions to various forms of genetic engineering.

None of these conditions for success is equally evident in the domain of the social sciences. First, the phenomena under study in the social world (human beings) assign meaning to their own actions. Second, many social facts are not amenable to precise definition, measurement, and feedback. Third, concerns which subvert the efficacy of any particular set of methodological controls intrude more easily upon social scientific research.

These difficulties lead some critics to argue that scientific methods of knowing and (presumably) controlling cannot comprehend the essential aspects of human behavior. Jürgen Habermas, for example, believes that the empirical sciences, as he construes them, are only one way to constitute knowledge, embodying an instrumental interest in "technical control over objectified processes."[24] Two other cognitive interests, practical and emancipatory, constitute knowledge differently, and they are characterized by different types of action. Our practical interests concern successful communicative interaction guided by consensual norms, whereas our emancipatory interests involve questions of power and the liberation of human energies. According to Habermas, the empirical sciences cannot adequately account for these latter two interests; rather, practical interests require interpretive approaches, and emancipatory ones suggest the need for critical social analysis.

The social world differs qualitatively from the natural world of the empiricist sciences, and a fuller understanding of social interaction requires that we recognize and account for these differences. The natural world, first of all, possesses no innate meaning or value; it merely exists to be dealt with in some way. Scientists (for that matter, all human beings) impose their meanings upon the natural world.

Social activities, in contrast, are carried out by thinking, purposive creatures. Human beings constantly give themselves covert directions (motive) and engage in covert responses (meaning) to their own and others' behavior. For this reason, social events cannot be equated with those in the inanimate or unreflective worlds. In some sense, the social world *does* possess innate meaning: the meanings that the participants themselves assign to their own behavior.[25]

Also, the meanings participants attach to their behavior cannot be understood *in vacuo*; rather, they take shape within a field of common meanings and must be so interpreted.[26] Scientific method, based upon an empiricist epistemology, does not appear to be able to account for such intersubjective meanings, because they cannot be facilely reduced to the "brute data" of individual behavior but must be seen within a context of mutually expected response. A positivist-inspired social scientific methodology, therefore, by focusing upon the overt behavior of individuals without regard for subjective content, necessarily obscures the meanings of the behavior for the subjects, along with the mutuality that shapes these self-assigned meanings.

Ongoing social action, additionally, is *prospective* in nature, for the participants look forward to some *to be completed* act. Scientific explanation (indeed, all explanation), in contrast, is *retrospective*, that is, based upon the observation and interpretation of *already completed* events. Such a retrospective stance is also adopted when we as social actors step out from the continuous flow of the *durée* and look back upon discrete actions that we conceive as already completed. The prospective stance adopted by participants in the ongoing life process contributes to a sense of indeterminacy and free will, in that whatever we plan to do, we feel we could choose to do otherwise. The retrospective stance, in contrast, contributes to ideas of determinacy and causation, because the events have been completed and cannot be altered. Their absolutely irrevocable contiguity to prior events suggests causal linkages.

Finally, the covert motive and meaning contexts of the actors may themselves be distorted.[27] Not only may actors deceive an observer as to their motives and meanings, but they may deceive themselves as well. People are not uniquely capable of "knowing" their own actions. This problem of "false consciousness" implies that the observer must adopt a critical stance in evaluating self-ascribed motives and meanings of the social actors. The more people labor under false consciousness, the more the critical observer's interpretations will diverge from those of the observed.

Such concerns do not mean, however, that the controls of scientific method are necessarily irrelevant to the foundation of communities of social scientific inquiry, though they do suggest that a consensus on the particulars of a set of methodological strictures may be more difficult to establish and maintain. Even if such a consensus is established, it most likely will not be as effective in limiting the range of response and maintaining solidarity within the community of social inquirers. Moreover, if some standards of logical empiricism, however specified, are to be applied in social analysis, then they must be incorporated in a perspective that accounts for the self-reflective characteristics of social phenomena as well.

Epistemological Instability in the Social Scientific Community

Science, in contrast to protoscientific activities in the commonsense world, systematically exploits the relations among explanation, experimentation, and feedback through the imposition of precise rules for formulating and linking statements and through rigorously defined experimental evidence. Insofar as the linkages are determinant and the feedback precise, scientific method may be used to establish shared meaning within a scientific community.

Although such methodological controls may have proven effective in structuring response in the natural sciences, interpretationalists question whether any controls based essentially upon logic and empirical validation can comprehend areas of covert motive and meaning. The social sciences, to be both *social* and *scientific*, must account for these covert motives and meanings when justifying (that is, controlling the response to) knowledge claims.[28]

Some representation of covert motives and meanings may, then, be considered an essential *epistemological* component of both social scientific and commonsense knowledge of the social world. Almost all of our knowledge of both contemporaries and predecessors rests upon typifications of the motives and meanings that appear to underlie their overt behavior and render it comprehensible. Even our self-knowledge, when we look upon our actions in retrospect, is essentially typical in form. Only in our ongoing experience of the *durée* or in some face-to-face relations when two people grow old together in an empathetic I-Thou relation can the typical character of self-knowledge or social knowledge be transcended.[29] Typifications also form a part of all social analysis, even though this might not be recognized or acknowledged by the analyst. All explanations of social behavior either explicitly state or implicitly assume that the actors give themselves certain covert directions (intention) and engage in certain covert responses (subjective meaning) when conducting their activities.[*30]

The debate as to whether scientific methodological controls are relevant to social explanation seems to arise from a confusion between *what* is done—the typification of covert motives and meanings—and the *way* it is done—rigorous observation and logical systemization.[31] What is done, typification, distinguishes the social from the natural sciences and associates social scientific explanation with commonsense knowledge of the social world. The way typifications are validated, through conformance with the dictates of some variant of scientific method, distinguishes social scientific typifications from those of the commonsense world and establishes an affinity between the natural and the social sciences. The purpose of method in both is the same: to provide some standards of logic and evidence that can constrict the range of response to explanatory propositions and thereby contribute to the development of shared meaning within a community of inquiry.

In developing their typifications, social scientists must devise a historical construct of the context within which the behavior took place. The elements of this construct must, in principle, be formulated so as to be transmissible to another independent

---

*The collective result is not necessarily the *sum* of individual intentions; to continue the mathematical metaphor, it is the *product* of them. Even when demonstrating how collective "irrationality" emerges from individual rationality (e.g., the "tragedy of the commons" or the "savings effect"), some account of individual motive and meaning is still implied.

observer. The objective of social scientists, analogous to that of their counterparts in the natural sciences, is not simply to formulate explanations, but also to have them accepted by other members of the community of inquiry. For this latter purpose, they must convince their colleagues that the proffered explanation accounts for the observed behavior (validation by correspondence to empirical evidence) and is compatible with other accepted explanations (validation by logical coherence).

Initially, such judgments of validity may seem analogous to the construction and interpretation of data in the natural sciences, but in practice disputes over validity may be more difficult to control in the social sciences because they also involve the typification underlying any particular explanation. Consequently, Alfred Schutz argues that the explanations proposed by the observer ought to be acceptable to those whose covert motives and meanings are being typified.[32] If we accept this contention, then social scientists need to consider whether the actors would recognize social scientific explanations as adequate representations of their covert motives and meanings. This concern for adequacy encompasses that of observational validity, for the actors' motives are unlikely to be adequately reflected by a typification that fails to account for the essential observable aspects of their social activity.

The most obvious avenue for evaluating the adequacy of a typification is to ask those being typified. This option is, admittedly, not entirely reliable, especially if the presumed motives are conventionally viewed as reprehensible, and, in any case, may be impossible. All typifications are retrospective constructs, even those made in the world of contemporaries, and many social actions have slipped far into the past. Under these conditions, the evaluation of adequacy involves making a construct of the historical context so as to gain additional guidance for deciding on a typification's adequacy.[33] The self-interpretations of the original actors may have more authority than those of our retrospective observers because they possess more information for making their historical construct. This advantage is pragmatic, not absolute. Observers may be better able to grasp aspects of the cultural situation to which the actors may not have been aware that they were responding. In this case, the typification, if presented to the actors, would presumably be recognized by them as revelatory of their actual motives.[34]

Consideration of the typical adequacy of social scientific explanation adds a dimension of ambiguity beyond that of judgments of observational validity. It requires an additional interpretational step. Whereas validity by itself involves the imposition of meaning upon observations of overt activities, adequacy involves checking the imposed meanings against the "inherent" meanings the actors themselves assign to their activities. Consequently, social explanations may be undermined not only by reference to observable aspects of the behavior not accounted for by the explanation but also through reference to the reconstruction of actors' own self-interpretations

The suggestion that the perspective of an outside observer may be better able to reveal the etiology of social behavior suggests a third factor involved in evaluating typifications, one that goes beyond considerations of both validity and adequacy. Actors may accept typifications of their behavior as being adequate, but both self-conception and that imposed by the observer may be based upon some delusion or "false consciousness." In such cases, critical theorists have a point in arguing that to base social scientific typifications upon a deluded sense of motive and meaning hardly provides a reliable foundation for our understanding of social reality.

The question of the "inauthenticity" of the actors' own self-interpretations raises the problem of a false knowledge that resists replacement by a more honest (or authentic) perspective. Authentic explanations go beyond concern for valid and adequate typifications to include some recognition of how the behavior typified reflects social and psychological forces of which the actors may not only be unaware but which they may actually distort or repress. Thus, a psychoanalyst uses a theory of repression and displacement to characterize how a patient distorts the motives underlying his behavior. Similarly, a Marxist applies presumed knowledge of the fundamental linkages between the forces and relations of production to illuminate how existing ideologies obscure perceptions of economic activities; and the critical linguist applies a construct of the ideal speech situation to identify the distortions that occur in communicative acts.

Once the basis of the critical position has been accepted, the criterion of authenticity guides the theorist in constructing explanations that not only account for the actors' covert motives and meanings but also critically contrast them with a construct of undistorted social activity.

Unfortunately, it appears easier to accept the principle that actors may delude themselves than to agree on a standard for identifying and correcting for such delusions. Indeed, the critical standard may itself be distorted in either its formulation or application and thus be subject to a further critique. Once the possibility of self-deception is admitted, it leads either to an indefinite critical regress that can be terminated only by a pragmatic consensus or by the discovery of an absolute ground of meaning. The former remains unstable, and the latter may not exist.

Natural scientists need to concern themselves only with the descriptive validity of their constructions of a nonreflexive world. Social scientists must recognize in addition the problems of interpretative adequacy and critical authenticity, the dimensions of which can only be indirectly assessed and pragmatically established. An apparently "valid" explanation can be undermined by challenging either its adequacy or its authenticity. The reverberations of instability, to be sure, flow both ways insofar as the introduction of reconstituted observations may call into question both the adequacy and the authenticity of a previously accepted explanation.

Social scientists concerned about the failure of the social sciences to establish a stable community of shared meaning have some reason to be discouraged. Not only can the basic perspective of *what* constitutes the relevant social facts shift, so also can the consensus on *who* should constitute them and *how* they should do so. We present our explanations as reflecting typifications of covert motives and meanings that are valid, adequate, and authentic. The instability at the foundation of our social knowledge suggests that any explanatory proposition is open to multiple epistemological challenges. Even when a provisional epistemological consensus is established, other characteristics of the social world erode the political efficacy of scientific method as a means of controlling the range of response and thereby establishing shared meaning in the social scientific community.

The Politics of Method
in the Social Sciences

The effectiveness of methodological controls in the natural sciences depends in part upon the availability of sufficient, precise, and unambiguous feedback as well as on a reasonably stable epistemological consensus. Insufficient feedback, or that contaminated by a good deal of "noise," makes it more difficult to apply exact rules for linking statements or to use empirical evidence to validate (or invalidate) knowledge claims. Any erosion of the effectiveness of these controls results in a spreading of response and a consequent weakening of "communal" ties.

The social sciences have never been able to develop or exploit methodological controls as effectively as in the natural sciences, in part because of the difficulties encountered in either eliminating or ignoring unwelcome feedback noise. These problems are *not*, however, points of absolute contrast with conditions prevailing in the natural sciences. In fact, the extent to which these problems are common helps to explain some of the instabilities of shared meaning in the natural sciences communties as well.

What is Fed Back? The Problem of Social Facts

Scientific method devises rules for systematically linking explanation with experimentation in an effort to control the range of response. The forging of these links depends, in part, upon the generation of precise feedback from the experiments. Feedback ultimately consists of statements of fact, but "facts," as we have suggested, may not be quite so solid as they seem, even in the natural world. In both the natural and the social sciences, facts are always interpreted or constructed out of an indefinite range of possible perceptions. In order to limit the range of response to their factual constructs, natural scientists depend in large part upon precise measurement and, if possible, controlled experimentation. In a controlled experiment, the facts produced are presumably less contaminated by influences considered ir-relevant to the relation under study. The limited range of feed-back produced by a controlled experiment structures the stimulus field in an effort to control response.

The opportunities for controlled experimentation, however, may be severely constrained, particularly in the social sciences. Some of these constraints are extrascientific in origin; for exam-ple, people may not be willing to be experimentally manipulated by either biological or social scientists (antivivisectionists extend this objection to experimentation on various animal subjects as well). Some problems, moreover, cannot be defined so as to be amenable to controlled experimentation. Ecological puzzles, whether in the natural or the social world, must, by definition, be examined in their settings in order to identify and interpret complex interdependencies.

Social scientists, as well as investigators of other living sys-tems, often face an unhappy methodological dilemma. The analysis of problems in their natural settings often fails to struc-ture feedback to any significant degree, and a method of optimal ignorance becomes increasingly difficult to implement. Alterna-tively, to abstract elements of such complex interdependencies in order to engage in controlled experimentation may not lead to optimal ignorance but merely to simple ignorance of critical influences. In many instances, of course, the issue is moot be-cause the possibility of even an oversimplified experiment is out of the question.

The successful imposition of precise controls linking experi-mental results with explanatory statements also requires accu-rate measurement. Amorphous data, even if the product of a controlled experiment, convey little reason to retain, revise, or abandon a particular explanation. Ironically, accurate mea-surement may itself be a source of explanatory instability, as when newly devised instruments of measurement produce unan-ticipated results.

In any case, many phenomena, especially in the social world, cannot be accurately measured according to interval, much less ratio, scales. Even efforts at nominal categorization founder upon ambiguous conceptualizations. Thus, social scientists often confront a second methodological dilemma: In order to deal with problems of significance, they must content themselves with imprecise indicators; when precise, their investigations sometimes seem confined to the relatively trivial. Amorphous data, of course, encourage variability in interpretation, and shared meaning erodes. The desire to control the range of response through precise measurement means that, where such indicators exist, they tend to displace consideration of "softer" data. The result is the underestimation of important residuals, as is exemplified by the concentration upon economic indicators as measures of national well-being.

What is Being Explained? The Problem of Social Explanation

Experimentally produced data, whether structured or unstructured, precise or ambiguous, do not exist *in vacuo*; rather, they both reflect and affect the structure of explanatory hierarchies. Ambiguous, noise-contaminated feedback not only contributes to variable interpretational responses to the data but also adversely affects the application of precise rules for formulating and linking explanatory statements. Instabilities of facts therefore contribute to instabilities of explanation.

In some fundamental sense, as we have argued, explanation begins as soon as we move from nonverbal to verbal behavior, that is, as soon as we categorize our perceptions. Such categorization, which may or may not be mistaken, often follows instantaneously upon perception; yet, sometimes, although we perceive a configuration, we hesitate before we are able to categorize it. So strong is our urge to categorize and order our response that we all probably experience considerable tension in such a situation.

Even at the level of these basic categorical statements, something has been added to the simple perception. Categories, as the first step in explanation, attach not to a particular perception but rather relate to a group of presumably similar perceptions.

"Presumably similar," however, does not mean necessarily similar. Two perceptions subsumed under the same category may be recategorized by the same observer at another time or by a different observer. The strictures of scientific method are intended, at least in part, to control such reclassification. Yet, the verbal structure of all explanations may be subverted at any point.

Explanation, of course, usually implies a higher level of generalization than that of the initial categorization of perceived sensations. Conventionally, scientific explanations relate empirically categorized phenomena to form ordered patterns.[35] Each generalization relating these phenomena may, in principle, be subsumed under a more encompassing generalization, and that explanation by another, and so on indefinitely until some arbitrarily chosen stopping point is reached.[36] The "covering law" model of scientific explanatory structures constitutes a special case of this hierarchical regress, one wherein the links among the statements are so defined that lower levels may be ineluctably derived from a higher, or covering law, statement. The applicability of this model depends, however, upon the prior existence of a consensus on rules of logic.

The higher we rise in an explanatory regress, even in a simple, well-founded classification scheme, the more comprehensive will be the generalization, and the more the empirical details will be obscured. The higher the level of generality, the more unstable the explanation often is, owing to the increased likelihood that inconsistent statements will be subsumed or contradictory data incorporated. Consequently, responses to a high-level generalization may be more difficult to control because different elements are perceived as significant. In a sense, then, a high-level generalization resembles a complex stimulus field, any part of which may elicit a response. As one moves "down" the explanatory regress, the degree of specificity increases, and the stimulus field becomes progressively narrower. Then, the range of response can be more easily controlled.

The rules of scientific method linking statements to some empirical referent and to one another in a systematic fashion attempt to limit potential drift. The appropriate logic for constructing and linking generalizations may itself be a matter of dispute, especially in the social sciences where some attention must be given to the covert motives and meanings of the actors. Moreover, the social sciences are commonly observed to suffer from several additional problems that further weaken the controls of logic and thus contribute to the erosion of shared meaning.

The first and most obvious of these problems concerns the complexity of individual human beings, the irreducible monad of the social sciences. Although it may be possible to identify certain genetic contributions to an individual's behavior, the complexity of social interaction cannot be accounted for simply through appeals to genetic patterning. Each individual is the unique product of both a genetic and a biographical heritage. The individual's biography consists, moreover, of a series of essentially haphazard, inconsistent, and unpredictable experiences, with the result that the persona (or self-image) imposes an artifactual coherence on an incoherent package. The reality of this incoherence may be demonstrated during times of stress, when our integrated self disintegrates into behavior that we ourselves may find unpredictable.

The degree of sharing should not be underestimated; indeed, it stands as the foundation of social scientific generalization. Each person, however, combines the common elements in a somewhat different fashion. No two people, for example, speak exactly the same language; each has his or her own personal style of speaking. Closely related styles may be grouped together as dialects and related dialects into a language. Nonetheless, speakers of two different dialects of the same language may have difficulty in understanding one another. Common language may be the foundation of cultural unity, identity, and, therefore, social generalization, but it is not an absolute foundation. Thus, the basic units of analysis in the social sciences appear to differ from one another more than do the members of other animal species and certainly much more than do the elements of the periodic table. These incongruities affect the stability of generalizations covering members of the same cultural grouping.

Cultural *diversity*, however, contributes another problem afflicting the stability of generalization in the social sciences. No cultural grouping is completely coherent and may, as we just noted, include subcultures that are relatively incommensurable with one another. If such conditions pertain within the same cultural group, cross-cultural generalizations would seem even more tenuous.

Certainly, some bases for cross-cultural comparison do exist, including partial sharing of values and origins, as well as the possession of presumably similar biological and, perhaps, psychological needs. Such sharings constitute something considerably less than identity, however, and any explanation striving for cross-cultural generality can often be undermined through the introduction of conflicting evidence.

Human beings, moreover, change their behavior. This capacity erodes the validity of explanations striving for generality over time. The underlying source of this problem may well be the capacity of the human brain for random response.[37] Not only do we find it impossible to determine exactly what element of a stimulus field a person selects for response, but we also cannot predict absolutely how a person might respond even if the particular stimulus could be identified. Institutions of social control (that is, all institutions) attempt to narrow the range of response as much as necessary for their own functioning through the direction of the learning process, the ascription and denial of value, and the manipulation of rewards and punishments. These controls have never been completely successful, even in so-called totalitarian systems. Ironically, from this perspective, the capacity for successful social generalization, whether scientific or commonsensical, depends largely upon the effectiveness of the mechanisms of social control devised to ensure predictable response.

Finally, social scientific explanations seem especially vulnerable to "contamination" from extrascientific concerns. All scientists bring to their research the psychological and cultural baggage that makes up their personalities. Further, external sources of power and funding influence the direction of much research. Science certainly is not value free in the loose sense of this phrase, although the subject matter of the natural sciences is, in some sense, free of inherent value. Value, like meaning, is not immanent but imposed by human beings upon the natural universe. In the social universe, in contrast, the observers must recognize that the activities studied have some value for those participating in them.

The rules of scientific method function to minimize the intrusion of presumably irrelevant values and biases whose impact would undercut the grounds of shared meaning in a field of inquiry by prompting essentially "unscientific" responses to a problem. Social scientists, unfortunately, often find it difficult to isolate themselves from such infection, for the problems they study more immediately affect their own lives and values. They are a part of the world they study in a way the natural scientists are not.

Given the complexity of the subject matter and the vagaries consequently affecting feedback, existing evidence may often be interpreted as supportive of different generalizations. At such points of competition, extrascientific values may intrude. A classic instance involved the interpretation of data from the intelligence tests administered to army recruits during World War I. Since immigrants who had lived in the United States longer than more recent immigrants performed better on the exam, some social scientists concluded that the quality of immigrants was declining. Since these latter immigrants were of Slavic and southern European extraction, these data, so interpreted, served as a convenient justification for the immigration quotas established in the 1920s. The prejudice against these nationalities prevented some analysts from recognizing that the test score discrepancies could be more plausibly explained by differences in the length of domestic socialization, rather than the inherent inferiority of certain peoples.[38]

Sometimes social scientists respond to the threat of "value contamination" by attempting to sanitize their research through excessive abstraction, a strategy which cuts off the explanation even further from the existential base of social knowledge and contributes to its stereotypicality. Another methodological dilemma, then, is that to conduct meaningful research about their subject—human beings and their interactions—social scientists risk being unduly influenced by extrascientific values and identities. To minimize such influences, they often seem to dehumanize their subjects into objects for manipulation and control.

The ambiguity of social facts therefore subverts the efficacy of any system of methodological controls over response. Principles of empirical validation rely primarily on structured stimulus fields to limit the range of response, but problems of measurement and controlled experimentation in the social sciences conspire to produce data that encourage interpretational variety. Rules for constructing explanatory hierarchies require, in turn, clearly defined statements that can be precisely linked to one another so as to channel the movement from one statement to the next. Ambiguities of interpretation, however, weaken the relations among statements, especially cross-culturally and over time. Consequently, instabilities of factual interpretation and explanatory construction continually erode the foundations of shared meaning in the social sciences.

Conclusion: Science and the Control of Shared Meaning

The relevance of scientific explanation to the understanding of human interactions separates into two issues, one of epistemology and the other of methodology. The self-reflective nature of the subjects under study constitutes an essential difference between the social and the natural worlds—a difference primarily accounted for by the typification of covert motives and meanings that underlies social explanation. The nature of typification, though, undermines the stability of our knowledge of the social world. Natural scientists need only to concern themselves with descriptive validity, whereas social scientists must, in addition, recognize the importance of interpretative adequacy and critical authenticity. Shifts in perspective can emanate from any or all of these three facets, rather than just one, as in the natural sciences. The implication, to combine Kuhn with Trotsky, is the possibility of a permanent paradigmatic revolution in our understanding of the social world.

The *general* relevance of scientific method to the study of the social world cannot be denied. Appeals to evidence and to rules for connecting statements are useful in structuring responses to any explanatory proposition. Yet the instability in the ground of our knowledge of the social world and the essential ambiguity of much of what passes for social fact combine to weaken the efficacy of any system of controls on response. The result is a "delta"[39] of social scientific explanations all contending for the consent of the presumptive community of scholars.

Explanatory pluralism is not entirely deplorable, however, and ways other than scientific method exist to build a consensus on shared meaning. The social construction of mutual response to complex experiences may demand multiple perspectives, as Nietzsche reminds us. To move too quickly toward the resolution of a problem by imposing controls revelatory of only part of this experience may yield only a false consensus that will either be quickly challenged or be maintained through force. Pluralism is preferable to the unwarranted assertion of Truth.

Unfortunately, explanatory pluralism tempts people to resolve issues of shared meaning through devices other than logic and evidence. Such "explanation" by other means, including coercion, presents us with a dangerous dilemma: A denial of the polysemantic nature of the social world can be sustained only by the recourse to coercion, but the admission of polysemy contributes to conflict and, again, to the temptation to use coercion to resolve disputes over shared meaning. To these issues of conflict and consensus we turn in the next two chapters.

Scientific method is one important way to make sense of some bits of human experience, useful where applicable, potentially disastrous when it is used in an attempt to monopolize discourse.[40] By recognizing the essentially political purpose of scientific method, we will be better able to evaluate its contributions and its limits in creating and sustaining communities of shared meaning.

COUNTERPOINT TO CHAPTER 2
Art as Antimethod

> Action is essentially destructive of all institu-
> tional studies; just as it compromises the purity of
> doctrines, it damages the integrity of structures,
> upsets the balance of relationships, interrupts the
> network of communication which the institu-
> tional historian struggles to identify, and having
> identified, to crystallize.
>
> JOHN KEEGAN
> *The Face of Battle*

UNIFORMITY, STABILITY, AND PREDICTABILITY in social explanation depend upon the existence of uniformity, stability, and predictability in human interactions, regardless of how these are to be assessed and incorporated into explanations and expectations. Without the assumption that ordered relations can be identified, all forms of social explanation, whether positivist, hermeneutical, or critical, would be futile.

In constructing their explanatory propositions, social scientists generally typify covert motives and meanings, whether through the reification of selected traits, as in the assumption of economic rationality, or through the aggregation of individual motivation, as in the creation of collective types like the "nation state." While typifications may be complex, contradictory, and indeterminate (as are, indeed, some of the personal types we construct in the everyday world), such unstable types eviscerate the coherence and comparability necessary for the social scientific enterprise. Consequently, even when social science typifications are only probabilistically related to empirical "reality," they retain an implicit commitment to predictability. An explanation of low probability, that is, one that fails to account for much of the observed action, will tend to be discredited, and ones of greater efficacy sought.

Predictability is a trait shared by comic characters in drama who, as Morse Peckham notes, "show a high degree of consistency (and an almost total consistency in farce), while exactly the opposite is the case in tragedy."[1] Likewise, when we encounter an individual in the everyday world who presents highly redundant personality traits, we recognize him as "a comic or absurd or grotesque or eccentric figure."[2] In this sense, the pursuit of consistency and constancy in social scientific typification becomes comic, and our typifications possess empirical validity only to the extent to which social life is a comedy.

Fortunately for our jobs and our journals, social life is enough of a comedy to support our endeavors. In the everyday world we seek order with all the fervor of the scientist searching for the "secrets" of the universe. We create patterns, impose continuities, depend upon predictabilities, and otherwise behave so that the social scientists among us have something to do. Indeed, this behavior is the foundation of shared meaning (mutually expected response) in the social world.

Unfortunately, both for social science and for our own peace, sometimes our patterns break, our continuities are interrupted, our predictions fail. Even our personas may threaten to disintegrate under stress. The collapse of shared meaning is the stuff of tragedy. Such collapse, however, is not the stuff of science. Rather the discontinuities of life become the anomalies of social science: data that do not fit and are ignored until they become so egregious as to mandate revision or renunciation of the purported explanation. Even when such a "revolution" occurs, the purpose is to reimpose a more adequate order, not to bear sustained exposure to chaos. In social science, therefore, while asserting that only empirical data are real, we orient ourselves to our explanatory typifications which necessarily obscure the essential individuality and discontinuity that can characterize the data (human behavior).

Well, then, so what? What does it matter that an unexplained residual of unpredictability remains, if the vast majority of behavior is routine and, thus, explicable? Indeed, in areas of routine (e.g., organizational behavior) social scientific explanations seem to possess their greatest reliability. Yet, even accepting the assumption that the proportion of unpredictability is small does not mean that it is inconsequential. Certainly the enormous resources that organizations expend to control behavior and to sustain continuity belie the insignificance of the threat of collapse posed by this residual. Even minor deviations, if pervasive throughout a complex, interdependent structure, can lead to organizational deterioration and even collapse.

Moreover, not all social life is so routinized as that within bureaucracies. In an area such as social violence, what the presumptive scientific explanations leave out is precisely that which holds the most meaning for those immediately affected. Take, for example, the following hypothesis:

The magnitude of political violence varies strongly and directly with the ratio of dissident coercive control to regime coercive control to the point of equality, and inversely beyond it.[3]

Where are the dead in this? Where are the bereaved? Where are the fear, the hatred, the envy, the contempt? Where are the agony, the psychic scars, the seething resentment, and the lust for revenge? Nowhere; nor should any of this be expected, for the purpose of scientific explanation is to impose order to stabilize meaning, not to inject the chaos of emotion. As Thomas Pollack aptly notes, "The more accurately we report the results of experience, the less we communicate our experience itself."[4] The more we try to impose a comic order on the social world, the more the tragic discontinuities of life will be excluded. As Walter Kaufmann remarks concerning philosophy, social science "helps one endure the sufferings of others by distracting one's attention from them."[5] The ordered abstractions of the social scientist are unable to comprehend the extremities of "life at the limits."*

If such meanings lie largely outside the boundaries of social science, must they necessarily be completely nontransmissible? Is there some "method" or "antimethod" that rather than structuring response would, in some sense, destructure it? We could, perhaps, acquire some understanding of the meaning of the

---

*The disorder of "life at the limits," as Kaufmann points out, is not always tragic. Dionysian ecstasy also occurs at the extremity of existence and is also not comprehended by social scientific typifications.

breakdown of shared meaning through first-hand experience, but the avenue of "participant observation" suffers from several significant limitations. First, participant observation is severely constricted in scope. Second, only the understanding of the observer is directly affected; others must make do with the dim reflection of the experience cast by research reports, which, themselves, are the beginnings of explanatory abstractions. Third, even as they participate in the discontinuous flow of the life process, observers are, after all, also observing, that is to say, abstracting and removing themselves from the process and seeking to impose order. Finally, participant observation in "life at the limits" can obviously be rather threatening to the observer and does not seem to be as accessible as other more orderly arenas of social existence.

Some forms of art, however, may provide an alternative avenue to increased understanding of the breakdown of shared meaning in the social life process. Art, of course, is a product of social behavior and, like any other behavior, becomes an object for social scientific explanation. Thus, the social sciences often tend to reduce art to their own level, either by "explaining" art products sociologically or psychologically, or by trying to turn artists into pseudosocial scientists and scanning their works for testable hypotheses or sociocultural data.[6]

Neither of these two courses is surprising, for social science is, to extend Edward O. Wilson's provocative argument, the "antidiscipline" of art.[7] The practioners of any discipline attempt to reduce the more complex discipline above them to their own terms. Thus, chemistry is so reduced by physics, biology by chemistry, and, more recently, the social sciences have confronted the reductionist assaults of the sociobiologists. The reductionist surge, however, can only go so far, as Wilson admits, before the loss of complexity cripples understanding. Art can, to some extent, be analyzed through the dry propositions of science, but artistic vision cannot be wholly comprehended by science. When left unreduced, art provides a way to gain some understanding of the residuals of meaning that fall outside the compass of social science. Wilson notes that "a broad scholar can be defined as one who is a student of three subjects: his discipline, the lower antidiscipline, and the subject to which his speciality stands as an antidiscipline."[8]

However laudable the goal of broad scholarship might be, it clearly presents both a substantive and a "political" challenge. To begin to master the substance of another field is difficult enough, but, in addition, the venturesome scholar must face the outrage of the guardians of disciplinary boundaries. Nonetheless, despite the risk of provoking those who shudder at the intrusions of outsiders, art may be used to complement the limited comic vision of social life available through scientific inquiry. To demonstrate this, it would be useful first to counter several misconceptions.

One misconception involves the equation of art with beauty. "Beauty" is one of the more ambiguous concepts of aesthetics. Edmund Burke makes a distinction between the sublime and the beautiful, the former inspiring feelings of tension, awe, and even terror, while the latter produces feelings of relaxation and love.[9] While some works of art may be beautiful, more powerful ones seem to be more aptly characterized as sublime.

A related misconception concerns the relation between art and order. Often art is described as exhibiting harmony or displaying a higher, purer form of order. Certainly art is characterized by a degree of order, but works of art gain their interest from the discontinuities that the artist injects. Indeed, Peckham argues that "art offers not order but the opportunity to experience more disorder than does *any other human artifact* . . . (emphasis added)."[10] Art certainly does not incarnate unadulterated chaos; rather, in comparison to other human creations, such as tools, art objects are characterized by a relatively greater degree of deliberate unpredictability and tension, which are the sources of art's capacity to delight, surprise, and even outrage us. We implicitly recognize the role of discontinuity whenever we condemn a work of art, whether a poem, musical piece, novel, film, or painting, as being "utterly predictable." Low-level art, whether greeting card verse, pulp novels, calendar art, or disco music, most clearly embodies the quality of predictability and, in this sense, order. The frustation of expectation—disorder— forms an important basis of the contribution of art to our understanding of the breakdown of shared meaning.

A third confusion abounds over the accessibility of art. Here "amateurs" can err by believing that art is more accessible than other areas of intellectual activity. Certainly, some art is accessible, but so also is some philosophy and some science. Little of accessible art, however, holds much interest. Art at the "higher" cultural levels serves the purposes of understanding better and, concomitantly, is more difficult to appreciate. Not coincidently, art at this level offers a greater experience of discontinuity, the very source of most interpretational difficulties.

Finally, some enthusiasts claim that art performs a *unique* semantic function; that is, art communicates meanings that cannot be acquired in any other way. The truth in this notion, I believe, is that art may be used to communicate meanings that are beyond science, because the canons of scientific methodology are restrictive. Art, though, draws upon the general repository of meaning in a culture.[11] Just because the meanings of art are part of the culture of the everyday world, however, does not mean they are readily accessible to those who function *only* in the everyday world. Rather, a person's life is severely circumscribed, and exposure to both art and science reveals levels of meaning only dimly apprehended through the prism, or prison, of mundane experience. Art can broaden, clarify, or intensify experiences which in everyday life are diluted by happenstance and limited by one's place in the world.[12]

The potential contribution of art to understanding, then, is not beauty, order, or unique truth. Rather, as a complement to science, art may serve to transmit that which is scientifically nontransmissible. Specifically, through art the social observer may gain a better idea of the subjective content suffusing social relations—content generally removed from the ordered propositions of scientific explanation.[13] Art may improve our comprehension of the complexity, contraditions, and tragedy of life that the comic structure of social science filters out.

Most basically, art, as noted above, offers the experience of disorder. Such an experience depends on the existence of order, for expectations cannot be frustrated until they have been generated; shared meanings cannot be undermined unless they have first been established. The discontinuities the artist injects into his work exist against a background of continuity. These discontinuities may be of both form and substance. Formal discontinuities are most clearly exemplified by the stylistic dynamism characterizing the arts, especially over the past two hundred years. The rapid innovations that occur within or, more radically, break with established stylistic forms seem to serve no obvious purpose, leading Peckham to label them "nonfunctional."[14] Sometimes an artist will break with preceding conventions to such an extent that even trained art perceivers will be confused and even outraged. Illustrations of such perceiver disorientation include the initial receptions given to Stravinsky's "The Rite of Spring" and Duchamp's "Nude Descending a Staircase." Even Georges Braque was initially disoriented by Picasso's "Les Demoiselles d'Avignon," denying that the painting was art.

In addition to the "external discontinuities" of stylistic innovation, a single work of art may establish certain patterns of expectation and then violate them.[15] Such "internal discontinuities" of form are evident in poetry where rhyme and rhythm schemes are established and then broken, or in music, where melodic themes are defined and then varied. The highly ordered music of Bach, for example, engages us not because of its continuities but because of its variations. One of the more important discontinuities offered by a painting is that between the painted configuration and the forms which it implies for the observer. Obviously, as the painting becomes more "representational," the experience of this type of discontinuity diminishes. Conversely, the greater the extent to which the painted configuration deviates from the implied form, the more difficulty perceivers will have in categorizing and responding to their perceptions and the more disoriented they will feel. Even relatively subtle discontinuities can stimulate anxiety.

In works of fiction, the artist injects discontinuities in the way the story is told. These discontinuities can take four major forms.[16] First, expected solutions to the problem of the plot can be interrupted. Second, characters can be developed in surprising ways. These two sources of discontinuity serve to emphasize the nature of fiction as a "time art." The stance adopted by the reader is essentially prospective in nature, that is, looking forward to action to be completed in the future. In this sense, the orientation of the reader is analogous to that of the participant in ongoing social action. In addition to the interruption of plot resolution and unpredictable character development, the author of fiction can also inject deliberate ambiguities into the narration of the story itself through the use of multiple or unreliable narrators. Finally, the author can disrupt expectations through modulating the tone of the story in ways that violate the preconceptions of the reader.

Formal discontinuities, both external and internal, generate for the perceiver a problem analogous to one existing in the everyday world: "What is going on here?" Formal discontinuities, to be sure, are not equally present in all art works, no more than confusion is a constant quality in life. When our expectations are interrupted in the everyday world, however, we usually search for a more adequate orientation or categorization. The same holds true with respect to our involvement with art, for "the distinguishing character of the [art] perceiver's role is search behavior focused on an awareness of discontinuities."[17]

A work of art can also present substantive, or semantic, discontinuities generating a second problem analogous to one in the social world: "What is the meaning of this?" "How are we to respond?" Just as cognitive and emotional tensions arise when we are unable to interpret the situation confronting us in the everyday world, similar tensions can be generated by substantive discontinuities in art. Problems of form and substance are, admittedly, intertwined, for we can hardly interpret the meaning of a situation (that is, respond "appropriately") if we are unable to establish the "facts." Knowledge of the facts, however, is no guarantee that the appropriate meaning will be assessed. The most common ways through which the artist frustrates the drive for meaning are by withholding information necessary to complete the meaning, thereby forcing the perceivers to complete it for themselves, and by deliberately suffusing the work of art with ambiguous, conflicting, or even subversive values.

The most important way in which art may complement social science, therefore, is by injecting back some contact with the anomalies, the ambiguities, and the tensions that, at times, impinge on shared meanings but are excluded by the ordered perspective of social science. Beyond this general contribution, art may also enrich understanding in a number of specific ways. Artistic vision can provide a form of contact with a wide range of human types and experiences far beyond what could be expected in our ordinary lives. Moreover, these "contacts" need not be stereotypical, as they so often are in both life and social science, nor simply idiosyncratic, irrelevant, unconnected, serial experiences. Rather, a universality can be attained "by the very richness with which this particularity is represented.... In a great work of art men are able to recognize that something is being shown that has a broad and therefore lasting significance and illuminates hidden features of many situations."[18] Through the creation of such "concrete universals," art can thereby fill the gap between the particularities of our experience and the explanatory generalizations of social science.

Art, moreover, can incarnate ideas and vividly expose abstract moral issues. Art serves this purpose best not through narrow didacticism, although some works of art do adopt this approach. Rather, art teaches "by presenting us with characters in situations (usually of conflict and crisis) that generally have a greater complexity than our own everyday experiences."[19] When this substantive presentation is complicated by deliberately withheld meaning and value ambiguity, the perceiver is channeled not only into unprecedented dilemmas but also into complicity in their ultimate resolution.

Moral dilemmas, diverse and unpredictable characters, complex and indeterminate situations that frustrate efforts at interpretation, these are the discontinuities that continually intrude upon the "human comedy." In the everyday world, as Peckham notes, we generally try to suppress these disparities, for they are "cognitively disorienting and emotionally disturbing."[20] In social science, these problems are suppressed because they tend to undercut the efficacy of the explanatory enterprise in establishing shared meaning.

Although art can offer the experiences of disorientation and complexity, it also serves to isolate the perceiver from the necessity of acting.[21] "The safer, the more protected, the human organism the more it can afford to be aware of disparities, to search for problems, to account for the disparity, to solve these problems, and to correct the original cognitive model by feedback."[22] The experience of disorder and even terror, largely screened out by the imposed order of typified meaning and motive, becomes more tolerable in the insulated setting of the art perceiver than in the everyday world. The limitations upon our comic modes of thought, then, may be partially recognized and transcended through the medium of art.

Art can therefore function as a paradoxical kind of anti-method: a deliberately structured experience designed to challenge and even break down our structures of meaning. The assumption that social life is orderly and can be adequately characterized by our explanatory propositions reflects the essence of a comic faith, "for comedy is a dramatization of the orientation that man is adequate to the conditions of experience, that, if he uses his wits, he can triumph over them."[23] Such a faith, to be sure, is not unfounded, for most of our social interactions are based upon relatively stable, accurate expectations about one another's behavior.

Even when orderly, however, tension and ambiguity suffuse social life; when order breaks down, the presence of heightened ambiguity and tension are central to the understanding of the implications of disorder for the participants. Social science filters such implications out, as it must, for they inject subjectivity and instability into the explanatory enterprise. Contact with certain forms of art can communicate some understanding analogous to the *Verstehen* of the sensitive participant confronting the experience of the deterioration of shared meaning. Indeed, since art allows the perceiver to transcend a particular time and place and can emphasize selected aspects of experience, it is superior, in some respects, to direct participation in the *durée*, especially one "at the limits."

3

CONFLICT:
The Struggle to Control Shared Meaning

Life itself is essentially appropriation, injury, overpowering of what is alien and weaker; suppression, hardness, imposition of one's forms, incorporation, and at least, at its mildest, exploitation—

NIETZSCHE

Introduction

J USTICE "MEANS NOTHING but what is to the interest of the stronger party."[1] These words, attributed by Plato to the Greek Sophist Thrasymachus, introduce one of the earliest statements of what might be termed the *coercion theory of shared meaning*.[2] If meaning is embodied in response, the determination of response determines meaning. Coercive constraints determine response; thus, meaning can be "nothing but what is to the interest of the stronger party." The weaker participant in a relationship must either respond according to the dictates of the stronger or suffer the consequences. Might makes meaning.

Politics, defined as the deliberate effort to control shared meaning, becomes an arena of ceaseless conflict in which the contenders struggle to impose their respective meanings upon one another. No shared meaning so established would be especially stable, however, as the oppressed would strive to free themselves from relationships in which they have no voice and from which they are alienated. The legitimacy of such arrangements would be in continuous dispute.

Marx echoes Thrasymachus's position in his analysis of capitalist society in which the ruling class uses the power of the state to enforce its interests. To paraphrase his famous dictum: the ruling meanings are the meanings of the ruling class. The condition of the proletariat, which he characterizes as alienated, contributes to a revolutionary upheaval which establishes new, and presumably more stable, shared meanings. The initial post-revolutionary period, the dictatorship of the proletariat, would still be characterized by constraint. In this instance, however, the meanings imposed will be those of the great majority upon a recalcitrant minority.

In contrast with the conflict and instability inherent in coercion theory, *consent theories of meaning* stress consensus, integration, and stability. Instead of the imposition of the will of the powerful, consent theories suggest that a preexisting convergence of response engenders the shared meanings underlying social arrangements. Conflict, if it occurs, signifies an abnormality or distortion in the body politic, a deviation from an ideal state of affairs wherein all members conduct their activities in a well-integrated, mutually acceptable fashion.

Plato, in rebutting Thrasymachus, develops a theory of a good society in which philosophers capable of recognizing the Good direct the policy of the state, a class of guardians protects the polity from internal and external enemies, and an artisan agricultural class provides for the material needs of the *polis*. Each of the three elements contributes to the maintenance of shared meaning by playing its expected role. The acceptance of one's proper position in society underlies Plato's conception of justice.

The "decline of ideology" thesis represents a more modern variant of Platonic consent theory. Assuming a consensus on social ends, politics could presumably be reduced to the consideration of the appropriate means to achieve these goals. Such questions are susceptible to scientific analysis; therefore, disputes over meaning should be relatively easy to resolve through the application of scientific methodological controls. Conflict, though not eliminated, becomes incidental to the consensual clarity of most issues. In its extreme technocratic form, politics (in this case, simply the determination of appropriate means) would be left to experts trained to resolve these issues. These technocrats, then, would be the functional equivalent of the philosopher kings.

Without agreement over the ends of social action, however, the consensual basis of technocracy could well degenerate into conflict and the coercive imposition of meaning once again. Plato avoided this possibility by positing a realm of absolute Truth. More contemporaneously, Jürgen Habermas argues that a "rational consensus" on ends may be established without appealing to either strategic action (i.e., constraint theories of meaning) or to absolute truths. Such a consensus, he believes, may be reached in an "ideal speech situation," in which the participants conduct a discourse over norms free from any kind of compulsion or systematic distortion like that arising from the unequal ability to make and dispute normative claims.[3] In an ideal speech situation, the consensus on norms that emerges would reflect only the compulsion of the better argument, rather than a superior power position.[4]

Consent theories of meaning often imply the existence of some standard of truth independent of the solipsistic interests of participants in a social arrangement. That truth may be the received wisdom of tradition (in a sense, a prepolitical consensus), Platonic forms, correspondence to "scientifically established" fact, or the rational consensus that presumably emerges from an ideal speech situation. Unequivocal standards, should they exist, serve to determine response not through the imposition of constraints but through the common recognition of the way things necessarily "are." The comprehensiveness of consent, to be sure, may be more or less exhaustive, leaving a periphery of conflict in any social setting.

The stability of consensually based standards of truth, however, can be undercut. Thus, traditional wisdom may be subverted through contact with unanticipated, exogenous intrusions or by its own internal contradictions. The existence of Platonic forms or the relevance of the ideal speech situation to actual discourse may be denied, as did Nietzsche when he denounced such abstractions as "the last smoke of evaporating reality."[5] Even scientific method cannot be applied unreflectively but requires some interpretation, contributing to the instability of scientifically established meaning, particularly as controls of logic and empirical validation weaken.

Yet the solipsism implied by extreme versions of coercion theory, in which shared meaning simply reflects the will of the stronger party, fails to account for the mutual interdeterminacy of response present in all relations, even those between master and slave. Coercion theory ignores the existence of natural and social "resistances" that, even though not unequivocal and absolute, do not lend themselves equally well to an indefinite variety of responses. Individualistic perspectives ignore the ways in which an "individual" exists only within multiple contexts of mutual meaning; indeed, the individual as an independent monad of social reality is as much a fiction as transcendent absolutes. Consequently, though no consensus is immutable, unconstrained sharing is possible, if tenuous, and certain conditions relatively independent of any particular individual's will or interests can serve to structure common response. Even our own actions can become "objectified" and confront us later with their own intractability.

Neither extreme coercion nor consent theories of shared meaning fully account for the existence of mutual predictability in human communities. Both extremes are naive: the former because it denies the existence of truth independent of the will and the latter because it conclusively confirms the existence of such truth. Coercion theories tend to underestimate the possibility of consensually based meaning, and consent theories overestimate the likelihood. Conditions, natural and social, may be more or less conducive to consensus. The efficacy of the controls imposed through scientific method, for example, depends upon the presence of precise, unambiguous feedback. When such conditions remain imperfectly fulfilled, responses begin to diverge, and conflicts over meaning develop. As these conflicts intensify, shared meaning (if possible under any circumstances) is increasingly likely to be manipulated or constrained into existence. Though coercion may be used to resolve conflict through conquest, the meanings so established remain unstable owing to the absence of any foundation for shared response outside of coercive constraint. Any weakening of these restraints, therefore, leads to a reemergence of conflicts over shared meaning.

The conditions conducive to the emergence or the reemergence of conflict within established social interactions may be viewed from at least three different perspectives: culture conflict, resource competition, and decision-making discordance. Although this analytical separation should not obscure the interconnections among the three, each perspective reflects differently on the conditions inducing conflict in society.

Culture Conflict

The identification of social collectivities depends upon some notion of a common culture. Certain individuals are seen as sharing basic attitudes, beliefs, and expectations to the extent that they form a group distinct from any other. Identification of the essential components of a community's culture reveals some of the roots of individual behavior and forms a primary basis for generalization in the social sciences.

Simply stated, culture consists of directions for a performance.[6] Cultural directives, whether stated in laws, embodied in customs, or incarnated in artifacts, serve to channel response in various contexts. These directives, then, structure stimulus fields in an effort to instruct the members of a cultural group in a set of "appropriate" responses. People share a culture to the extent that they respond to the same set of cultural directives in mutually expected and compatible ways.

Shared meaning, it must be emphasized, does not necessarily imply identical response to the same stimulus field. Rather, shared meaning involves conformance with mutual expectations. In some highly routinized interactions, such as road behavior, mutuality does approximate identical response (e.g., all drivers travel on the right side of the road in two-way traffic). In other circumstances, shared meaning consists of common expectations about the appropriate behavior for each party in a complex relationship. The priest and his congregation share expectations concerning their different responses within the same context—the celebration of a mass.

As mutuality of response declines, conflict increases. In routinized behaviors, this may mean that people whom we expect to act as we do respond differently (e.g., the drunk or the Englishman coming at us on our side of the road), or those whom we expect to act differently respond in the same way (e.g., the Catholic reaction to the radical Protestant claim that each person is his or her own priest). To a great extent, order is based upon distinctions made in common, leading to different but mutually supportive responses.

The peculiar paradox of modern culture may lie precisely in its creation of responses that are excessively similar, contributing to the breakdown of the system of distinctions and degrees necessary under conditions of scarcity. The generation of "mimetic desires," as René Girard labels them, encourages competition over resources as much as the more obvious case of conflicting desires.[7]

Most cultural directives presume and predict that to follow them enhances the chances for survival. All cultures, though, suffer to some degree from internal incoherence. People, moreover, may be viewed as participating in many, overlapping cultural communities, some subsuming others, which compete for their loyalty, generating a kind of "external" incoherence. They often encounter, therefore, ambiguous or conflicting directions as to appropriate response in a particular situation. This incoherence leads to conflicts over meaning. The inconsistency, inadequacy, and indeterminacy of cultural directives each adds, in an interrelated fashion, to the severity of cultural conflict.[8]

Inconsistency

Inconsistency develops whenever contradictory directives apparently apply to the same situation. Examples abound from the trivial to the profound. Consider, for instance, the confusion characterizing certain commonsense maxims:

> "Look before you leap," but "He who hesitates is lost."
> "A stitch in time saves nine," but "Haste makes waste."
> "Absence makes the heart grow fonder," but "Out of sight, out of mind."
> "Many hands make for light work," but "Too many cooks spoil the broth."

Inconsistent directives, though, are no joke. In the 1960s, many young Americans were not amused by the conflict between the formal ideals of citizenship, equality of opportunity, and justice, which they learned in school, and the expectations and practices of the dominant groups in the United States with which they were ultimately confronted. "New Left" attacks on domestic racism, economic inequality, and foreign military intervention were prompted less by any conversion to a "foreign ideology" than by the radicals' attachment to the formal values commonly expressed in the contemporary American culture.

At a more profound level, the successful repression of spontaneous, aggressive impulse, required for the smooth functioning of complex, interdependent, socioeconomic structures, depends, at least in part, on having some outlet for the expression of such energies. The directives within an industrial society for worker discipline, precision, and punctuality conflict with (and contribute to the need for) the dependence of that society on various forms of narcotics as a source of stability. Yet, the essentially private rituals of rebellion embodied in the restricted consumption of narcotic substances become fundamentally conservative in implication, as long as the workers confine their "rebellion" to nonworking hours. When the consequences percolate into the workday, however (e.g., the problem of drunkenness among Soviet workers or the "Monday morning" automobile from Detroit), this inconsistency undermines the smooth functioning of the economic system. Moreover, the toleration of one narcotic, alcohol, and the proscription of others create a further inconsistency and stimulate more conflict.

Finally, the extent to which inconsistency can lead to widespread turmoil is amply illustrated by the recent conflict in China between two sets of comprehensive ideological directives, one subsumed under the rubric of "revolution" and the other under that of "modernization." This conflict incorporated numerous overlapping inconsistencies, including red vs. expert (revolutionary purity vs. technical expertise), equality vs. hierarchy, political movement vs. bureaucracy, and agitation vs. technical education. Interestingly, the forces of modernization have apparently emerged victorious, although the other directives continue to be latent in the culture.

People who find themselves at the nexus of competing communities may encounter particularly severe inconsistencies, especially if the issue involved concerns the fundamental ground of identity. The intensity of conflicts between national and subnational loyalties in countries as various as Canada, Lebanon, and Nigeria illustrates the contentious potential of these external inconsistencies. The conflict between impersonal standards of performance and familial demands (contributing to nepotism) might be an example of such conflicts at the individual level.

Inconsistent directives, then, contribute to the breakdown of shared meaning. The availability in any culture of a variety of incompatible directives competing for behavioral allegiance creates a complex and contradictory stimulus field, thereby weakening the capacity of any directive to channel response and encouraging a delta of potentially conflicting behavior.

Inadequacy

The inconsistencies confronting every person reflect and contribute to the problem of adequacy, that is, whether a particular directive actually does improve chances of survival.* The presence of contradictory directives suggests that no single directive addressing a given situation is likely to be fully appropriate at all times. Sometimes we should look before we leap, but, again, hesitation, on occasion, leads to loss. Similarly, the legitimacy of most political orders seems to depend in part upon the formal articulation of ideals which the system presumably incorporates, but these ideals often generate expectations which the pragmatic requirements and frailties of everyday politics inevitably frustrate. As Sophocles portrays in *Antigone* and other tragedies, the competing demands of different moral communities to which we belong may place us in situations where any decision outrages the gods, that is, proves inadequate.

The potential inadequacy of all cultural directives, whether or not they are consistent with one another, stems from the inherent instability of all categorical statements. Like other categories, cultural directives, even the most specific, abstract to

---

*Survival is viewed not so much as the ultimate value, but rather as the necessary condition for the realization of any other temporal value.

some extent from the existential situation to which they purport to serve as a guide. They "slip, slither, and slide" above the world, creating the continuous possibility of negation based on some aspect which they failed to take into account. The more abstract the directive, the greater ease and probability with which a counterclaim can be made. Thus, the adequacy of the directive "Stop for red traffic lights" is easier to sustain than "Look before you leap," because it is tied to a rather well-defined context. Nonetheless, the range of response to specific and highly redundant traffic laws suggests that even they are not perceived as perfect guides for behavior.

Any effort to impose an internally consistent set of cultural directives, if such were possible to devise, seems likely to result in the imposition of inadequacy upon a social arrangement, ultimately threatening its survival. But to accept the inevitability, indeed the desirability, of contradiction leads to instability and the unpredictability of response, encourages conflict, and disrupts smooth interaction. In order to survive in the present, shared meaning must be stabilized; in order to survive into the future, shared meaning must change to meet new demands, must confront its inadequacies. A social order founded upon completely stabilized meaning has no future, whereas one committed to innovation (which encourages the deterioration of shared meaning) may well have no present.*

Indeterminacy

Inconsistent cultural directives combined with doubts about the adequacy of any particular directive result in underdetermined response. Both, in effect, weaken the capacity of any directive to channel behavior. Inconsistency deconstructs the cultural

---

*A totally innovative society would be a contradiction, as any ongoing social arrangement demands some stability of shared meaning. Ceaseless innovation on the part of all parties in all areas of interaction would end all mutuality.

stimulus field, and doubts about adequacy undermine the plausibility of any particular directive. Such doubts, of course, encourage the innovation of alternatives presumed to be more adequate, leading to further inconsistency. The availability of competing alternatives, moreover, reinforces challenges to the adequacy of any particular directive. The fact that the adequacy of a dominant directive or any innovative alternative to it can be finally determined only after the fact lends a certain tension to the human condition.

The incoherent nature of culture contributes to the incoherence of the individual persona. Each person's biography, shaped by the inconsistencies of culture, combined with the capacity of the brain for variable response, further reinforces the likelihood of a range of behavior developing in any particular cultural context. All people try to impose coherence on their own behavior, a coherence reflected in our essentially fictive self-images. At times, this coherence breaks down, especially when we are under stress.[9] At such points, our behavior may startle ourselves as well as others.

Inconsistency, inadequacy, and the resultant indeterminacy of response are, obviously, matters of degree. During times of relative stability, internal cultural inconsistencies may not be readily apparent, the multiple communities to which we belong may be relatively compatible with one another, the degree of adequacy may be sufficient to ensure the survival of both the individual and the social order, and the indeterminacy of response may be largely contained within a narrow enough range so that smooth, relatively predictable interaction can be sustained. At the other extreme, the extent of the inconsistency may be so great as to belie the notion of a common culture. The adequacy of the dominant directives may deteriorate to a point where survival is clearly threatened, and behavior may become so indeterminate as to undermine most interactional arrangements and even threaten the coherence of the fictive persona. Between the two extremes of perfect order and perfect collapse occur more or less significant and intense cultural conflicts, that is, conflicts over the appropriate basis of shared meaning or mutual expectations in interactions.

Resource Competition

In some general sense, establishing meaning, in either the material or the social worlds, can be seen as an aggressive act. If meaning is embodied in response, then to create meaning necessarily imposes on the world in some way, though not always with the results intended. Even apparently quiescent reactions to external circumstances may still be construed as attempts to shape the world according to our needs and preferences within the limits of the resources we have available. To respond to the world requires some power resources, if only our lives. Death alone brings surcease from the quest for meaning.

Power Resources

Conflict over the appropriateness of alternative directives entwines inextricably with competition for the power resources that provide the means to respond in the world. The notion of power *resources* suggests something of an exchange perspective on social relations, where the participants (whether individuals or groups) control certain resources which they manipulate and exchange for one another or consume for their own sake.[10] Undoubtedly, the variety of resources relevant for social exchange could be enumerated in several different ways, and the following categorization is intended, therefore, to be illustrative rather than definitive:[11]

1. *Economic Resources*. These consist of both the inputs and the outputs of the processes of economic production. Conventionally, the inputs encompass land (including all natural resources), labor (including the skills of the laborer), and capital goods (the tools used in generating and combining land and labor). Economic outputs comprise those final goods and services that provide for material well-being.

2. *Political Resources*. The specifically political resources include both authority and legitimacy. Political authority signifies

the right to speak for a community and announce community policy.*[12] The vote, for example, is an authority resource, although intermittently exercised, as are positions in elective or bureaucratic organizations. Legitimacy, a somewhat more nebulous notion, involves the participants' perceptions of the worthiness or rightness of the authorities. Legitimacy may be demonstrated by the degree of allegiance and the extent of the support freely given to the regime (that is, in the absence of any concrete inducement such as the threat of punishment or the promise of a material reward, but solely out of feelings of moral obligation). Legitimacy is the resource controlled by the politically relevant subjects in an authority relationship, in that subjects may exchange allegiance for the regime's conformance with certain broad standards of rightful rule. Since not all the subjects are equally relevant to the continuation of most authority relations, legitimacy, like authority, may be unequally distributed among the population. The concepts of authority and legitimacy need not be confined to narrowly construed governmental relations but may be extended to any hierarchical relation. Thus, it would be appropriate to speak, at least in a restricted sense, of the legitimacy of the authority holders in a business firm and family.

3. *Status Resources.* In most social relations, some participants are esteemed, and others defer to them and follow their directions. People acquire esteem in a variety of ways, largely depending upon the values dominant in their culture. Esteem may be derived from accidents of birth (as in a hereditary aristocracy), feats of strength or bravery, economic success, personal achievement, and so on. Status constitutes a source of power because others follow an esteemed person out of the belief that he or she can better identify the appropriate response in a particular situation.[13] Thus, the esteemed person is believed to be capable of defining shared meaning. This element of faith distinguishes status from more materialistic resources. If the

---

*The right to announce policy is, in the sense developed thus far, the official right to define the nature of shared meaning. Whether authoritative definitions have any impact on actual responses is, of course, another matter.

followers ever question the actions dictated by the esteemed person, asking for justifications, then status has begun to erode as an effective power resource.

4. *Information Resources*. As social arrangements grow more complex, accurate and readily accessible information becomes increasingly important in the formulation of adequate response. Control over information, therefore, may be seen as a special kind of power resource needed for the effective and efficient use of other power resources. The ability to gather and, conversely, to withhold information can be a factor in the relative power position within and between organizations.

5. *Coercion Resources*. Physical coercion, or its threat, is commonly considered to be the resource of last resort, to be used only when other resources have failed to shape response in the desired fashion. Basically, coercion includes all acts intended to harm others or their value possessions.* So defined, the range of coercive acts extends from the slight and subtle to the extensive and overt. Coercion resources provide the capacity to harm another. In some fundamental sense, the possession of a minimal amount of physical strength can be construed as a coercion resource (and, perhaps, as an economic resource as well). Other resources, such as economic and information resources, may be bent to essentially destructive purposes. For purposes of clarity, the category of coercion resources should be restricted to those means, such as weapons, that are primarily designed to harm.

6. *Organization Resources:* Organization may be viewed as the amplifier of other resources.[14] Almost everyone controls some small resource reserve, but solitary action seldom has much impact on the shape of socially shared meanings. Organization brings disparate resource holders together and directs them to a common end. Generally, the ability to act in concert creates for the group a greater potential power than that of the sum of the parts acting separately. This synergistic effect, however, depends upon the quality of the organization and the value of the resources it brings to bear upon external relations.

---

*This definition of coercion, and some of its attendant ambiguities, is elaborated in the next chapter.

The achievement of internal discipline reflects the successful manipulation of power resources within the organization.

Each of these resources may be used to shape meaning (response), whether through the promise of reward (especially economic resources), the threat of punishment (especially coercion resources), or by structuring the stimulus field in various ways (especially authority, status, and information resources). The mere possession of power resource does not, however, guarantee a determining impact on the structure of shared meaning. Rather, our capacity to shape response depends upon at least three factors: the relative distribution of available resources, the value of a particular resource in exchange with others (i.e., a highly valued resource will command more of other resources when exchanged than would one of lower value), and the skill with which we manage our resources (a "power-rich" person may squander away this advantage, while one with significantly fewer resources to begin with may shrewdly manipulate them for maximum advantage). Through the manipulation of our available resources, we engage in the deliberate effort to control shared meaning, that is, politics.

Conflict over Meaning and the Competition for Resources

The manipulation and exchange of power resources may not involve conflict if they occur within already established shared meanings validating a particular distribution and channeling the patterns of exchange. The existence of such shared meanings need not imply an equality of power. In a master/slave relation, to draw on a rather extreme example, each party controls some resources, though presumably vastly disproportionate in size and value.* If both share certain expectations about their respective

---

*Exactly who possesses more can be debated. The slave's direct familiarity with the material world could be seen as a potential source of power equal to or even greater than that of the master's. Thus we have the well-established tradition of the "master" who is actually controlled by his servant or slave.

roles, however, there may be no conflict as long as each party lives up to the other's expectations. Indeed, certain revolts and rebellions have apparently been inspired less by a chiliastic vision of a new dispensation of liberty and equality than by a simple desire to restore previously held rights and obligations.

Some breakdown over shared meaning, then, is a necessary condition for conflict over the distribution of resources. Neither the fact of scarcity nor the fact of unequal shares is sufficient by itself to generate resource competition. Once shared meaning begins to disintegrate, then competition for control will intensify, as the concerned parties all seek to affect which meanings will be imposed (or inculcated) and which will be denied. Since meaning is never perfectly shared, the competition for resources is continuous.

The character of culture conflict, however, does not completely determine the nature of the competition over power resources.[15] Competition will also be affected by whether the resources over which we struggle are relatively or absolutely scarce. This distinction is *not* identical to that between renewable and nonrenewable resources. Renewable resources comprise those whose supply can be continuously replenished, including agricultural products and the labor pool. Noneconomic resources such as authority roles, legitimacy, and status also appear renewable in this sense. Renewability, to be sure, is a matter of degree, in that some resources may be more easily replaced than others. The ease of renewability of agricultural products, for example, depends upon the fertility of the soil and the skill of the farmer. Highly skilled labor is more difficult to replace than unskilled. A regime that loses the faith of the people in a key area may find it impossible to recover its lost legitimacy. All renewable resources, whether land, labor, or legitimacy, are subject to exhaustion and can become nonrenewable unless they are carefully husbanded.

All resources are scarce, or else they would not be power resources but free goods.[16] The availability of *relatively* scarce resources may, however, be meaningfully expanded through increases in productivity without causing a deterioration in their value. Supplies of food or legitimacy, for example, could be expanded, leading to an improvement in everyone's position at no one's expense. *Absolutely* scarce resources consist of those whose supply is definitively set, or those whose expansion in supply leads to congestion and the consequent deterioration in value. Prime ocean-front property is an example of a naturally fixed resource; the number of authority positions is a socially prescribed absolute scarcity. The problem of overcrowding and congestion can be illustrated by the value of a car in rush-hour traffic or that of a liberal arts degree in the current employment marketplace, or the worthlessness of a piece of "confidential" information that everyone knows.

An absolutely scarce resource, however, may still be renewable. Thus, as presidents die or are defeated, they can be replaced, but the United States has only one at a time. A charismatic leader, though, may be both absolutely scarce and nonrenewable. Alternatively, a nonrenewable resource may not be absolutely scarce, except at some theoretical limit, as long as technologies of use keep improving. A renewable resource whose value declines in proportion to the extent it is shared may approach a condition of absolute scarcity. Relative scarcity also may be considered a matter of degree. The supply of one resource may be relatively more difficult to expand than another, in which case the latter is less relatively scarce than the former. In addition, certain resources may be subject to more rapid deterioration in value as a result of expansion in supply than others.

The significance of absolute scarcity for resource competition lies in the probable intensification of conflict over shared meaning as meanings themselves are pursued through the competition for absolutely scarce resources. Fred Hirsch argues that the inability of these sectors to expand in terms of real value helps to explain some peculiar characteristics of politics in advanced capitalist states. First, despite apparent increases in material well-being (a trend that may well have played itself out), many people seem to feel ever more alienated, frustrated, and powerless.[17] This "paradox of affluence," as Hirsch terms it, becomes more comprehensible once we recognize that increased material affluence does not necessarily guarantee access to other sectors where power resources are absolutely scarce. Rather, the price of these absolutely scarce resources is simply driven up, or their value once possessed declines as a result of congestion. Indeed, the expansion of material affluence over the past century may well have contributed to the breakdown of mutually acceptable distinctions and the rise of mimetic desires, consequently directing competition into precisely those sectors of absolute scarcity, such as positions in socioeconomic hierarchies.

The heightened conflict over absolutely scarce resources contributes to a second peculiarity of contemporary politics. Despite the continued rhetoric that general improvement in economic well-being results from growth (the "expanding pie" or "trickle-down" thesis), increasingly sharp conflicts arise over questions of distribution.[18] The "distributional compulsion" inevitably arises under conditions of absolute scarcity, because the possibility of real growth is nil, and our position can improve only at someone else's expense. Conflicts over meaning, therefore, engender a competition for resources that is essentially "zero sum" (or even negative sum) in nature. Ironically, the principle of equality of opportunity reinforces conflicts over absolutely scarce positions; such conflicts were limited when the access to these positions was restricted. The failure to achieve a collective consensus on what constitutes a "fair" distribution of resources further intensifies competition in this area.

Third, contrary to the ideological obeisance paid to laissez-faire policies, capitalist regimes have become increasingly involved in the regulation and collective provision of these absolutely scarce resources.[19] "Reluctant collectivism" results from the begrudging recognition that the only way those who did not arrive first are going to have some control over or access to these resources is through public control and allocation. Examples of this control include policies ranging from the creation of national parks to the "fairness" doctrine in broadcasting. Collective provision, allocation, and guaranteed access do not solve the problem of absolute scarcity, however. In addition, the use of these resources must often be regulated to prevent deterioration of value due to congestion and overcrowding.

Breakdowns of shared meaning give rise to conflicts over the appropriate structure of response in a given social arrangement. This, in turn, engenders competition for the power resources needed to impose meanings (responses) on others and to protect oneself from such impositions. As the character of these resources approaches absolute scarcity, the competition over them tends to grow more severe. The consequent disputes over distribution, control, and access, as well as the appropriate bases for regulation, create a growing burden on governmental and quasi-governmental organizations. These demands suggest a third perspective on conflict: the concordance and discordance which characterize the authoritative decision-making process in all ongoing interactional arrangements.

Discordance in the Decision Process

Conflicts in the decision process may be viewed along a continuum that runs from extreme concordance to extreme discordance. Concordance is extreme if those participating "seek and attain unanimity in decision, making all the value sacrifices necessary for such outcomes."[20] Extreme discordance is evident when individuals adopt competitive and antagonistic attitudes toward one another, each seeking to maximize his or her own preferences, and mobilizing all available power resources to attain that preference, regardless of the consequences for the interactional arrangement.[21]

Concordance and discordance may be further illustrated by the contrasts shown in the table on page 74.

When a high level of concordance characterizes the decision process, the participants approach a condition of organic solidarity, and no one feels alienated from either the process or the outcome of the collective determination of shared meaning. As decision behavior grows progressively more discordant, the solidarity of coalitions declines. Individual interests become increasingly perceived as diverging from the collective outcomes. Participants, therefore, begin to see themselves as personally winning or losing in particular issue areas, and the losers come to feel alienated from the outcomes of the decision process. At the midpoint between the two extremes, personal preferences

Concordant and Discordant Decision Behavior

BEHAVIOR AREAS	CONCORDANCE	DISCORDANCE
1. Conflict resolution	Conflicts among decision makers, if allowed to surface, are resolved amicably and quickly.	The resolution of differences tends to be rancorous, difficult, and slow.
2. Decision rules and decision-taking	Even highly polycratic decision rules tend to produce outcomes smoothly.	Even if decision rules require only narrow agreements, outcomes tend to be fewer and are tough to produce.
3. Stability of coalitions	Coalitions among decision makers tend to be stable.	Coalitions tend to fall apart over trifling conflicts.
4. Amount of agreement on decisions	Decisions tend to be made unanimously or by large majorities.	Decisions, if made, tend to be by narrow margins.
5. Collegiality	Decision makers tend to prefer collegial decision-making bodies, even if they are not required.	Decision makers tend to operate through systems of "dispersed monocracy," to the extent they operate as groups at all.
6. Divisive issues	Issues known or suspected of being highly divisive tend to be subliminated into the realm of "non-decision-making."	The divisiveness of the issues has no relation to the extent to which they are pressed.
7. Amount of conflict	There is little conflict over issues where one might expect sharp conflicts.	Sharp conflicts appear over issues that involve low personal stakes and thus where one would not expect them to develop.
8. Collective responsibility	Decision makers manifest collective responsibility in the sense of publicly supporting, or at least not dissenting from, collective decisions with which they disagree.	Decision makers often carry their disagreements into the public arena, attempting to generate pressures in behalf of their preferred positions.
9. Collective identity	Decision makers generally use the collective "we."	Decision makers tend to disavow decisions taken even by groups of which they are a part.

SOURCE: Harry Eckstein and Ted Robert Gurr, *Pattern of Authority: A Structural Basis for Political Inquiry* (New York: John Wiley and Sons, 1976), pp. 136–37.

and collective harmony relate in a delicate balance.[22] Further increases in the level of discordance contribute to alienation and sap the cooperative capacity of the decision makers. The level of conflict among them can ultimately approach a *bellum omnium contra omnes*. The dichotomy between concordance and discordance replicates, at the level of decision making, the general antinomy of consent versus coercion theories of shared meaning.

Discordance in decision making develops, therefore, as shared meaning decays. The process of decay is a concomitant of cultural conflict that, in turn, results in intensified competition for scarce power resources. The competition for resources, especially those approaching the condition of absolute scarcity, can be regulated only by the collective decisions of authoritative bodies. But the capacity of decision makers to reach a collective consensus is undercut by the same forces that increase the demand for such decisions.

Culture conflict, resource competition, and decision-making discordance are something other than three clearly differentiated, casually sequential forms of conflict and something more than simply three perspectives on the general nature of conflict in social arrangements. Instead, they are perhaps best seen as three "corresponding planes" of conflict. As in the medieval world view, where disturbances in the body politic would be replicated in the natural world and the heavenly spheres, conflict on one plane is interactively linked to that on other planes. The successful resolution of conflict on one plane, therefore, necessarily carries over to the other planes as well.

Containing Conflict

The interconnections among the three planes of conflict raise the problem of where to intervene to resolve or, at least, contain conflict. If power resources are not absolutely scarce, conflicts over meaning might be partially accommodated and limited through real growth. Incommensurate interests at the cultural level might then be satisfied by a distribution of resources that would leave each somewhat better off, if not perfectly fulfilled (the happy situation of a "positive-sum" game). Such a containment of the apparently incompatible economic interests of workers (higher wages) and capitalists (higher profits) has been achieved, at least temporarily, in the advanced industrial economies over the past century.

Resource expansion, however, can provide only a partial redress. Historically, growth has been possible in some sectors, but not those characterized by absolute scarcity. Moreover, the belief that an expanding economy could moderate all conflicts through the satisfaction of economic interests seems to assume these interests are limited. Unfortunately, the reverse seems to be proving true, for "the attempt to create social stability by satisfying the demands of interest groups merely brings into existence more interest groups and increases the amount of social instability."[23]

In any case, as people become relatively satisfied in those sectors where meaningful growth through increased productivity has been possible, they tend to develop interests in precisely those areas where it is not possible. Finally, if the arguments of the "limits-to-growth" school have some merit, even those sectors in which growth has been possible may now be approaching exhaustion. Consequently; it appears increasingly improbable that conflicts over meaning and the multiplication of incommensurate interests can be managed through resource expansion. Indeed, the social and material limits to growth may well reinforce these conflicts.

Nor does it seem probable, or particularly desirable, that conflicts over meaning and the consequent competition for limited resources can be resolved simply by authoritative fiat. First, culture conflict and resource competition probably contribute to considerable discordance in the decision structures themselves. Second, assuming that the structures remain relatively intact and insulated from the wider discontinuities, their decisions resolving conflicts, in the absence of a new consensually based shared meaning, must necessarily be imposed upon some, or even most, of the participants in the social interaction. Every set of authoritative decision makers, in the absence of infinite resources, "must be selective in responding to the interests of the population under its control, and ultimately that selection can be maintained only by force."[24]

Yet, unless the multiplication of contending meanings can be primarily contained in some other way, force alone seems unlikely to suffice. Indeed, the use of force to maintain stability in the teeth of incommensurate meanings is a reasonable definition of a coercive tyranny, one that resolves conflict through conquest.

The fact that no extant society has degenerated completely into a war of each against all indicates that conflict has been contained, to some extent. Alternatively, the fact that no social arrangement is completely free from conflict suggests that such containment has been, and perhaps must necessarily be, imperfectly accomplished. Once conflict begins, it reverberates throughout the planes of correspondence. Similarly, consensus over meaning radiates into the areas of resource competition and decision making. A strong value consensus may sanction a particular distribution of available resources and undergird concordant decision-making behavior. Consensually based shared meaning limits or channels response in some mutually accepted and expected ways without the recourse to material rewards (resource expansion) or coercion (imposed fiat). Three mutually reinforcing avenues to consensually shared meanings may be pursued: (1) affective identification, (2) rational consensus, and (3) procedural regulation.

Affective Identification

Apart from the direct use of coercion or bribes, shared meanings are established and maintained through the ceaseless repetition of regulatory and performatory directives concerning the character of appropriate response. In short, we are told again and again how to behave in a myriad of life situations. All human behavior, in a sense, is aggressive in that it imposes meaning upon the world. The level of aggressiveness or energy release, however, must be controlled to ensure smooth social interaction, and regulatory directives "give instructions regulating the flow of energy or aggression."[25] Given the essentially physiological purpose of regulatory directives, it may be that they trigger essentially automatic, biologically encoded, responses in human beings.

Regulatory directives can be easily seen in the arts, especially music, where they can be presented without any propositional content. The high pitch, volume, and tempo of rock music, for example, clearly function as directives to release energy. The political implications of regulatory signs in music can be readily seen by listening to the essentially "aggressive" quality of most national anthems. As Nietzsche ironically notes, "How good bad music and bad reasons sound when one marches against an enemy"[26] Other examples of regulatory signs include the effects of different colors on behavior (thus, convalescents tend to improve more rapidly in "cheerful" or energetic green or yellow rooms, whereas deep blues and browns act as depressants).

More significant for continuous social interaction are the regulatory signs embodied in speech and gesture. One of the reasons a play must be seen in performance to be fully appreciated is simply because in reading a script we are largely denied the direction of these regulatory signs. Gesture and tone of voice guide our response.

Whatever the biological foundation of the response to these regulatory directives, they do not occur as pure entities in abstraction but within socially constructed contexts. The structure of regulatory directives changes according to the requirements for given levels of energy release in particular interactions. Norbert Elias argues that the evolution of manners coincided with the development of complex socioeconomic structures which required highly structured behavior.[27] Human impulsiveness, therefore, had to be contained, and its repression became an essential component of the "civilizing process." Similarly, Nietzsche forcefully states that when human beings found themselves "enclosed within the walls of society and peace," aggressive instincts had to be turned inward or internalized (thus anticipating Freud).[28]

The other major, and more obvious, method of channeling response in a social interaction is through performatory directives which, as the name suggests, instruct us as to the content of appropriate performance.[29] These, too, tend to be highly redundant, in order to instill the correct response. Of course, the redundancy of regulatory and performatory directives alone fails to account for shared meaning, not only because of the problems of inconsistency and inadequacy afflicting all cultures but also because we need to suggest why people might wish to behave "appropriately"—follow directions—in the first place.

One simple answer to this conundrum of motivation is that "appropriate" behavior leads to the collective validation of our individual worth. The foundation of our personal sense of worthiness is unstable, and thus our self-value can never be definitively established or finally fixed. Consequently, our need for validation is "an insatiable maw" devouring whatever signs of worth we can grasp.[30] This insatiable need helps to impose a continuous source of control on our behavior. Thus, a major source of shared meaning is the desire to be considered competent in our activities. Even when the directives are ambiguous, we will anxiously search for the behavior that will be judged by others as appropriate.

The desire for validation through collective judgments of our competence suggests why we actually seek to live up to one another's expectations. Through the mutual desire for mutual validation, shared meaning is generated. The allure of a tradition-bound system, where each member accepts his or her position and the behaviors appropriate to it, results in part from its promise of a clear and unambiguous ground for mutual validation. "Tradition-directed" people, to borrow David Riesman's typology, can be assured of continuous validation regardless of their position in the hierarchy, as long as they conform with its prescriptions.[31] The plight of the "other-directed" people involves the continuous search for guidance as to what constitutes appropriate response in each of the multiplicity of situations encountered in the segmented modern world. Only the "inner-directed," those who have internalized a system of self-validation, can be free from this form of social control.

Yet, despite the ability of the desire for collective validation to establish shared meaning, it cannot guarantee the complete resolution of conflict for a number of reasons. First, the relatively inner-directed person will be less susceptible to the blandishments of social validation or denigration. Of course, even the inner-directed, true believer may need the psychological support of some other like-minded souls and thereby be affected by their judgments of appropriateness. This points to a second problem, however: the possibility that a person may find validation within a group that stands largely alienated from the dominant meanings of the community. Consequently, though the need for validation may prevent a Hobbesian war of each against all from ever coming to pass, it may well contribute to conflicts between groups (a wide range of discourse exists between the poles of complete harmony and total chaos). Finally, the desire for approbation may not be sufficient to overcome either the inconsistencies or inadequacies of all our efforts to categorize and respond to the world. The good intentions of the approval seeker may be unable to resolve conflicts arising out of ambiguous social contexts.

Rational Consensus

Our need to be considered competent accounts in part for the relative effectiveness of regulatory and performatory directives in structuring mutually expected response without the recourse to the inducements of material rewards or punishments. Even though approbation provides an instrument of mutual control based upon something beyond purely instrumental calculation, it cannot ensure conflict resolution between contending parties whose members find sufficient validation within their respective groups. In such circumstances, the ability to demonstrate that one's position is "correct" or "true" offers an attractive alternative to reliance on bribery or coercion to contain conflict.

Presumably, if disputes arise over questions of "fact" or "efficient" means as opposed to ultimate ends, they would be subject, at least in principle, to some rational resolution satisfactory to the concerned parties. Thus, Arnold Brecht, in formulating his position of scientific value relativism, argues that questions of value may be answered scientifically in relation to "(a) some goal or purpose for the pursuit of which it is or is not useful (valuable), or to (b) the ideas held by some person or group of persons regarding what is or is not valuable."[32] The former entails empirical, "economic" analysis, and the second, logical derivation from certain givens. Ultimate values, whether chosen by the will or grasped through intuition, cannot be scientifically demonstrated.[33] Unfortunately, disputes over "ultimate" values, "ways of life," or "models of man" are precisely the kinds of conflict that threaten social arrangements most severely. If a rational consensus can develop only in debates over efficient and effective means or logical deduction from already agreed-upon premises, its contribution to conflict containment would be quite limited. The limits would be even more severe once the difficulties associated with deducing precise entailments of vague commitments (as to the general welfare) or determining effective or efficient means in complex, ambiguous settings with imperfect information (the ecological dilemma) are taken into account.

Brecht's essentially "noncognitivist" position prompts the fear that questions of ends are to be thrown to the winds to be resolved not through strength of argument but merely through strength. Cognitivists, at least as far back as Socrates and Plato, assert, to the contrary, that moral statements are about objective states and can be demonstrated to be true or false. For the cognitivist, then, the possible scope for rational consensus as a means of conflict resolution expands considerably.

A reformulation of the cognitivist/noncognitivist debate may better reveal the character of and possibilities for rational consensus in politics. The creation and maintenance of shared meaning depend upon controlling the range of response to particular sign configurations encountered in common in order to establish accurate expectations about one another's behavior. If a rational consensus is to emerge out of a normative conflict, the range of response to normative statements must be structured by "reason" as opposed to other conceivable, and presumably less satisfactory, means. Noncognitivists construe the realm of reason quite narrowly. Carl Hempel, for example, states

a sentence makes a cognitively significant assertion, and thus can be said to be either true or false, if and only if either (1) it is analytic or contradictory—in which case it is said to have purely logical meaning or significance—or else (2) if it is capable, at least potentially, of test by experiential evidence—in which case it can be said to have empirical meaning or significance.[34]

Moral discourse, as Brecht observes, may draw upon these strict forms of structuring response up to a point, but not when contention develops over ultimate principles or what Paul Taylor terms "ways of life." Taylor, in contrast to noncognitivists like Hempel and Brecht, believes that an appeal to a particular way of life "can be justified in terms of a rational choice among different ways of life."[35]

The possibility of a rational consensus emerging out of a conflict over ultimate commitments depends upon the extent to which we can argue for our commitments and persuade others to accept them. Such arguments cannot use conventional deductive logic, for there are no higher principles from which we can deduce our position. Carl Wellman suggests, however, that an ethical position can be defended through forms of inductive and what he terms "conductive" reasoning. Induction argues from particular cases to a general conclusion in ways somewhat analogous to procedures in the empirical sciences.[36] These particular cases, though, need not be empirically observed but may consist of thought experiments that exemplify and support the general principle.[37] Conductive reasoning occurs when "(1) a conclusion about some individual case (2) is drawn nonconclusively (3) from one or more premises about the same case (4) without any appeal to other cases."[38] As such, it is a form of reasoning that is neither strictly deductive nor inductive.

In justifying our ethical claims we can draw upon all of these forms of reasoning to meet challenges to our position. Successful justification would lead our opponents to withdraw their objections. The purpose behind these more broadly construed forms of reasoning is not to demonstrate indubitably a logical truth but simply to structure the responses of others. Deductive logic, within its sphere, may be the most effective way of controlling response through reasoning. Inductive and conductive arguments, although they impose weaker controls, also can structure response.

A defense of our own position from challenges will not be sufficient to persuade the adherent of a radically opposed value system or way of life. Any hope of persuasion in these circumstances depends upon providing an "internal critique" of the

opposing position which "would show that the philosophy de-
feats its own purposes."[39] Internal critique could conceivably
draw upon all forms of reasoning, as well as pragmatic consideration of probable consequences, in an effort to channel an
opponent's response.

The strict cognitivist position that a rational consensus can
emerge only through deductive reasoning and empirical exemplification narrowly construed restricts the realm of reason as a
form of verbal control too severely. In addition to deduction and
empirical evidence, ethical positions may be buttressed by inductive reasoning based on thought experiments, conductive
reasoning, and consideration of likely consequences (practical
reasoning). In part, a more expansive role for rational persuasion may result from the fact that people generally do not hold
to completely consistent hierarchies of value. Pluralistic, inconsistent cultural directives may contribute to conflict, but,
ironically, they may also provide grounds for persuasion, even
when two people find themselves holding to incommensurate
positions in one area.

The rational kingdom of ethical persuasion, to be sure, is not
imminent, for the *possibility* of persuasion neither guarantees its
inevitability or even its likelihood. Rational controls may be
called upon in a wide range of ethical conflicts but with no certainty of success. Admittedly, the ineluctable nature of the move
from one sentence to the next weakens as we leave the narrow
sphere of strictly defined deductive logic. Broadly construed
categories, moreover, tend to be more unstable than narrower
ones because they subsume a wider and potentially diverse
range of phenomena. The common assertion of the universal
applicability of ethical standards may, ironically, be a major
source of instability and conflict in moral discourse, as people
can easily differ over the relevance and interpretation of such
general categoric statements. Rigorous argumentation is politically convenient if you can achieve it. Richard Rorty observes

if the purposes you are engaged in fulfilling can be specified pretty
clearly in advance (e.g., finding out how an enzyme functions, pre-
venting violence in the streets, proving theorems), then you can get it.
If they are not (as in the search for a just society the resolution of a

moral dilemma, the choice of a symbol of ultimate concern, the quest for a "post-modernist" sensibility), then you probably cannot, and you should not try for it.[40]

In addition to clarity of purpose, the nature of the categories that form ethical as opposed to empirical statements is also significant. Although the categorization and interpretation of natural signs are not immanent, natural signs seem to possess a kind of reality independent of any particular human community, unless we adopt a position of extreme solipsism. Consequently, when exemplifying a categorization of a natural sign, we may be able to refer ultimately to a phenomenon that exists outside any particular community of shared meaning. Humanly produced signs, in contrast, possess no reality outside some humanly produced community, some form of human life.

Substantive ethical categories, then, presuppose a context of shared meaning in a way that natural categories do not. Efforts to sever ethical categories from the context that informs them tend to drain them of their content. Nietzsche, for all his admiration of Socrates, believed the Greek philosopher's attempt to rationally ground ethics abstracted from the Greek cultural ethos produced just such results:

Positing proofs as the presupposition for personal excellence in virtue signified nothing less than the disintegration of Greek instincts. They are themselves types of disintegration, all these great virtuous men and word-spinners.

In praxi, this means that moral judgments are torn from their conditionality, in which they have grown and alone possess any meaning, from their Greek and Greek-political ground and soil, to be denaturalized under the pretense of sublimination.[41]

Natural signs, although they take on meaning only within human communities, that is, only when they are embodied in response, possess an intractability independent of any particular community that can limit the range of response and thereby help to resolve conflicts. This intractability does not determine a particular response so much as prove progressively more resistant to the responses that increasingly fail to account for these external constraints. The meanings of good and evil, however, are wholly defined within human communities and possess no necessary communal transcendence.* They do, of course, constrain action insofar as they have been accepted, but these constraints are not grounded in anything outside the particular human community.

The belief in an afterlife where an all-knowing God rewards and punishes according to absolute standards of performance appeals, in part, because it provides a ground for the meaning of substantive ethical terms independent of any particular form of life. Ironically, the extent to which human behavior is the product of genetically encoded proclivities might also provide an independent ground of meaning: Signs that appear to be cultural products might turn out to be natural signs after all. Sociobiology claims to reveal a way out of the hermeneutical circle of culture.

Ethical categories are not the only ones confined entirely to human communities of shared meaning. Political terms such as legitimacy and authority (which are often ethical at the root) are of the same nature, as are the categories of aesthetics, such as beauty or artistic value. Conflicts over the meaning of humanly produced signs can be resolved through rational persuasion only within a deep contextual consensus, which, to borrow Tracy Strong's term, we might call the realm of the unquestioned.[42] The possibility of persuasion, including the persuasion of an opponent who holds to a fundamentally different way of life, assumes such a deep consensus. Included in this realm of the unquestioned cultural context would be some presumption about a basis for communication, a willingness to criticize and be criticized, and a mutual recognition of some minimal critical principles.[43] If these areas of unquestioned mutuality are ever questioned by one or both parties to a conflict, the possibility of rational discourse leading to even a tentative consensus evaporates. Ultimately, maintenance of a deep consensus may reflect a fundamental desire for validation—a need to be understood, even by those with whom we differ. We may fail to question the

---

*Another way of stating this is that we are wholly responsible, as human beings, for the meanings of good and evil. This observation will be further explored in the next chapter.

validity of our presumably common language (or the translatability of different languages) and may submit to certain rules of discourse simply to maintain contact. Although the strict noncognitivist position, then, appears too restrictive, with respect to the realm of the unquestioned, it appears to be correct, for without such fundamental sharing, communication, let alone conflict containment, would be impossible.

A deep consensus is necessary but not sufficient to bring about a rational consensus on a way of life or ultimate principles. Rational control on response, even when broadly construed, cannot guarantee the emergence of shared meaning. The resort to coercion (or bribery) in order to establish mutuality remains a continuous temptation in situations of social conflict. As an alternative, however, conflict can also be contained through procedural regulation.

Procedural Regulation

In the absence of a substantive agreement on meaning and purposes, conflicting parties may accept a decision "because it is made by the proper authorities in accordance with the proper rules and procedures."[44] The probability that those participating in an interaction possess some incompatible values suggests that the scope of such authoritative decision making should also be limited. A well-ordered society, under these conditions, may need to be composed of a plurality of communities on which the imposition of shared meaning would be strictly delimited. In most areas of incommensurability, the communities must agree to disagree.

Procedural regulation of these limited transcommunal decisions does not so much resolve conflict (as do coercive conquest, the conversion represented by affective identification, or the rational consensus reached through some form of discourse) as control it. The possibility of procedural regulation of conflict depends upon a number of factors.

First, the reality and necessity of the conflict, at least within limits, must be recognized by all the contending parties. What often happens is that each side sees the other's position in terms of its own world view, rather than from its opponent's perspective. The opponents and proponents of gay rights or abortion, for example, are not simply adopting conflicting positions on a simple proposition but are structuring their worlds in significantly different ways. The supporters of abortion on demand do not see themselves as advocates of mass murder, nor do their opponents see themselves as working to suppress women's rights. Similarly, gays do not identify themselves as apostles of perversion, nor do their opponents believe they are advocating the suppression of human freedom. Until an issue can be defined so that all sides share a recognition of what is at stake, they are unlikely to realize the reality and necessity of their conflict.

The opponents must also grant each other the right to exist. Pluralist values cannot be reflected in the social arrangements if any participant is committed to converting or conquering those with whom they differ. But why might opposing value communities care to demonstrate such toleration? Perhaps an argument could be developed from a proposition analogous to John Rawls's depiction of the limiting conditions of an "original position."[45] If no value community knew what its relative power position would be in the final state, each might support a principle of mutual toleration in their desire to avoid the worst alternative: their group being eliminated. More pragmatically, if no value community has sufficient power to eliminate or convert those with whom it disagrees, it may be willing to accept toleration as the "satisficing" alternative. Some groups of true believers, of course, might well prefer to go down fighting rather than vitiate in any way the values through which they justify their existence. Absolutist dichotomies of good and evil diminish opportunities for rational persuasion and vitiate the tolerance needed for procedural regulation.

Finally, the incompatible value communities must come to an agreement over the formal and informal procedures used to regulate the conflicts among them. Conceivably, the plurality of communities could grow in toleration of one another and still be unable to agree on procedural norms. The distinction between procedural and substantive issues is often arbitrary, and the choice of procedures may have substantive consequences (thus, the appeal of the so-called "mixed state," although this solution may simply obscure, rather than neutralize, the impact of procedures).

Differences over procedures, moreover, cannot be resolved procedurally; thus, a consensus on procedures must emerge some other way. One possibility would be to submit the problem to free and open discourse, but, if a rational consensus cannot be reached on key substantive norms, it may not be forthcoming on procedural ones either. Ultimately, shared procedural norms may have to emerge, at least in part, through affective identification and even some constraint, that is, the desire or necessity to live together.

In those areas where fundamental meanings overlap, conflicts that arise may be resolved through free discourse reaching a rational consensus. The existence of value communities that cannot resolve their differences through free discourse does not necessarily result in uncontrollable conflicts. These may still be resolved through affective identification or regulated by procedural validation. The possibility for either affective resolution or procedural regulation probably depends upon the depth of the differences characterizing the conflicting value communities and the extent to which they must interact in the areas of conflict. A society characterized by significant value disagreement may still be relatively conflict free, as long as these differences are seen as private matters of conscience and an essential consensus (either affective or procedural) exists in those areas of public concern. Alternatively, a relatively broad consensus does not guarantee social peace if the value communities still conflict on critical matters of mutual interest.

COUNTERPOINT TO CHAPTER 3
On Revolution and Nihilism

REVOLUTIONS DEVELOP out of the polarization of meaning in contexts demanding mutuality. The areas of discord cannot therefore be defined as private matters but must be ones demanding common recognition and resolution. Jon P. Gunnemann argues that such a politicized polarization arises when a significant portion of the population challenges the prevailing theodicy of a sociopolitical order.[1] Following Thomas O'Dea, Gunnemann observes that human beings inevitably confront four contexts of social evil: scarcity, uncertainty, powerlessness, and human perversity.[2] His secularized use of the concept of theodicy thus involves "not justifying God but justifying evil and legitimating social inequities" that arise from and sustain the four contexts of evil.[3] A theodicy does not concern all aspects of social interaction but obviously affects certain matters of central importance and mutual interest.

Gunnemann develops an analogy with Kuhn's notion of a paradigm, arguing that just as scientific revolutions are characterized by paradigm shifts, social revolutions involve shifts in theodicies. The established theodicy is progressively undermined by "anomalous evils" which it cannot plausibly justify. Anomalies alone, however, cannot produce a revolution; rather, a new paradigmatic solution to the problem of experienced evil must be developed and accepted by a significant segment of the populace as a more adequate justification of the inevitable patterns of domination and subordination. Once a "theodic shift" has occurred, there is no easy return to the earlier theodicy. "For those undergoing a transformation of consciousness in a revolution, this irreversibility takes on all the characteristics of irresistibility and even of necessity."[4]

When a theodicy is challenged, disputes over the nature of good and evil can no longer be adjudicated. The absence of any neutral ground means that "revolution poses a kind of moral dilemma that undercuts the usual starting points for developing a political ethic."[5] As Gunnemann notes, "An appeal to the order of creation or natural law will not be persuasive to those who believe that creation and nature are about to be transformed radically."[6]

Revolutionary conflicts, from this perspective, exhibit four problems: First, the issues involved cannot be privatized, because they involve patterns of mutual domination and subordination. Second, the possibility of affective identification is nil, for the opposing sides see each other as the embodiment of evil. Third, a rational consensus cannot be achieved, owing to the absence of any consensual ground on which to base a free and open discourse. Finally, a consensus on procedures cannot be developed as long as neither side can entertain the possibility of compromise. Only coercion and conquest remain.

The threat of nihilism for politics is even greater than revolutionary dualism. Nihilism leads to the atomization, rather than the polarization, of shared meaning. At least in situations of revolutionary dualism, the contending sides share meanings with their comrades. Complete value atomization is perhaps even less likely than total polarization, but, as social interactions become more atomized, the foundation of shared meaning decays as surely as it would under progressive polarization.

One hundred years ago, Nietzsche foresaw the consequences of what he termed "the death of God"—that is, the loss of a common faith in an absolute ground of meaning. As the "tide of faith" recedes, human beings would face the task of reconstructing value and meaning beyond the illusions of previously determined good and evil. This responsibility, as Nietzsche's own decline into insanity implies, easily leads to nihilistic disintegration.

Richard Rubenstein sadly notes that the bloody history of the past century demonstrates

that rights do not belong to men by nature. To the extent that men have rights, they have them only as members of the polis, the political community, and there is no polis or Christian commonwealth of nations. All that men possess by nature is the necessity to participate in the incessant life and death struggle for existence of any animal. Furthermore, unlike other animals, men have no fixed instinctual structure that regulates their behavior and limits their aggression against members of the same species. Outside of the polis there are no inborn restraints on the human exercise of destructive power.[7]

Any reversal of the entropic thrust of nihilism must come, therefore, from human beings creating their own shared limits and mutual responsibilities. This is the challenge of the politics of the future.

4

THE POLITICS OF DEFINITION:

Explaining Coercion in Utopia

> "Just" and "unjust" exist, accordingly, only after
> the institution of the law.... To speak of just or
> unjust *in itself* is quite senseless; *in itself*, of
> course, no injury, assault, exploitation, destruc-
> tion can be "unjust," since life operates *essen-*
> *tially*, that is in its basic functions, through
> injury, assault, exploitation, destruction and
> simply cannot be thought of at all without this
> character.
>
> NIETZSCHE

*This essay has appeared in a somewhat different form as "Coercion, Force, Violence, and
Utopia" in Arthur L. Kalleberg et al., eds.,* Dissent and Affirmation: Essays in Honor of
Mulford Q. Sibley *(Bowling Green, Ohio: Bowling Green University Popular Press,
1983), pp. 49–66.*

The Politics of Definition

DEFINITIONS ARE TOOLS, not truths, their value determined in use, not in terms of their approximation of some transcendent ideal.[1] This pragmatic view of definition highlights its essentially political function: successful definition shapes mutual response and thereby helps to establish and maintain communities of shared meaning. Disputes over appropriate definition are thus political conflicts.

The politics of definition, to be sure, may involve clarity and logic, which are, after all, instruments of control. The utility of such controls over response presupposes, however, the existence of a fairly fundamental consensus on language and principles of critique within which logical discourse can proceed. In the absence of such a consensus, and even with it if the problem being construed is sufficiently vague, definitional debates often draw upon more overt instruments of power.* The dolorous history of doctrinal disputes among religious or ideological factions amply illustrates the potentially bloody character of definitional conflict.

The natural sciences, given the frequent presence of a scholarly consensus on the means and ends of inquiry, often approximate the rational ideal of definition. Political science, in contrast, seems afflicted by a surfeit of tools ostensibly de-

---

*We must not forget that logic, too, is a form of power, perhaps in its way more obnoxious than others. When defeated by someone's superior argument, we not only are controlled but feel the fool, as well. At least when we are overcome by coercion or bribery, we can still believe, in our heart of hearts, that we were right. Reason may fail so often because human beings resist conclusions that entail not only defeat but also a confession of incompetence.

signed for the same purpose. Even under circumstances where apparent analytical clarity can be proposed in defining political terms, the distinctions made often disguise an ongoing, substantive process of considerable complexity and fluidity in the wider society of which the scholarly community is a part. The interconnected concepts of coercion, force, and violence provide a central example of these links between analysis and politics.

Two verbal strategies can be followed in combating polysemantic concepts. First, a term could be construed so broadly as to cover almost every conceivable variation. This seems to be the case when Samuel Dubois Cook says "to coerce is to compel or restrain the human will by an outside agent."[2] He then elaborates:

Coercion may be physical or nonphysical (psychological, spiritual, intellectual, aesthetic), violent or nonviolent, public (official) or private, individual or collective, overt or covert, legitimate or illegitimate, positive (rewards or promise of benefits) or negative (punishment, or threat of deprivation), formal or informal, etc.[3]

The breadth of Cook's definition contrasts sharply with the narrower focus of Christian Bay who limits coercion to acts involving "physical violence" or sanctions strong enough to deter an individual from a strongly desired course of action.[4] Bay thinks that coercion is "the supreme political evil."[5] Given the breadth of his definition, if Cook had concluded the same thing, he would condemn the vast preponderance of human behavior. Consequently, he argues that coercion is "ethically neutral," its moral quality being determined by "its purposes, forms, processes, consequences, and alternative possibilities inherent in the objective situation."[6]

The strategy of definitional inclusiveness, of course, manages polysemy by incorporating it. Once accepted, discussion inevitably focuses upon the multitude of different "forms" of coercion and their respective implications. The second approach reverses this bias by attempting to split off those meanings which appear unessential in an effort to hone the concept into a sharper tool of inquiry. This is the strategy we follow in distinguishing coercion first from what it is not and then attempting to delineate what it is. Once some apparent definitional clarity has been established, we then proceed to "deconstruct" it by arguing that each distinction made depends upon a complex consensus in the wider political community—a consensus that is in a constant state of challenge and flux. When the politics of definition in this area has been clarified, we explore the extent to which it is possible, or even desirable, to eliminate coercion in utopia.

Defining Coercion

In defining coercion, the associations which are better accounted for by other concepts need to be bracketed in order to concentrate on those elements that appear more essential.

Coercion is not simply a matter of harm. Human beings can be harmed by many events, including natural conditions as well as the activities of others. Natural events certainly do *constrain* human activities, but to say that a flood or a hurricane coerces people seems inappropriate.[7] The concept of coercion is better confined to something human beings do to one another.

Coercion, however, needs to be distinguished from humanly imposed constraints. Coercive actions, or their threat, *may* constrain behavior, but they need not; in any case, constraints also emerge from other sources such as habit or conscience. Moreover, people are continually constrained by the accidental or incidental side effects of the activities of others. Similarly, a parent who stops a child from running into a busy street is protecting, not coercing, him. To equate coercion with all constraint seems unjustifiably broad and misleading.[8]

Likewise, those commentators who suggest the possibility of "coercive bribes" construe the concept too imprecisely.[9] People may be induced to act in ways they would not otherwise consider through a variety of means, some of which are coercive. Enticements, however, if accepted, leave an individual better off *in his own judgment*, a rather odd consequence to term coercive.[10] The concept of "power" seems sufficiently broad to embrace both positive and negative inducements without stretching coercion in the same fashion.

Finally, the definition of coercion should not be made dependent upon the behavior of the coerced. Michael Bayles, for example, argues that coercion "is an achievement word; it denotes success."[11] Accordingly, if a person refuses to comply with the wishes of the coercer and absorbs the consequences, then coercion has not taken place, although it has been attempted. This rather interesting distinction, however, unduly emphasizes the behavior of the victim at the expense of that of the perpetrator. Moreover, it asserts that the intention of the coercer is to change the behavior of the victim. This *may* be the case when a coercive sanction is threatened, but when it is actually imposed, the coercer may be less concerned with the victim's subsequent behavior than with other matters like redressing a perceived wrong or deterring similar behavior on the part of others. Further, to argue that coercion has not occurred unless the deterrence succeeds would impose an impossible task of empirical verification on the definition. To construe coercion as necessarily changing the behavior of the coerced seems again to be identifying it with the more diffuse concepts of constraint or power.

Coercion, then, is a human activity, not one of the physical universe; it can constrain, but it might not; it is a form of power, but not the only one; coercive threats are different from coercive acts, and both threats and acts may have multiple consequences, intended and unintended. None of these factors, however, identifies any essential, distinguishing characteristic of coercion.

Many definitions of coercion, consequently, tend to conflate the concept with others that are more broadly construed. After bracketing these associated ideas, one irreducible monad remains: coercion harms a person. Coercion, therefore, belongs to that class of human activitites that harms people. Coercion must be further distinguished from those actions that harm others either accidently or incidently. Coercion, from this perspective, is a form of human action where the perpetrator intends to harm the victim. Secondary intentions may accompany this primary purpose, such as the intent of altering the behavior of the victim and/or others in some fashion, but the distinguishing characteristic of coercion may be defined as intentional harm.

Organizations may be considered externally coercive if their primary purpose, like that of the military, is to inflict harm on others. All institutional arrangements constrain the activities of those who take part in them, and coercion may be one of the means used to control the behavior of the members of an organization. However, unless coercion or its threat is the major method of controlling behavior, as perhaps it is in a prison, it would be inaccurate to describe an institution as internally coercive. Admittedly, observers of different ideological persuasions might interpret the same set of social arrangements differently. A laissez-faire economist would see the condition of workers in a capitalist economy as the consequence of impersonal market forces, while a Marxist would consider the workers' plight as the result of deliberate exploitation to maximize profits.

"Force" and "violence" can be considered the two basic types of coercion—the difference between them depends upon what constitutes "acceptable" coercion within social relations. Violence consists of those acts of coercion that violate the boundaries defining the acceptable use of coercion, whereas force denotes those acts that lie within the boundaries of acceptability. The notion of "acceptable coercion" implies a judgment that the benefits of the coercive act outweigh the harm done, as when the police use force to apprehend law breakers or a violently insane person is confined.

This process of term splitting yields a simple progressive differentiation as shown in the diagram. Unfortunately, the analytical clarity of the diagrammed definition is undercut by considerable operational obscurity. Indeed, an examination of the ambiguities attendant on the meaning of these distinctions in practice reveals some of the dimensions of coercion in social relations.

Although the imposition of meaning is something that humans do in human communities, this task seldom proceeds with confidence-inspiring clarity or consensus. Human beings invest enormous energy in efforts to determine meaning (i.e., appropriate response), but with varying degrees of success. Politics, as we have argued, may be defined as the process through which shared meanings are established, altered, or abandoned within communities.

Consequently, the existential meanings of the distinctions between harmful and harmless actions, intentional and acciden-

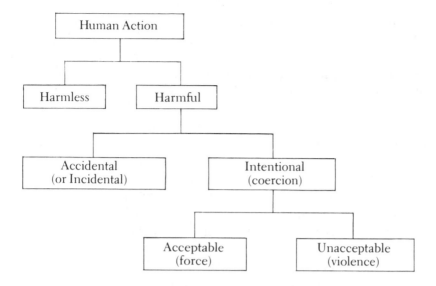

Coercion: A Diagrammed Definition

tal harm, and unacceptable and acceptable coercion are established essentially through political action and are, therefore, inherently dynamic and conflictual. Yet, conflict and dynamism need not imply total chaos; in fact, they seldom do. How the meanings of these distinctions are established, challenged, and changed within communities, however, is central to our understanding of coercion in social relations.

Harm

Reason, Locke asserts, teaches that "no one ought to harm another in his life, health, liberty, or possessions."[12] Reason, unfortunately, teaches no such thing; indeed, it often instructs the opposite. Locke's assertion, however, does reflect what is conventionally, if not universally, perceived as a "hierarchy of harm" descending roughly from loss of life, through loss of limb or health, then liberty, and finally to loss of possessions. Of course, even this rough hierarchy founders upon the reef of individual and cultural variance. A person may well prefer death to torture or loss of a limb to the confiscation of all of his possessions. No transpersonal Benthamite calculus exists for definitively establishing degrees of comparative harm. Most of us would probably agree, however, that the loss of any or all of these four constitutes harm, and many would add other violations as well.*

What, though, does "loss" mean? Presumably, a person cannot lose what was not previously possessed. John Donne aside, each man's death does not diminish me, at least not in the same way that it diminishes the deceased. If my neighbor is robbed, he suffers the loss, not me, except possibly through the decline in my sense of personal security, but my loss differs from his.

Previous possession alone, though, is insufficient to establish a loss. If my neighbor takes back what was stolen from him by the thief, he does not thereby harm the thief, for the thief was not entitled to the goods, and my neighbor was. Pure restitution, if it could be determined, is not harmful; only if some additional penalty is imposed would harm be done to the thief. Only when a person suffers the loss of something to which he was previously entitled has he been harmed. †

Entitlements to possessions, like other shared meanings, are established in human communities, and, like other forms of meaning, questions of entitlement may be shrouded by ambiguity and dispute. In a situation where entitlement is unclear, it becomes debatable whether harm has been done. The hierarchy of harm noted earlier may reflect not so much the recognition of "intersubjectively transmissible" degrees of harm, as the clarity of title. Thus, titles to life and limb seem fairly well founded, whereas those to liberty and property are somewhat more nebulous.

Nevertheless, even in areas where title seems well established, it still may not be absolute, unambiguous, or universal;

---

*Since the discussion of these rights is simply intended to illustrate problems with making certain distinctions, no effort is made to provide an exhaustive list of what human beings may view as harmful.

†I choose to use the word *entitlement* rather than *right* because I think it is less likely to imply some transcendent ultimate, and it can be applied to areas where the concept of right seems somewhat grandiose.

debates over meaning can still occur. The abortion controversy aptly illustrates this point. Those who advocate abortion on demand hold that the fetus, being part of a woman's body, possesses no independent title to life; therefore, the termination of the pregnancy cannot constitute a harmful act. Indeed, to prevent a woman from doing so if she wishes is viewed as harmful in that she suffers a loss of liberty and, perhaps, other possessions.

Those who oppose abortion adopt a quite different perspective. They see the fetus as possessing a title to life from the moment of conception and believe ending that life is an act of murder. The fact that the fetus temporarily occupies a woman's body and gains sustenance from it is incidental. Parents, they would argue, do not have the right to terminate their offspring merely because the children are totally dependent on them and are a source of considerable inconvenience.

A third, intermediate position is also possible. A fetus can be conceded to have a claim to life, and abortion, therefore, harms it. Nevertheless, abortions may be accepted under certain strictly defined circumstances, such as to save the mother's life. Such an intervention would then be a case of "justifiable homicide."

Harm, then, even in terms of the deprivation of something apparently so fundamental as life, does not have any political reality until so recognized by a community. Animals who die for human purposes suffer no harm in this sense except insofar as they have been bestowed with certain entitlements by the community. Those who empathize with the sufferings of animals butchered for food or used in medical experiments probably think not at all about the millions of microbes slaughtered when they take antibiotics. Microbes, unfortunately for them, are rather remote from our consciousness, whereas chimps and other "higher" life forms partake more closely of our humanity and thus are granted, at least by some people, certain entitlements of which they may be deprived. Man is the measure of all things in the sense that all entitlements *within* human political communities can only be derived *from* human communities.

If the meaning of harm is derivative from the community even in an area apparently as absolute as the "right to life," the concept becomes progressively more disputable when other

Lockean rights are considered. Title to limb or health relates quite closely to questions of life but with some additional ambiguity. We may, after all, have part of our bodies removed for the benefit of the whole. Surgical removal of a diseased organ could be calculated as the acceptance of a lesser harm to avoid a greater evil. Yet, it appears equally plausible to focus only on the benefit gained. Most people do not view doctors as harming them to prevent greater harm but simply as helping them preserve their health. This is not to say that they cannot or should not recognize the harm done to them, merely that they need not and probably do not see harm in this situation.*

When the presumed benefits of medical treatments are challenged, however, questions of harm do arise. Recently, doubts have been raised about certain forms of elective surgery, chemotherapy, and radiology, and people are more inclined to consider questions of harm in these areas where none existed before. Nevertheless, the harm, if so defined, is still perceived as incidental or accidental, regrettable but not coercive.

Another related consequence of the divisibility of limbs is that harm to a person's health can be a matter of degree. One cannot, in any socially significant sense, be more or less dead; one can be more or less tortured. Losses suffered to liberty and property are also questions of degree. Problems of establishing and comparing the extent of the losses to various persons' health, liberty, and property add yet another ambiguity to culturally derivative notions of harm. Debates develop over what point of change in an individual's health, liberty, or property harm actually occurs.

Determination of harm to liberty and property are further complicated beyond the question of degree. Concepts of life and limb have at least one foot, so to speak, in a biological reality independent of culture. Notions of liberty and property, however, appear to be completely culturally dependent. A person's

---

*If one accepts an organic view of the state, then an analogous argument might be developed: The individual may be lost for the benefit of the whole. In an extreme organic state, the individual would have no entitlements to anything. Harm could be done only to the collective. The individual might still be protected, but only because it is in the interests of the organic community to do so.

title to liberty or property and the degree to which this title may have been violated are impossible to determine until some common agreement as to the meaning of these terms has been reached. Granted that some debates do occur over clinical definitions of death or health, these disputes lack the breadth or significance of the arguments over the nature of liberty or property.

Generally, liberty seems to imply some idea of space; most basically, a literal space within which to move, more figuratively, "space" to express a range of opinions or engage in a variety of behaviors.[13] Positively, liberty may suggest the possession of the resources necessary to utilize available space. In any case, space is always restricted to some extent; in no community are either liberties or the resources needed to realize them unlimited. Harm to a person's liberty, therefore, involves the imposition of restriction *beyond* those that have been conventionally established. Of course, the definition of the "appropriate" limits on liberty, and thus where harm begins, is often what is in dispute.

The concept of property is also culturally dependent, and questions of harm to property relate to how property is construed. The range of this particular problem extends from Proudhon's dictum that private property is theft, to Robert Nozick's assertion that taxes are theft. In contexts where private title is clearly defined and commonly accepted, harm is relatively easy to identify, but in the case of community property or so-called "free goods," just who is harming whom, or whether anyone is being harmed at all, is more difficult to establish. People tend to exploit and pollute resources held in common because of the difficulty in establishing individual responsibility. The concept of harm is further attenuated when stretched to cover damage to the collective in the absence of demonstrable damage to specific individuals.

One final complication seems worth mentioning: the interconnectedness of the human enterprise and the resultant possibilities for indirectly affecting others. Interdependency could be used to argue that no title is absolute, not even to life, for a person's actions necessarily affect others. To take one's own life, to exploit one's own property, to abuse one's own body, therefore, indirectly harm others, and this indirect harm could justify limiting entitlements.

The concept of harm, then, emerges somewhat unsteadily from the ongoing efforts of human beings to establish shared meanings within communities. Whether a harm is perceived as being done depends on whether an entitlement exists at all, and if it does, to what extent. In relatively stable communities, a widely shared consensus may exist, but even under these conditions, the consensus will seldom go unchallenged for very long.

Intention

Harm, once established, must be intended to be considered coercive; that is, coercers must direct themselves to harm the victim. This condition adds the next layer of ambiguity to the concept of coercion, for not only are such directives commonly covert and difficult to assess, but the consideration and coherence informing the directives also varies, and the "coerciveness" of the harmful act partly depends upon this "degree of directiveness." Acts that are identical in terms of their consequences for the victims (e.g., they are dead) can be evaluated as having different significance. Somewhat arbitrarily, five levels of directiveness may be distinguished:

Accidental Harm. An accident occurs when the harmful event is unforeseen, essentially random, and unavoidable. A child darting in front of a car whose driver is in conformance with all rules and norms of safe operation of the vehicle is killed accidently. The child has been harmed (according to communally accepted titles) but has hardly been coerced.

Incidental Harm. Related to accidental harm, but worth distinguishing from it, are harmful consequences that may occur as a secondary concomitant to an action. The harm is not the intention of the action, but it is recognized beforehand as a possible outcome. An example would be a patient who dies on the operating table. All surgery involves risk, but normally the medical staff would not be judged as coercing the deceased.

Negligent Harm. Harmful consequences are sometimes judged to be avoidable, even though they were not specifically intended by the perpetrator. For example, if the driver of the automobile had not been speeding or if the surgeon had not been intoxicated, the deaths of the victims *might* have been avoided. The possible consequences of speeding or drinking could be foreseen and, thus, avoided, but this is a question of probability and introduces another area of judgment. Negligence implies a degree of culpability; nonetheless, it seems dubious to consider negligent harm coercive.

Diminished Capacity Harm. In one sense, negligence contributes to a diminished capacity to *avoid* doing harm. At this next level a directive to harm is present, but that directive is mitigated by some factor that diminishes the capacity of the perpetrators to recognize the implications of their actions. Insanity and passion are two arguments of diminished capacity. The idea of diminished capacity, admittedly, implies some notion of "full" capacity and thus is a matter of degree. This level of intentional harm seems plausibly labeled as coercive, although culpability would be lessened.*

Full Capacity Harm. "Premeditation" is the concept most commonly associated with the highest level of intentionality, but this presumes the premeditation is done with the exercise of a person's full mental capacity. Harm that is the intention of full capacity premeditation, however that might be ascertained, implies the greatest degree of culpability and is the clearest form of coercion defined as intentional harm.

Another's intent, especially in the complexity suggested above, is impossible to know directly. Nevertheless, people cannot avoid assessing intent in responding to the social world. This paradoxical plight injects an additional element of instability into social relations generally and, in particular, into the interpretation of harmful acts. "Appropriate" response depends upon the interpretation of intent which is not directly accessible. Indirectly established intent, however, need not be based upon haphazard and essentially subjective guesswork. A motivational construct can be formulated by drawing upon a careful (and intersubjectively transmissible) analysis of the cultural matrix

---

*In fact, in a court of law, culpability may be deemed less for some instances of diminished capacity (e.g., an insanity plea) than negligent harm.

within which the act occurs.[14] Such analysis permits a plausible narrowing of the intentional range, which, even if it does not establish definitive truth, at least sets forth "probably" intent. Such reasoning proceeds overtly in a court of law and more or less consciously whenever human beings try to interpret one another's covert motives and meanings. Yet no matter how carefully we conduct our analyses, there will always remain a gap between the interpreted and the actual intent. This, in turn, suggests the possibility that any two people may assess intent differently. Divergent opinions in this matter mean that even though agreeing that a harmful act has occurred, these two people may differ as to whether the action should be termed coercive.

An epistemological objection may also be raised here to the biases of "methodological individualism."[15] By focusing upon individual intent, our approach to conceptualizing coercion misses those social arrangements whose consequences are harmful, even though the individuals who embody the arrangement in their responses do not specifically intend harm at any point. Rather, they are simply doing their assigned task within a system of mutual expectations. Systems of shared meaning can produce collective results different from any specific intention.

One response to this difficulty might be to argue that in most cases those directing such harmful social arrangements are aware of and do intend the harmful consequences. This leaves open the question of the extent to which the contributing cogs should be held culpable for the collective consequences of their actions. In those cases where all the participants and perhaps even the victims remain ignorant of the harmful effects of their systems of shared meaning, the arrangements might be termed exploitive or oppressive, as opposed to specifically co-ercive. Coercion could then be confined to the level of individual relations.

Such distinctions, obviously, are pragmatic, and we need to remain aware of the potential biases of any particular approach. In any case, our purpose here is not to resolve this methodological dispute but to illustrate the political dimensions of definitional arguments.

Acceptability

Intentionally harmful acts range from the essentially trivial (e.g., mild forms of parental discipline) to the devastatingly destructive. Moreover, desirable or not, coercion suffuses social relations. A distinction between "force" and "violence" may be based upon whether or not a particular coercive act is considered to be "acceptable." Such a definition explicitly recognizes that the meanings of force and violence are socially established and admits the possibility that two people may evaluate the same coercive act differently.

Despite, or perhaps because of, the possibility for disagreement, one function of politics generally and of the modern state in particular is to determine the boundaries defining the acceptable use of coercion. The state does not so much claim a monopoly on the "legitimate" use of coercion as the ultimate responsibility for demarking the boundaries governing the use of coercion.[16]

In a relatively stable social order, the commonly agreed-upon definition of acceptable coercion, whether set through custom or law, is usually biased in favor of the status quo. Acts of greater harm will be tolerated if perceived as essentially defending the established distribution of resources and values. Alternatively, coercive acts that are seen as undermining the established order will tend to violate the boundaries. This does not necessarily mean that "anything goes" as long as it is defensive, or that all redistributive coercive acts will necessarily be deemed violent. The definition of force may be biased, but the extent of that bias may vary. In fact, one possible definition of an "open" society is one where "establishment" coercion (e.g., police powers) is strictly regulated, while certain forms of redistributive coercion (e.g., industrial strikes) are tolerated. The factors affecting the distinction between force and violence are illustrated in the accompanying diagram.

The distinction between force and violence requires four further clarifications: First, "acceptable" does not imply conformance with a universally agreed-upon standard of the good. The word was chosen, instead of possible alternatives such as

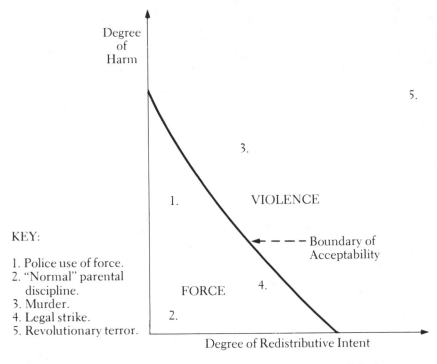

Factors Affecting the Distinction between Force and Violence

"legitimate" or "justifiable," in order to emphasize its situational character; that is, acceptability is determined by the dominant systems of shared meaning in a culture. We may argue, therefore, that the use of force by a tyrant is evil and unjustifiable, while the use of violence against a tyrant is justifiable and good. Acceptability in any particular social order is therefore determined empirically, albeit with inevitable interpretational ambiguity.

Second, the boundary between force and violence, even in a relatively stable social order, is not always clear-cut. Inevitably, disputes arise over the acceptability of certain acts of coercion, and, in modern systems, a major purpose of adjudication is to make such determinations.

Third, the boundary, based as it is on conventionally established criteria, can change over time and vary from place to place. The increasingly stringent restrictions placed on harsh parental discipline illustrate this process of change in the United States over the past century.

Fourth, if the consensus over the definition of the boundary disintegrates, then the distinction between force and violence collapses. The complete dissolution of shared meaning in this critical area casts the community back into a Hobbesian state of nature where each individual is his or her own judge as to what is acceptable. This Hobbesian extremity, however, is probably only of hypothetical interest, as people will still share meaning within groups even while contending over the carcass of the wider community.

To regard an act of coercion as acceptable may also be viewed as involving the suspension of a conventionally recognized entitlement. Within limits, parents may suspend certain entitlements of their children, ones derived primarily from the children's participation in the small community of the family. Other entitlements, such as that to life, are generally recognized as deriving from the children's membership in a wider community of shared meaning, a community in which the intentional killing of a child would be an act of violence. Acceptable coercion or force, then, is determined by what entitlements exist within a community and the circumstances under which they may be suspended. These conditions are both variable and open to dispute.

Coercion, force, and violence have no meaning outside of a community; to establish their meaning, or any other meaning, takes a continuous political act of considerable complexity. To be coerced means to be harmed, but harm can occur only with the loss of an entitlement, and entitlements exist only within communities. Harm is also a concept of degree, but the degree of harm is at least partially rooted in nontransmissible perceptions. Coercion presumes that the harm was intended, but intention, too, is a question of degree and can only be indirectly assessed. The distinction between force and violence depends upon the concept of acceptability, which itself may be more or less consensually established and fluctuates over time and space. Finally, all these meanings are open to challenge and change.

One might wonder, given this complexity, how any consensus is established. Without belaboring the issue, two paradoxically related answers may be suggested: (1) People do not think very much about what they are doing, yet (2) they invest enormous energies in their efforts to do it. Human beings tend not to recognize the extent to which they are responsible for the meaning of the world, even though the point of all political behavior is precisely to establish such shared meaning.

Coercion and Utopia

The threat and practice of coercion pervade human relations, a condition that stimulates a variety of responses. Hobbes was so frightened by his vision of unrestrained, reciprocal coercion that he was willing to submit to a highly coercive bondage to escape it. The Leviathan, in the terms developed previously, acquires legitimacy to the extent to which it establishes and effectively defends a restrictive distinction between force and violence; it uses force to contain violence.

Other theorists judge coercion in terms of the ends for which it is used beyond the coercive control of coercion.

Illegitimately lodged and used, [coercion] is a deadly weapon of human enslavement, oppression, and exploitation. Legitimately institutionalized and utilized, it is a unique agent of human freedom and the enlargement and enrichment of human experience. It can be a tool for the exploitation of the weak by the strong, but it can equally serve both for the protection of the weak against the strong and for the humbling and weakening of the strong and the strengthening and elevation of the weak.[17]

Finally, some see at least extreme forms of coercion, whether defined as force or violence, as an absolute evil. Mulford Sibley, for example, argues that "violent coercion" (that which takes or severely harms life) is so inherently evil that it necessarily corrupts the ends for which it is used, whatever their merits.[18]

Yet, as Robert Paul Wolff notes, even those who argue that coercion can be justified, still view it as an evil that needs to be minimized and not as ethically neutral.[19] Harm, however defined, is unpleasant, at least for the victim. Consequently, a place where people do not harm, or if they harm, they do not coerce, or if they coerce, they do not unacceptably violate one another, holds out considerable allure.

Utopianism, at its best, attempts to raise the level of critical consciousness, introduce new meanings, and move the political community in some specific direction (either toward a eutopian or away from a dystopian projection). Such speculation, it must be emphasized, takes place within some community of meaning. No "metacommunal" position exists from which to criticize and expound, for critics can move from one community of meaning only to another more or less closely related to the first.

Utopian thought, especially that which attempts to project a "happier place," is commonly criticized for attempting to impose a rationalistic coherence from above on communities of meaning that emerge organically, incrementally, and indeterminately from below. Nevertheless, utopian critiques and projects may be used to expand recognition of the theater of possibility in a community, even if they seldom succeed in remaking a social order.

Before considering the dimensions of a place free from coercion, two misleading antinomies may be usefully abandoned: Coercion is not the direct antithesis of either reason or freedom in social relations. Reason reflects the drive to order, explain, and ultimately control the world, and coercion may be the resort of reason when other means fail. The imposition of reason upon a recalcitrant "reality," whether the physical universe or the social world, can be enormously destructive. As Richard Rubenstein argues with respect to the Holocaust, we cannot understand the use of coercion of even genocidal scope until we recognize the extent to which it may be a "reasonable" solution to a difficult problem.[20]

Nor should coercion be considered the simple antithesis of freedom, at least freedom defined as the absence of restraint.* The relation of coercion and freedom so defined is somewhat more complex. Coercion may be used to restrain, but it is

---

*The concept of "freedom" is examined further in Chapter 7.

neither the only nor necessarily the most effective form of restraint. Other mechanisms for channeling behavior, whether
external inducements or internalized habits of obedience, may
be far more successful, especially since they are less likely to be
recognized as restraints. Whatever its other demerits, when
coercion is used to control behavior, at least there is little likelihood of mistaking what is going on.

Coercion, then, is not the best, but merely the last, resort of
someone attempting to control the behavior of others. Its absence from a social relation does not necessarily signify the presence of freedom; ironically, the reverse may be true. A social
arrangement that tolerates a fair degree of freedom of action
from its participants may have to accept a certain amount of
coercion as a concomitant for loosening the bonds of other
restraints.

The Absence of Harm

A "harmless" place is either a horror or a dream, either a society
without entitlements or without flaw. Where there are no entitlements, there can be no harm. Such a condition may appear so
pathologically extreme as to merit little consideration, but this
conclusion would be dangerous. Although the full realization of
such an arrangement seems unlikely, its partial incorporation is
a fact of social existence: Not all the elements of the environment are granted entitlements within the community. Harm
may be limited by restricting the coverage of the concept of
harm. Where entitlements are not presumed, there can be no
consciousness of harm.

Given the debates concerning the rights of the unborn or of
animals, it might appear that the concept of harm is being extended to incorporate wider circles of existence. The history
of the twentieth century, however, confounds such optimism.
If entitlements have a meaningful existence only within communities organized to defend them, it is possible to eliminate entitlements through expulsion from the community. The
German Jews, for example, were first cast out of the community
and only later destroyed. Perhaps the initial act harmed them,

but the full enormity of the Nazi innovation is that the extermination of the Jews did not involve any harm within the Nazi
community of meaning. Of course, harm may have been
done in terms of the wider world community ("crimes against
humanity"), and certainly it was harmful in terms of the Jewish
community. While the Holocaust was proceeding, however,
the behavior of the "world community" indicates that the
Jews were considered outcasts by more than the Germans.
The participation of the Jews in their own destruction, moreover, suggests that even they accepted, at least to some extent,
the meanings of their exterminators.[21]

If limiting entitlements, in some sense, simplifies the task of
limiting harm, then expanding entitlements may increase the
probability of harmful events. Even assuming complete knowledge and perfect benevolence (two truly utopian assumptions),
harm could still occur as a result of scarcity. Thus, a doctor
might still be faced with a situation where either the mother or
infant must die. Only by eliminating scarcity as well would the
possibility of tragic harm be avoided. A society of limitless
knowledge, benevolence, and resources is, of course, heaven.
No harm is done, therefore, in either heaven (the realm of no
limits) or hell (the realm of no rights).

The Absence of Coercion

In a world of both certain entitlements and limits, some harm is
inevitable, but it need not be coercive harm. To be coercive, the
harm must be intended, which assumes that people can "intend"
anything at all and that they will at times intend to harm. When
stripped of its metaphysical connotations, intention simply
means that people's actions reflect directions they give themselves. Intending is a form of behavior—verbal behavior—
though it is usually covert.

To intend anything, however, also implies that one *could*
have intended to do something else. If people's actions are
merely the instruments of forces beyond their control or even
conception, then their sensation of self-directiveness is an
illusion. Such a determined condition resembles, but is not

identical to, having one's behavior structured through the manipulation of external constraints. Placing choice in chains, however, does not deny that human beings still retain the capacity to intend otherwise, or even to act otherwise, if willing to accept the costs of defiance. Complete determinism denies precisely this capacity, and human behavior becomes essentially similar to events in the physical universe; therefore, any harm humans inflict upon one another has the same cognitive status as other harmful events in nature. It would be as inappropriate to term harmful human behavior "coercive" under conditions of absolute determinism as it would earthquakes and other consequences of fate.*

Such a world is envisioned by B. F. Skinner. A society where behavior is perfectly determined through conditioning is not only "beyond freedom and dignity" but beyond coercion as well.[22] Harm could still be inflicted and punishments meted out, but notions of coercion, force, and violence, as we have defined them, would exist only as convenient fictions useful to the process of operant conditioning. In theory, harm resulting from "breakdowns" in conditioning, as opposed to that arising accidently, incidently, or as a consequence of scarcity, could be minimized in a completely deterministic community. "Walden Two" is a happy place for Skinner in part because harm is minimized and coercion impossible. His utopia is rightly considered a perfect totalitarian order.

In order to coerce, in the sense used here, people must have the capacity to choose to do or avoid doing harm. If the capacity to choose, to intend anything, is assumed, could a world be imagined where people would freely choose not to harm one another? The answer, it would seem, depends on the function of coercion in social relations as much as upon whether one believes human beings to be inherently "evil" or flawed. Coercion,

---

*I am not attempting to solve all the problems raised by determinism, problems which remain largely unresolved by modern philosophy (see Richard Taylor, "Determinism," *The Encyclopedia of Philosophy*, volume 2, pp. 359–73). Rather, I am attempting to indicate some of the implications for the concept of coercion that come from assuming a position of "hard determinism."

as noted earlier, is one way, perhaps the ultimate way, of imposing meaning on the world. As Morse Peckham rather cynically notes:

The only final way to prove that [a person] is indeed mistaken is to kill him. Throughout human history it has been a very popular way of defeating an opponent in arguments about meaning. Certainly it has an almost irresistible charm.[23]

Whether a parent is disciplining a child during toilet training or armies are slaughtering each other in the mud of the battlefield, human beings coerce each other primarily because of disputes over meaning. In order to minimize or eliminate coercion, meaning would have to be definitively established to the satisfaction of all the concerned parties through ways short of coercion. This is what politics is all about—the effort to determine shared meanings. Political "success" is achieved when shared meanings are satisfactorily established through devices other than coercion, such as affective validation, bargaining, rational argument, or procedural regulation. Yet, none of these means of conflict resolution or regulation seems able to contain conflicts that arise from fundamentally incommensurate values that cannot be effectively compartmentalized and which engender competition over absolutely scarce resources (see Chapter 3). Moreover, even when shared meanings are established, they will eventually be undermined by inadequacy. Unless we assume a *perfect* fit between the mutually expected responses and the demands of the environment, all shared meanings can be destabilized by introducing elements of the situation for which they do not account. Even if the fit were perfect, shared meaning could still be undermined by cultural inconsistency and behavioral indeterminacy. The temptation to resort to coercion as a way to structure response is continuous, especially as the frustration over the failure of the other devices grows.

Another reason for the continued possibility of coercion in a free society relates to an earlier point. As restraints on behavior are relaxed, the range of behavior spreads.[24] No guarantee ensures that all aspects of this behavioral variation will be tolerable within a social arrangement. As theologians of "free will" have been noting for centuries, to be free implies the capacity for "sin." In the absence of other constraints, coercion may be necessary to protect the community from ultimate dissolution.

The Absence of Violence

If coercion cannot be eliminated, can it be contained? This objective is fundamental to the distinction between force and violence: to limit coercion to "acceptable" forms. Acceptable forms of coercion are determined empirically; the question whether these forms are desirable requires a subsequent normative judgment.

Coercion, for example, might be effectively contained in a system of "imperfect" totalitarianism, that is, a system that defines all, or nearly all, forms of state-directed coercion as being acceptable. Assuming the state possesses extensive coercive capabilities, it may well be able to enforce such a boundary. The totalitarian control is imperfect, however, because the state's reliance upon force signifies that other means of controlling behavior have failed. The use of regime terror, then, is a tribute to the continued presence of freedom (as deviance).

Unlimited state coercion is not a definition of acceptability that most political theorists would find desirable. Sibley, for example, condemns capital punishment as an intrinsic evil regardless of what justifications the regime provides or what legal niceties have been followed.[25] Acceptable coercion for Sibley would proscribe certain extremely harmful acts no matter who, regime or citizens, perpetrates them. Such a limitation, though, seems to presume an absolute entitlement—e.g., the right to life—that cannot be suspended under any circumstances. An "absolute" entitlement can exist only if recognized by and incorporated in a community. Once established, the temptation will always exist to qualify it (e.g., self-defense), and the debates over meaning will continue.

Apart from a notion of an absolute entitlement, arguments for limiting state coercion could be based upon principles of proportionality, due process, or pragmatism (i.e., unlimited state coercion causes destruction far in excess of any presumed benefits). These arguments are more judgmental than that from an absolute entitlement, which at least possesses surface clarity. Consequently, they are subject to continual dispute. Questions of proportionality can never be definitively resolve for, as Walter Kaufmann notes, a person's "just deserts" can never be incontrovertibly determined.[26] Concepts of due process are clearly rooted in culturally relative conditions. Arguments from pragmatism can be more or less well defended, but their truth or falsity can never be demonstrated, for following one policy negates the possibility of ever knowing the consequences of alternatives.

A second question, beyond the methods of limiting state coercion, concerns whether certain forms of coercion directed against the state should be accepted. The dominant distribution of values and resources, after all, also reflects an explanation or related set of explanations, and as such confronts the problem of adequacy. If the established order is necessarily imperfect, the need for change must be recognized. Coercion is one means at the disposal of those disputing over explanations. Granting the use of this means (however limited) to the side of the status quo, while denying it to the advocates of change, presumes that the status quo is more adequate than the alternatives. Such is the position of the conservative—not to deny the possibility of change altogether so much as to tip the scale in favor of what is.

Not surprisingly, those less convinced by the relative merits of the established order tend to favor equalizing the "debate," at least to some degree. If the system does not accept some forms of "innovative" coercion, the more radically inclined may well advocate violence. In the United States, and other reasonably open societies, certain forms of strikes and boycotts are tolerated even though their intent is clearly redistributive.

Interestingly, the major forms of redistributive coercion that appear to be accepted tend to be those that use the strategy of withheld behavior rather than direct attack. A refusal to cooperate, like a general strike, can be tremendously coercive, but the

harm is done indirectly. Theorists of the strategy of noncooperation argue that such coercion is less destructive of the warp and
woof of social relations and is less likely to corrupt otherwise
noble ends than direct attack.

Consequently, although the elimination of harm and coercion seems a highly improbable and even dubious objective,
perhaps an appropriate goal of utopian political action is to advocate a distinction between force and violence based on the
difference between the strategy of withheld behavior and noncooperation and that of direct attack. As Gene Sharp notes,
however, the credibility of such "indirect" coercive techniques
suffers from the myth of efficacy that surrounds strategies of
direct attack.[27] To be effective, admittedly, noncooperation
must involve something of value being withheld. The value of an
individual's or group's contribution to a wider community is partially a function of the degree of interdependence characterizing
that community. The more interdependent a social relationship,
the more effective a strategy of withheld behavior becomes, and,
for the same reason, strategies of direct attack become more
self-destructive. It is against those who are independent of us in
all other ways that the strategy of direct attack holds out its
greatest promise.

Noncooperation is not inherently good, for it may be used for
purposes as evil as the worst of conventional violence. But, in an
increasingly complex and interdependent world, it may be the
coercive alternative that becomes not only increasingly possible
but also more conducive to the survival of the species.

Conclusion: On Human Responsibility

The concepts of political philosophy tend to be dry, dead
things—"mummies," as Nietzsche once called them.[28] The
formal definitions of coercion, force, and violence offered here
are really no more lively than most. In order to vivify them, I

have argued that the formal meanings take on life only in communities of shared meaning through a process filled with flux, conflict, and uncertainty. Richard Rorty remarks:

If there is one thing we have learned about concepts in recent decades it is that to have a concept is to be able to use a word, that to have a mastery of concepts is to be able to use a language, and that languages are created rather than discovered. We should renounce the idea that we have access to some superconcepts which are concepts of no particular historical epoch, no particular profession, no particular portion of culture, but which somehow necessarily inhere in all subordinate concepts, and can be used to "analyze" the latter.[29]

Definitive assertions of absolute entitlements, unambiguous intentions, and clear-cut distinctions between force and violence are, at best, "noble lies" and, at worst, an evasion of responsibility.[30] We produce the distinctions; we endow the rights; we formulate the norms. Yet, ironically, as individuals, we do not completely control our fate, for the human "we" consists of communities of shared meaning extending over space and through time. What we as individuals can do is limited by the objectification of the shared meanings that are produced by our mutual interactions.

Though we can never free ourselves from the shackles of community-imposed meaning, we can reforge them, link by link, through a process appropriately considered political. The Greeks recognized that politics was central to the life of their communities, for through politics shared meanings could be preserved or transformed, even if they could never be transcended. To accept responsibility for the communities of meaning of which we are a part is to embrace politics. To recognize the paramountcy of the political is, ultimately, to accept life over death.

COUNTERPOINT TO CHAPTER 4

Complexity, Shared Meaning, and Violence

THE COLLAPSE of European overseas empires and the emergence of a plethora of new Asian and African states after World War II prompted social scientists to extend the range of their concerns beyond the confines of the Western political experience. Initial efforts to develop "theories" incorporating the so-called modernizing societies and developing polities tended to err, however, through both excessive optimism and continued, if more subtle, ethnocentrism. The path of development was commonly conceived as a unidirectional recapitulation of the Western experience (i.e., industrial development, social modernization, and political democratization). This naiveté eventually gave way to both disappointment over the "developments" that actually occurred in many of the Third World states (i.e., economic stagnation, social pathology, and military autocracy) and a certain skepticism concerning the fate of the presumably developed states.*

Yet, whatever the doubts about the positive nature of events in the Third World or the ultimate efficacy of modern social arrangements, change has undoubtedly taken place. These changes generate new challenges, especially for politics. Perhaps the pattern of change that places the greatest burden on politics is the "transformation from relatively undifferentiated roles and structures to more differentiated ones, from functionally diffuse to functionally specific modes of organization."[1] Under the impact of such changes, interactions become more specialized, segmentalized, and compartmentalized, participants grow more interdependent, and the overall patterns of

---

*The problem of the future of the modern world will be discussed more fully in the final chapter.

social arrangements become more complex. The emergence of greater social complexity, of course, is commonly associated with processes identified as attributes of modernization such as urbanization, industrialization, expanding literacy, and secularization/rationalization of people's world view.

The processes of complexification, however, do not resolve political problems; they contribute to them. Increased complexity, if it is not to degenerate into entropic meaninglessness, must be coordinated. The coordination of complexity in any interactional arrangement poses a problem of shared meaning; that is, people must be able to form stable, accurate expectations about each other's behavior. As a society grows more complex, the problem of generating and maintaining shared meaning also becomes more demanding. Not only might political capabilities be unequal to the exigencies of increased complexification, but also, as Fred Riggs argues, the consequences of political failure are far more serious in a complex than in a relatively simple social structure.

Riggs illustrates his point with an idealization (see the diagram, "The Politics of Complexity").[2] To place this argument within the context developed in this essay, I am making an equivalence between integration and politics and between differentiation and complexity. The vertical axis represents the dimension of political "success," and the horizontal axis represents the dimension of complexity. Boundary lines AB and AC define the limits of integration and malintegration at each level of social complexity. Riggs observes that a perfectly coordinated simple society is, in some sense, less integrated than a perfectly coordinated complex society (somewhat analogous to the point that a large vessel contains more when filled than a smaller one). A similar situation pertains if two societies of differing complexities are in states of "perfect" collapse. Perfection, whether benign or perverse, is seldom attained in this world; thus, extant societies fall within these limits. Consider, for example, two societies, S_1 and S_2 (which could be the same society at different times). S_1 is *relatively* more integrated than S_2 but *absolutely* less integrated; that is, the political processes in S_2 succeed in coordinating more complexity than those of S_1, but the demands posed by the increased complexity are greater still. Similarly, the consequences of total collapse would be more

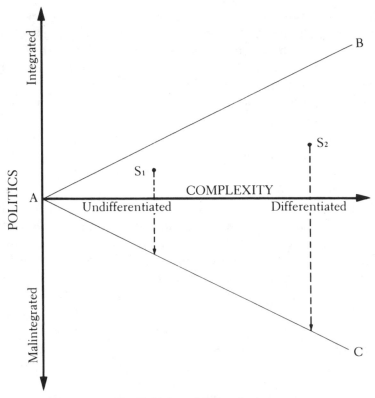

The Politics of Complexity

calamitous in S_2 than in S_1, primarily because the increased interdependence of the participants in S_2 makes it more difficult for them to isolate themselves from breakdowns in shared meaning.

These relationships may be elaborated further by adding a third dimension, that of violence, producing the pyramidal model shown. The pyramid is bounded by four intersecting planes ABC, ABD, ACD, BCD (BCD is an arbitrary termination). This model illustrates the relation between disintegration and violence. The collapse of a more complex society S_2 (disintegrating down the line BC) generates greater possibilities for violence than the collapse of a simpler one (disintegrating down line bc).

Violence consists of coercive acts that violate the boundaries defining the acceptable uses of coercion in social relations. A

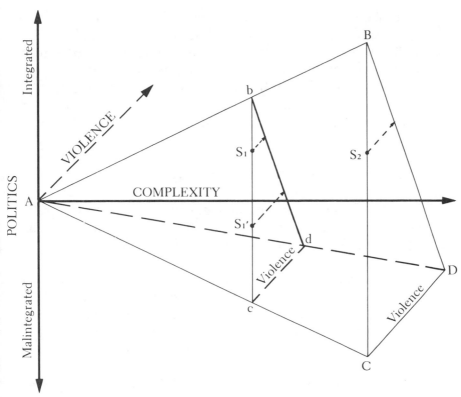

Politics, Complexity, and Violence

well-integrated society does not necessarily eschew coercion; indeed, strictly controlled coercion continues as a tool of integration if applied within limits reflecting a well-established consensus.

Violence can be seen as a function of both complexity and integration. If a given level of complexity is assumed, a decline in relative integration increases the likelihood of violence for several interrelated reasons (S_1 decays to S_1'; the dotted arrow represents the increased potential for violence):

1. Disintegration progressively weakens the consensus on the norms and rules governing the uses of coercion. A complete breakdown of this consensus would mean that the distinction between force and violence becomes meaningless, and the situation would be one of a Hobbesian war of each against all. A

partial decline implies that an increased number of people no longer share the previously prevailing definition of the boundary between force and violence and would therefore become more willing to use severe coercion to accomplish their ends.

2. The decay of a political consensus would also weaken the effectiveness of those organizations charged with boundary maintenance at the very time challenges to those boundaries are on the increase.

3. The decay of the systems of shared meaning increases the possibility of conflict as previously accepted interactional arrangements are called into question.

4. The density of interdependent interaction, however, remains the same, limiting the possibilities of withdrawal (i.e., simplification) as a strategy for moderating conflict.

If the absolute level of the integrative capacity remains the same while the complexity of the society increases, the destructiveness of the violence will tend to increase (S_2 as compared to S_1). Destructiveness is a function of complexity for at least three reasons:

1. Increased complexity is generally, although not necessarily, associated with enlargement of scale, both in terms of geographic size and, especially, population. Thus, the numbers of people affected by violence tend to grow with increased complexity.

2. Growing interdependence, a necessary concomitant of complexification, means that acts of violence become difficult to isolate; rather, their effects tend to reverberate throughout the system.

3. Increased power also tends to correlate with complexity, both in terms of organization and technologies, raising the destructive capabilities of the potential combatants.

Political success, in terms of creating and maintaining systems of shared meaning capable of sustaining a given level of interactional complexity, is a multidimensional problem. The integrative capacity of established shared meanings is relative to the shifting challenges confronted and, in turn, affects the potential likelihood and destructiveness of violence.

5

ORGANIZATION AND EXPLANATION:

Structures of Shared Meaning

From a doctoral examination. "What is the task of all higher education?" To turn men into machines. "What are the means?" Man must learn to be bored. "How is that accomplished?" By means of the concept of duty. "Who serves as the model?" The philologist: he teaches grinding. "Who is the perfect man?" The civil servant. "Which philosophy offers the highest formula for the civil servant?" Kant's: the civil servant as thing-in-itself raised up to be judge over the civil servant as phenomenon.

NIETZSCHE

This essay is forthcoming in a somewhat different form as "Organization and Explanation: New Metaphors for Old Problems" in Administration and Society (1984). Reprinted by permission of Sage Publications, Inc.

SHARED MEANINGS EMERGE out of continuous interaction; politics, the deliberate effort to control shared
meaning, is best conceived as a process as well. Significant
aspects of our interactive arrangements, however, become so
redundant and predictable that we begin to grasp them as establishing a "structure." Structures of shared meaning, which exist
only through our collective and mutually expected responses,
become objectified and assume a "reality" that appears to transcend our individual participation. We find ourselves as members
of, or subject to, organizations.

The significance of these structures of shared meaning has
not escaped social analysis, but a consensus on how best to
understand them has. At the risk of developing simply another
perspective (which would be of some value), we suggest that
organizations, especially complex organizations, may be best
thought of as if they were explanatory structures. Clearly, this
approach contains an element of metaphor, but most organization "theories" appear to have a suggestive metaphor at their
core. Initially, then, the use and potential abuse of metaphor in
political analysis deserves some consideration.

The Use and Abuse of Metaphor

Metaphors pepper political discourse. Leaders prowl as lions
and foxes; political machines manufacture electoral support;
actors play roles in political dramas; and the state dominates
the social world like a Leviathan. We systematize our metaphors
and label them models, maps, and simulations. It appears that
we can no more escape metaphorical characterizations of the
world than we can dispense with language itself in explanation.
Metaphor helps us economize in our explanations; it provides,

as Colin Turbayne observes, "two ideas *as* one (emphasis in the original)."[1]

Gilbert Ryle suggests that we commit a "category mistake" when we represent "the facts... as if they belonged to one logical type or category (or range of types of categories), when they actually belong to another."[2] This statement, as Turbayne notes, is a good definition of metaphor. The temptation to cross categories, especially when characterizing social and political arrangements, can be attributed to a number of factors. At the level of style, the use of metaphor indicates a certain poetical impulse. Poetry is often richly, although not uniquely, metaphorical, and metaphorical images, selected for vividness of impact, may well enliven otherwise drab social scientific prose. The use of metaphor, however, represents more than the triumph of form over substance, for metaphors may also contribute to our knowledge of the world. The relatively unknown and unfamiliar may become more comprehensible when characterized in terms of a more familiar world.[3] Eugene Miller, for example, suggests that political metaphors provide "a way of moving from the observable or sensible to the political."[4] We perceive only contiguous events; we cannot observe the relations those events presumably signify. To represent such relations, we import into the statements of our observations, terms characterizing what we cannot see, such as "cause," "force," or "authority." Such terms are commonly rooted in metaphor, although the roots are often obscure.

The substantive contribution metaphors may make to the intelligibility of the social world also suggests the pitfalls of metaphorical reasoning. Metaphorical characterizations are not neutral—they structure the ways we constitute the world of sense apprehensions.[5]* We need not embrace a radical

---

*Eugene Miller develops what he terms a "manifestationist" view to counter the extreme verificationist and constitutivist views of metaphor. Metaphor, he argues, makes manifest some hidden but intelligible structure. This position, he concedes, assumes "political things have an intelligible structure." That may be, but the only way we "know" the structure is through the linguistic reconstructions of our observations. It is hard to see how the manifestationist view escapes a certain perspectivism. Whatever the structure might "be," we can still "see" it in a variety of ways. See Eugene F. Miller, "Metaphor and Political Knowledge," *American Political Science Review* (March 1979): 169.

perspectivism to recognize that metaphors, by their nature, must necessarily emphasize some aspects of the situation being characterized, while obscuring others. Metaphors, whatever their virtues, cross categories, thus making the synthesized category doubly unstable. All categories may be undermined by pointing to observables not adequately subsumed. Metaphorically constructed categories, moreover, may be subverted from either side of the categorical construct. To assert that "man is a wolf" can be challenged by those siding with either wolves or men. To commit oneself to a metaphorical characterization of observation may well be illuminating, but the perspective so granted is necessarily unstable and vulnerable. Metaphorical "investments" purchase a potentially misleading and unstable world view.

A powerful metaphor, ironically, may be particularly dangerous. "The line between make-believe and belief," Turbayne reminds us, "is thin," and we can easily slip from category crossing into category trespassing; that is, we may take the metaphorical for the literal.[6] The failure to distinguish between procedure (metaphor) and process (that being metaphorically characterized) can afflict the greatest minds. Descartes, who along with Newton promoted the enormously influential geometric/machine metaphor, apparently came to believe that the world and even the human body were not merely like machines, they literally were machines: "In short, enthralled by his own metaphor, he mistook the mask for the face, and consequently bequeathed to posterity more than a worldview. He bequeathed a world."[7]

One heir to this legacy of Descartes and Newton is, of course, organizational theory. Organizations are often characterized, more or less systematically, as machines. Frederick Taylor went so far as to incarnate the Cartesian man-as-a-machine metaphor in organizational behavior. The influence of the machine metaphor reflects its dominance in the modern world view, where it defines not only the allocation of facts but also the classical characterization of science itself (i.e., the deductive relation of events, the reduction of physical explanation to casual explanation, and the identification of deduction with computation).[8] Organization theorists, like so many other social scientists of the past century, wanted to enter into what they took to be the mainstream of legitimate science. Embracing the machine metaphor provided them both an idea for theoretical elaboration and a certain sense of scientific legitimacy.

The machine metaphor is not, of course, the only one occurring in organizational theory; others also exercise considerable influence. Among the more significant is the twentieth-century cybernetic variant of the machine metaphor: the organization as a self-steering mechanism. Additionally, like the wider society of which they are a part, organizations have been treated as both organisms and as dramas. A recent survey of the literature reveals other organizational metaphors, explicit and hidden.[9]

Now nothing is intrinsically wrong with metaphorical thinking. At the core of most research programs lies a suggestive metaphor systematized into a model and then developed into an empirically testable theory. Yet the presence of multiple metaphors suggests a possible need for reconstruction. Competing metaphors may well emerge from the perspectivism implied in metaphorical thinking. Since all metaphors reveal and conceal at the same time, what one conceals may give rise to another. The organic metaphor in organization theory, it would appear, developed in response to the limits of the machine model. Yet plurality does not imply equality among competing metaphors. Metaphorically guided inquiry may constitute the world in a variety of ways, but not all metaphors prove equally valuable. Metaphors cannot be judged to be definitively "right" or "wrong"—they are not "mirrors" of nature but, as Turbayne suggests, resemble "portraits" which incorporate certain features while neglecting others.[10] A particular metaphorical portrait, however, may be judged superior to others if it proves more suggestive of theoretical applications. Some metaphors, moreover, may prove more comprehensive than others, in terms of subsuming them and going beyond.*

With such considerations in mind, we explore a new organizational metaphor: organizations may be treated *as if* they are explanations or, more precisely, explanatory structures. Explanation, as used here, involves more than "neopositivist" concern

---

*Two radically incommensurate metaphorical constructions, therefore, could not be directly evaluated as to comprehensiveness. There is no way of deciding which world view is more complete unless one can subsume the other.

for logical construction and empirical validation; it implies interpretive and critical elements as well. The explanatory metaphor, consequently, subsumes the insights of the machine metaphor, including its cybernetic variant, in addition to those of other organizational metaphors. It appears, moreover, that the explanatory metaphor possesses a certain *prima facie* superiority. Organizations are composed not of gears and cogs, microprocessors, or cells, but of human beings engaged in verbal and nonverbal behavior. Explanations also consist of verbal behavior guiding nonverbal behavior. Explanations and organizations, then, appear to relate to similar types of activity to an extent not duplicated by many other organizational metaphors. The suggestiveness of this metaphor can be illustrated by demonstrating how it represents fundamental organizational characteristics, serves as a basis for a typology, and isolates certain forms and processes of organizational change.

Organizations as Explanations

All organized behavior depends upon shared meaning, as evidenced by mutually expected responses, contributing to smooth interaction. Yet the concept of "organization" commonly connotes something more than established patterns of predictable interaction. Predictable relations, after all, could be transitory, open-ended, essentially egalitarian, and largely unregulated. An organization (complex or simple), admittedly something of a reification of certain patterns of repeated behavior, may be distinguished from the more inclusive notion of organized behavior as being a relatively stable interaction among fairly well-delineated participants whose relations are coordinated (at least in part) by authorities capable of enforcing their directives.[11]

Any organization may be reduced to the responses of those who constitute it. These responses, however, are "mutually expected"; individual actions, therefore, take shape under the influence of these mutual expectations. The participants create and sustain an organization through the outpourings of their energy in the world. Each member's outpourings, however, affect and are affected by the actions and expectations of the others with whom he or she interacts.[12] In such a dialectical fashion, the interacting responses of the participants both create and are created by the organization.*

Purpose

All organizations organize the same thing: shared meaning (mutually expected response). Whatever other tasks they undertake—producing toasters, collecting taxes, conquering neighbors—organizations depend upon the structured responses of those who comprise them. By routinizing responses, organizations establish shared meaning by guaranteeing mutually fulfilled expectations.

Explanations, too, attempt to control shared meaning by channeling response in various ways. Basically, "an explanation makes something intelligible or comprehensible."[13] Behaviorally speaking, something is intelligible when we "know" how to respond to it. Intelligibility is demonstrated by "appropriate" use, whether of a concept, a tool, or a complex social setting. An explanation, therefore, attempts to guide behavior in certain ways through a variety of means. Scientific explanation strives to structure appropriate response through appeals to logic and empirical evidence, while other forms of explanation draw upon alternate means, not excluding coercion, to control the range of response (cf. Chapter 2).

Organizations incarnate explanations.[14] Every explanation is a potential organization, and every organization is a behaviorally manifested explanation (or complex set of explanations). Not all explanations become organizations, for they may be reflected in patterns of behavior that are not stable, shared, or authoritatively coordinated; indeed, they may have no impact on anyone's behavior.

---

*This interdetermination of individual responses contributes to the notion that an organization, or any grouping, constitutes an "entity" greater than the sum of its parts. Organizations *are* greater than the sum of their parts, because the parts are metaphorically "multiplied," not "added," together. To paraphrase the cliché, an organization is *equal* to the *product* of its parts.

Hierarchy

Something becomes intelligible when related to other things already known. The degree of intelligibility or, perhaps more accurately, the surety of our knowledge, depends upon the strength of the relationship established. The strongest relationship is a deductive one, where specifics may be indubitably derived from general principles. A sense of intelligibility may also be established when specifics are only probabilistically related to general principles or simply fit into an accepted pattern.[15] The thrust of most explanations, however, is toward the hierarchical subsumption of the more particular under the general, if only in terms of probabilistic or tendency statements.

Organized behavior exists when specific responses fit into a pattern of mutual expectations. Formal organizations, as a species of organized behavior, possess heirarchical structures analogous to those of formal explanations. "Who says organization," asserts Robert Michels, "says oligarchy,"[16] But Michels's "iron law" exaggerates, because organizations need not imply oligarchy, at least not in the restricted sense of a tightly knit, highly centralized rule of a tiny, self-perpetuating elite. Some organizations may be so structured, just as some explanations may be rigorously controlled by deductive logic. Other organizations may be less highly structured, or even primitive in nature, internal relations may be only probabilistically established, and the organization itself may be constituted out of competing explanations.

Even simple explanations involve some degree of heirarchical subsumption. The most basic form of explanation, that of categorization, still stands at a higher level of generality than the phenomenon being categorized. The organizational equivalent of a categorization, admittedly, would be so undifferentiated that it might well be described as incipient. A categorization, though, may create a significant, two-tiered hierarchy, like the ones reflecting the distinctions between master and slave or citizen and alien.

Complex organizations more clearly resemble an explanatory regress, in that each lower level of the organization is subsumed by a higher one until some essentially arbitrary termination point is reached. An extensive regress, however, need not imply a high degree of coherence, consistency, or centralization. The organization of the federal government of the United States, for example, has no clearly defined termination point. Harry Truman may have commented that the "buck" stops with the President, but federalism, the separation of powers, and the myth of popular sovereignty combine to produce an organizational regress with multiple branchings and contending termination points. This arrangement, as its critics have noted for two centuries, sacrifices a certain amount of coherence for the sake of other values. A too neatly structured governmental "explanation," in the minds of at least some of the authors of the Constitution, was an invitation to tyranny.

Organizations commonly contain competing elements, as if structured from related, though somewhat incompatible, explanations. One obvious tension arises from the competition between administrative and substantive tasks, where the "experts" from each area contend to subsume the other under the imperatives of their own task.[17] The often cited contrast between formal and informal organizations resolves itself into the tensions that arise from a particular member's responses being subject to competing explanatory directives. For example, should an employee be hired on the basis of ascriptive ties or universalistic critieria? Should the employee conform with the norms of an informal group or with the official directives of the formal heirarchy? Seeing such tensions as the product of contending explanations addressing the same essential context helps to reduce the tendency to reify formal and informal organizations into concrete entities.

The higher the position occupied in the hierarchy, the more familiar a person will be with an organization's general functions and operations, knowledge constituting the "intelligence" of authority. Such intelligence has its costs, however, since the higher the position, the less an official is likely to know about the particulars of operations at the lower levels, contributing to the ignorance of authority and the "intelligence" of democracy. Analogous to the conditions prevailing at the higher (theoretical) levels of an explanatory regress, the activities of those functioning at or near the top of an organization are more diffuse and less amenable to precise evaluation.[18]

Top-level participants, consequently, are more likely to suffer losses of meaning than those at lower levels; that is, they more frequently encounter situations where they will be initially at a loss for a response, contributing to pressure, anxiety, and their somatic side effects. Ultimately, organizational leaders must respond—determine some meaning—for that is the burden of their positions and why they receive generally high compensation. Often such responses must be made in the absence of sufficient information or, even worse, upon the basis of contradictory information. In contrast, those near the bottom of a hierarchy usually find their behavior to be much better defined. For these workers, organizational meanings are well established, even if they may often be alienated from them.

Empirical Frontier

Each organization also possesses a more or less clearly delineated "empirical frontier" beyond which lies the "reality" that it attempts to subsume (explain) and control. At this lowest point of the organizational regress, the directives and procedures of the organization are ultimately tested. From these "experiments" comes the evidence fed back (presumably) to check the governing directives and the assumptions that support them. If the results of the organization's experiments at its frontier are ambiguous, contradictory, or distorted, they will provide only limited guidance for the decision makers who must ultimately evaluate the effectiveness of the current directives.

If scientific method delineates the most systematic exploitation of the links among explanation, experimentation, and feedback, systematic organizations might be thought to imitate scientific procedural controls.[19] A highly developed organization, from this perspective, would resemble a rigorously defined, logically integrated, scientific explanatory structure.[20] (1) Coherent, consistent orders (the explanatory hypotheses) would be derived from clearly conceived organizational regulations and objectives (laws). (2) These orders would be precisely elaborated as they progress down the hierarchy (exemplification); until (3) they specify behavior at the organizational frontier (experimentation). (4) The consequences of the organization's operations at the frontier would (ideally) produce unambiguous feedback by which the utility of the original directives could be evaluated (validation or invalidation). (5) Finally, this evaluation would be used to guide needed refinements in operational directives (normal scientific incrementalism).

Most extant organizations fall considerably short of this ideal, principally because goals are multiple and often conflict, behavior is weakly structured, and feedback, especially negative feedback, is blocked. Some serious epistemological doubts, moreover, can be raised about the adequacy of this "positivist" model of a highly developed organization.*

Epistemological Assumptions and Organizational Types

Positivist Organizations

Modern bureaucratic organizations, as Max Weber idealized them, approximate the structure and method of a positivist scientific explanatory regress. Twenty years ago Sheldon Wolin pointed out this similarity: "To the theorist of organization, the patterns of such [bureaucratic] structures supply a 'logic' to human behavior comparable to the way methodological procedures guide intellectual inquiry."[21] Positivist bureaucracies, Richard Rubenstein observes, "can be best understood as a structural and organizational expression of the related processes of *secularization, disenchantment of the world,* and *rationalization* (emphasis in the original)."[22] These processes, not coincidently, are also closely associated with the rise of positivist science. The positivist organization imitates the procedural

---

*Martin Landau, in condemning those who argue for more "authentic" organization, reaffirms the "principle of scientific management" emphasizing "knowledge" and "rationality." He does not seem to recognize that the content of these terms is what remains problematic.

controls of this model of inquiry in an effort to replicate in the area of organizational concern the apparent success of the natural sciences. As Weber states,

The peculiarity of modern culture, and specifically of its technical and economic basis, demands this very calculability of results. When fully developed bureaucracy also stands, in a specific sense, under the principle of *sine ira ac studio* [without anger or zeal]. Its specific nature...develops the more perfectly the more the bureaucracy is "dehumanized," the more completely it succeeds in eliminating from official business love, hatred, and all purely personal, irrational, and emotional elements which escape calculation.[23]

Positivist organizations in emphasizing the standards of efficiency, calculability, and impersonality, force "the imposition of new norms of behavior that are, in fact, the norms of mechanics as a subdivision of physics."[24] The controls of positivist method were devised to enhance the reliability of the explanations produced and, ultimately, the ability of the scientist to predict and, perhaps, control the phenomenon under study. Analogous controls on bureaucratic behavior are similarly intended to improve the technical effectiveness of the organization in fulfilling its assigned tasks, which also involve prediction and control. The claim of "scientific" management, as Alasdair MacIntyre notes, justifies bureaucratic authority.[25]

Disintegration constantly threatens all patterns of social interaction, and the more complex and closely defined the behavior, the more effort must be expended to maintain it. Positivist organizations demand precisely predictable behavior in order to ensure the calculability of results. Precise predictability, in turn, depends upon narrowly channeled responses, for even minor deviations, if pervasive throughout the organization, can contribute to deterioration or even bring about collapse.

The control of behavior, then, becomes an obsessive concern of positivist organizations. Substantial resources must be devoted to the tasks of discipline and surveillance, the functional equivalents of the controls of logic and empirical validation in the construction of explanations, in order to restrict behavioral drift. This overwhelming preoccupation with order encourages the emergence of a bureaucratized society where, as Michael

Foucault comments, the "prisons resemble factories, schools, barracks, hospitals which all resemble prisons."[26]

At the extreme, these scientized organizations displace the more diffuse values of justice, freedom, happiness, love, and even hate and replace them with the values of precision, stability, discipline, reliability, calculability, and impersonality.[27] As with positivist explanations, bureaucratic organizations are not really "value free"; rather, certain values structure response to the exclusion of other influences deemed disruptive to the bureaucratic (explanatory) enterprise. This exclusion leads to the fragmentation of the bureaucrats' personalities, as aspects of their character which threaten impersonal operations are repressed.

Positivist organizations, consequently, resemble a particular, and essentially limited, perspective on the nature of scientific explanation. These bureaucracies replicate within the sphere of organizational operations the reductionist tendencies of positivist science. Undoubtedly, much contemporary science, wedded to technology for the past 150 years, has shifted from "contemplative to manipulative rationality." Indeed, physicist Herbert Bernstein insists that modern science has largely dropped the "goal of understanding the world in favor of being able to calculate, predict, and control."[28] The rise of manipulative science parallels and reinforces the growth of manipulative organizations.

Positivist norms, however, do not appear to be a wholly adequate base for either scientific explanation, especially in the social world, or, by metaphorical extension, social organizations. Other explanatory considerations and other forms of organization may be better suited to subsume both the explanatory and the organizational environments. Specifically, the positivist characterization of the scientific enterprise tends to ignore factors that escape precise calculation, fails to recognize the interpretive aspects of science, cannot account for covert motives and meanings of actors in the social world, and does not encourage the critical revelation of prevailing misconceptions and delusions. Though all highly developed organizations must incorporate elements of scientific method, these methods entail something beyond conventional positivist prescriptions.

Another perspective challenges the dominance of the reductionist, manipulative stance in the natural sciences. The *ecological* approach encourages a certain skepticism about the desirability of intervening in the environment on the basis of only what is immediately evident and easily calculated. As Garrett Hardin states, the ecologist always asks, "And then what?"[29] What happens after the intervention? What are the longer-term implications? The ecological perspective, then, encourages the recognition that "we can never do merely one thing."[30] "Controlled" experiments are only hypothetical constructs; applied experiments can never fully control, or even isolate, all the critical contingencies and consequences. Neatly structured explanatory hierarchies, therefore, may not be adequate guides for action in the natural, much less the social, world.

Once admitted into consideration, the implications of such softer variables would undermine the stability of an explanatory hierarchy defined in more rigid, calculable terms, leading to an increased dispersion of response among the participants in a research community. The links among the elements of the explanatory structure tend to weaken under these conditions, contributing to a more flexible, multiply-terminated explanatory regress. The ecological approach seems to increase the possibilities for deviance and disorder, thereby weakening the foundation of shared meaning and widening the sphere of conflict. The members of a community of inquiry would have to struggle to establish new bases of shared meaning accounting for the softer, noncalculable consequences of ecological assumptions.

Superficially, such explanatory instability would not appear to provide a foundation for a form of organization superior to the orderly, precise, manipulative model of Weberian, positivist bureaucracy. The most extreme form of irrationality, though, may well be the failure to recognize the limits of manipulative rationality.[31] While it may be that positivist organizations are well suited for particular types of problems—those that can be isolated, meaningfully not hypothetically, from nonquantifiable influences—the limits of their effectiveness are rapidly reached in environments where these more qualitative and less easily controlled dimensions cannot be excluded. Ecological orientations, despite the increased possibility of disorder, may be more appropriate to areas of operation that remain embedded in a wider web of relations. By patterning itself after such a model, an organization could increase its sensitivity to multiple interconnections and potential implications that tend to be neglected by positivist organizations.

An ecologically sensitive organization, to be sure, does not abandon concern for feedback validation and organizational logic, nor does it eliminate organizational hierarchy. Rather, the adoption of a more holistic approach complements positivist organizational norms and contributes to a more flexibly structured organization characterized by a more diffuse structure of authority, a greater toleration of dissensus, and a certain openness, within limits, to innovation.

Beyond the general concern for longer-term environmental impact and flexible structures of operation, ecological norms may be manifested in specific ways as well. Defining a role as multifunctional rather than unifunctional reflects a clear shift to a more holistic, ecological perspective. A policeman, for example, might no longer be characterized merely as a law enforcer with a badge and a gun but may also share some of the functional attributes of a criminal psychologist, lawyer, social worker, and expert in community relations. The well-known Kalmer Plan of the Volvo automobile company, wherein work groups are given the responsibility for a complete job such as installing the engine, provides another example of a more holistic work environment replacing positivist specialization. Although such shifts in role definition recognize the complex setting of individual behavior, multiple roles can contribute to ambiguity and even role conflict. Ecological organizations, like their explanatory counterparts, involve certain costs, as well as potential benefits.*

---

*Interestingly, according to Robert Presthus, a Detroit worker team that spent several weeks in the Volvo plant concluded that they preferred the American system "because it required less thought and concentration." This reminds us that positivist organizations, with their emphasis on precise definition of tasks and responsibilities especially at the lower levels, appeal to those who wish to avoid the ambiguity necessarily associated with the adoption of a more ecological perspective. See Robert Presthus, *The Organizational Society* (New York: St. Martin's, 1978), pp.21–22.

Comprehensive instances of a shift to more ecologically sensitive organizations involve altering the positivist structure of authority (i.e., centralized, strictly hierarchical, with clear superior/subordinate relations). Schemes to involve workers in management decisions, whether in Socialist Yugoslavia or in the United States, alter, though they certainly do not eliminate, organizational authority structures. Similarly, the creation of an independent ombudsman system, capable of intervening in a bureaucracy's operations on the behalf of clients, affects the standard conception of the authority structure of a bureaucracy, as well as its relation to its environment.

Adequate Organizations

Explanations of social behavior, in contrast with those of the inanimate or unself-conscious worlds, not only must incorporate a concern for empirical *validity*, but also must give some account of interpretative *adequacy* and critical *authenticity* (cf. Chapter 2). Validity depends on whether an explanation provides an acceptable account of what are judged to be the relevant facts. The adoption of a more ecologically sensitive perspective broadens the construction of "relevance." The second concern involves whether actors would consider the proffered explanation to be an adequate representation of their covert motives and meanings. The final concern, that of authenticity, questions the nature of these covert motives and meanings in order to assess whether they might reflect delusion or "false" consciousness. These two additional considerations broaden the epistemological basis of social explanation beyond the reductionist assumptions of positivism. Presumed social knowledge, therefore, may be challenged on three grounds: adequacy, authenticity, and validity. Insofar as these considerations are necessary components of our social knowledge, positivist explanatory constructs do not eliminate their effects so much as keep the observer in ignorance of them.[32]

Social organizations, in addition to incorporating the broader standards of a more ecologically defined validity, may also reflect analogous concerns for more adequate and authentic operations. Typically, the Weberian, positivist model, insofar as it is approximated, is criticized for alienating both those who comprise it and the clients it presumably serves. This does not mean that such organizations fail to establish shared meaning; rather, the meanings they establish so segment the lives of both personnel and clients that they fail to identify with the actions they undertake (or have inflicted upon them). Clients are treated as mere "cases" that possess only certain organizationally relevant characteristics and whose other attributes are ignored, if not suppressed. Bureaucratic roles are defined as highly specialized and strictly controlled, while other aspects of the official's identity are excluded.

At its extreme, positivist bureaucracy leads to a potentially obsessive concern with control, ignoring more subtle questions such as legitimacy. Conditioning replaces more broadly construed socialization, and bureaucrats are motivated through the manipulation of concrete rewards and punishments rather than through appeals to broader social norms. Orders coming down the hierarchy replace the development of an independent superego (thereby fomenting the occurrence of the "I was only following orders" syndrome). Finally, what Ralph Hummel terms "id satisfaction" replaces ego satisfaction, as mastery is denigrated in favor of routinized contributions to the collective effort.[33]

Adoption of the ecological model would help to mitigate some of these alienating tendencies. Concern for the "adequacy" of the organization's definition and procedures would go further still in that greater attention would be paid to the covert meanings and motives of both bureaucratic officials and their clients. In organizational theory, the human relations and the institutional schools, rooted in an organic metaphor, tend to see effective organizations as incorporating such interest in adequacy. Wolin neatly epitomizes this perspective as viewing an organization as representing

a complex response to a particular historical environment, an institution which constantly adjusts to the needs, sentiments, and emotions of its members, and the members to it. The primary function of these organizations is not to produce profits in the most rational manner possible, nor to delight the production engineer by virtue of its efficiency. Instead, it is to promote the values of social stability, cohesion, and integration.[34]

The generation of such emphathic identification demands more dramatic efforts than those made in conventional training programs. Some devices, such as sensitivity training and encounter-group therapy, aim to reduce prejudices and increase official understanding of clients and subordinates. Therapeutic sessions of this sort have also been used to break down racial stereotypes and thereby improve relations between officials and the minority communities with whom they interact.

The role reversals of the Chinese Cultural Revolution, wherein factory managers were forced to work on assembly lines and government officials were sent out to the fields, exemplify more radical programs to increase empathy, as well as combat the rigidification of an emerging hierarchical structure. These reversals were intended, at least in part, to break down some of the status barriers between organizational superiors and inferiors and develop in the more privileged sectors a better understanding of the position of the masses. Similar, though less dramatic and disruptive, techniques are in evidence when a criminal court judge sentences himself to jail for a weekend or welfare workers attempt to live for a month on a welfare check.

Such programs may indeed lead to some increase in empathy, although at a certain cost, but they hardly serve to institutionalize concern for the covert motives and meanings of those involved in (or with) an organization. Empathy alone cannot be relied upon to provide an adequate representation of these characteristics. To interpret covert motives and meanings within an explanatory typification, we must often go beyond empathy and devise a historical construct of the context within which the action takes place in order to gain additional guidance on how to interpret the action appropriately.[35] Organizationally, such an approach implies a greater concern with the whole context within which officials function or which clients reflect. Organizational intelligence therefore needs to be more broadly construed than it would be in the segmentalized structure of a positivist bureaucracy. By giving greater attention to the wider setting of organizational behavior, an ecological organization concerned with adequate operations attempts to provide a better account of covert motives and meanings.

Organizations embody adequate values insofar as they strive to lessen the stereotypicality of role definitions. We cannot, of course, be expected to know and respond to all people as "whole" persons; some "reductionism" is inevitable in almost all social interactions. More appropriate organizations, however, would recognize a wider range of individual characteristics as relevant for operations. A modest, although not trivial, example of this tendency is the increasingly wide adoption of the policy of maternity (and paternity) leaves or flexible-hours programs. These policies, in effect, admit the existence of extraorganizational roles and needs that deserve some consideration when structuring organizational operations.

Just as concern for adequacy can undermine the stability of any purported positivist explanation, more adequate organizational norms inject diffuse and potentially conflicting considerations into the surface rationality of positivist bureaucratic operations. Presumably, any disruption of organizational logic will be offset by improved morale and productivity, but the existence of such benefits can be established only after the fact. At some point, as the excesses of the Cultural Revolution indicate, the attempt to induce "adequate" attitudes may threaten the overall integrity of the organization.

Authentic Organizations

The problem of authenticity in social explanation raises some difficult questions of critical social theory: specifically, whether the covert motives and meanings of social actors, and the explanations that attempt to typify them, reflect a "false" consciousness. The problem of false consciousness admittedly begs the question of how we are to distinguish between "false" and "true." We find it easier to accept the possibility of delusion than to agree on an intersubjective standard for defining, recognizing, and correcting such errors.

The need to posit and defend such a standard might be avoided, however, by concentrating on the process of criticism rather than the substantive criteria used. Thus, if we accept the possibility (probability, inevitability) of distortion in our knowledge of ourselves and our relations to others, we might embrace the stance of continuous self-criticism, regardless of what particular standard we might apply. An organization that embodies a similar recognition of potential inauthenticity would also be committed to a process of continuous critique of its structure, functions, and perhaps even its formal goals and assumptions.

"Institutionalized" criticism may take two forms, restricted or unrestricted. The restricted alternative involves the application of a standard of evaluation that cannot itself be criticized. The Chinese model of self-criticism or the monastic tradition of confession and penance are two examples. In each case the participants judge their own performance and vow to improve upon their shortcomings. Even the overall organization may be subject to criticism for deviating from the primary goals and purposes for which it was created (e.g., Luther's condemnation of the Roman Church or certain Marxist critiques of the Soviet Union), although this type of systemic criticism can easily lapse into "heresy." Similarly, a positivist organization committed to responding to negative feedback though without ever questioning its own organizational presumptions may be considered to be a "critical" organization in this limited sense.

Unrestricted criticism places no limit on the critique; even the very foundation assumptions of the organization may be challenged. At the theoretical limit, all points of the organized consensus on meaning could be criticized at all times. Such a limit is never going to be reached, for an organization as a stable pattern of responses could not be maintained under the corrosive conditions of basic, constant, and comprehensive critique. More pertinent is the case where no element of the organized consensus is immune from criticism, but the consensus is not being challenged at every point at all times.

An authentic organization encourages innovation and structural change, recognizing that all adaptations are inadequate to some extent (just as all explanations fail to comprehend fully what they presume to subsume). Of course, whether any alteration actually improves organizational authenticity can be known only after the fact, if then. As in the case of critical theory, a critique of an organization may indeed identify certain "delusions," but unless we assume that the critique itself cannot err, then it too must be considered only a partial perspective, possibly even more deluded than the one it replaces, and certainly not immune from further criticism.

Although an organization that institutionalizes critique may lack a clearly defined hierarchical structure of authority and the logical coherence associated with the model of a positivist bureaucracy, its commitment to innovation closely resembles that of the contemporary scientific enterprise. The provisional character of all organizational routines replicates the hypothetical character of all scientific knowledge. As in the sciences, though, the commitment to innovation is not unqualified, for, if it were, there would be no shared knowledge or organization, only deviance. Innovations not only must be generated but also must achieve acceptance, whether in the scientific community or by the other participants in the organization. An innovation that fails to gain some measure of acceptance remains a simple case of individual deviance which will be ignored or even suppressed.

An organization (or an intellectual community) that attempts to institutionalize an unrestricted critique in order to encourage innovation away from inauthentic and inadequate routines (or explanations) encounters a dilemma: Failure to develop commonly accepted standards for evaluating the conclusions of a critique may contribute to the uncritical incorporation of these conclusions and, ultimately, to the deterioration of the shared meanings that underlie the organization or community. However, the development of too stringent a standard for critical acceptance may undercut the function of criticism at a later point. There seems to be little significant difference between suppressing the possibility of critique and suppressing its conclusions. Moreover, just as the critique cannot be uncritically accepted, neither can the standards for evaluating a critique, and so on. Adoption of an openly critical stance, whether within a field of inquiry or in an organization, implies a "critical regress" that can be terminated only arbitrarily. Indeed, such Nietzschean skepticism can finally be turned back upon itself, and we can become skeptical as to whether our assumption of the inadequacy of all human efforts to attain the truth is correct.

Organizations "embody" explanations. Scientific explanations as the most highly developed (because of their systematic combination of explanation, experimentation, and feedback) provide the model of organizations in their most highly developed form. Organizational logic replicates scientific method, in that it tries to develop a systematic organizational analog of explanation, experimentation, and feedback.

Yet, as we have argued, the character of appropriate scientific method remains a matter of some dispute. If we choose to adopt a positivist image of science, with its emphasis on manipulative rationality, strict explanatory hierarchy (nomothetic theory), precision, and control, then the Weberian model of bureaucracy would seem to be the most highly developed. If, however, we take a more ecological perspective, the nature of a "good" or "valid" explanation or organization alters somewhat, for it becomes important to incorporate some factors that may not be easily quantifiable and that may disrupt the coherence of the explanatory or organizational hierarchy. An ecological organization adopts a more holistic stance toward the environment in which it functions, contributing to a more diffuse, context-relevant structure and increased responsiveness.

Adding considerations of adequacy and authenticity further modifies the character of an acceptable explanation in the social world. Adequacy heightens concern for the actors' own meanings; in an organization this leads to increased empathy and a consequent reduction in the stereotypicality of bureaucratic roles and client "cases." Finally, concern for explanatory authenticity, especially in social explanations, encourages the adoption of a critical stance in judging knowledge claims. Depending upon the definition of the limits of the critique, this stance encourages explanatory innovation. A critical organization, similarly, structures into its operations a process by which established routines can be challenged and replaced by ones deemed to possess greater authenticity. Ironically, the scientism reflected in positivist bureaucracy is probably not particularly suited to the incorporation of innovation through continuous critique. The emphasis on reliability and control militates against any strong commitment to constant questioning and re-working of established patterns.

Different organizational characteristics, reflecting alternative explanatory concerns, may be better suited to different environments.[36] Weberian, positivist bureaucracy may be effective in managing a "placid" problem area that can be meaningfully isolated from multiple environmental influences without engaging in a vulgar reductionism. Such organizations might be required for tasks demanding considerable precision, though they would still run the risk of internal alienation.

If the organization cannot be insulated from wider, heterogeneous influences, and the consequences of intervention become less certain, the ecological model increases in relevance. Concern for a fuller range of human motives and meanings also becomes more important as the operations of the organization affect more aspects of human existence. Educational and welfare services exemplify the heightened heterogeneity of function and consequences that seem to call for more "adequately" oriented organizations.

An organization might find it advantageous to institutionalize self-critique according to an unquestioned standard in a situation where a high priority is placed on ideological élan and purity. One example, as the Chinese case suggests, would be that of a revolutionary organization attempting to carry out a social transformation. Finally, the disruption implicit in the implementation of an unrestricted critique might be functional in a hostile and rapidly changing, "turbulent" environment. Under these conditions, an organization capable of sloughing off irrelevant routines may have the best chance of survival.

These "types" of organization (positivist, ecological, adequate, and authentic) should not be seen as mutually exclusive categories, no more so than a concern for adequacy and authenticity eliminates the relevance of empirical validity and logic in social explanation. Rather, each more qualitative dimension incorporates aspects of the less qualitative while adding further considerations. Thus, authentic organizations must provide an account of the covert motives and meanings of its personnel and clients before engaging in a critique. Similarly, a concern with covert motives and meanings necessarily implies a more ecological perspective.

Explanatory Modification and Organizational Change

Organizations channel response in order to establish and maintain systems of shared meaning (mutually expected response). The more complex and interdependent the meaning systems established, the more an organization's energies will be devoted to restricting the range of behavior. This concern with control, which to some degree characterizes all organizations, develops not out of a malevolent conspiracy of oligarchic authorities bent on domination but from a desperate scramble for survival.

The controls on behavior within an organization are analogous to the controls on response incorporated in explanatory structures. Charles Perrow suggests we think of three different types or levels of control:

direct, fully obtrusive ones such as giving orders, direct surveillance, and rules and regulations; bureaucratic ones such as specialization, and standardization, and hierarchy, which are fairly unobtrusive; and fully unobtrusive ones, namely the control of the cognitive premises underlying action.[37]

Directives serve as the explanatory hypotheses of an organization derived more or less deterministically from governing rules and regulations (laws). These rules, in turn, are related through the "theories" embodied in the organization's hierarchical and functional structure. Finally, underlying this structure are the shared cognitive and value assumptions that provide the paradigmatic foundation for the organization. Supporting this array of controls is a variety of more or less overt rewards and sanctions.*

---

*The overt sanctions available in an organization need no elaboration. More subtle ones, especially those supporting a system of shared premises, commonly involve forms of ostracism. Perrow remarks that "this is why social class, ethnic origins, and social networks are so important—they make it more likely that certain kinds of premises will exist." (See Perrow, *Complex Organizations*, p. 152). In a scientific community, a paradigmatic consensus is supported by analogous controls on socialization and recruitment.

Failure to control the range of response leads to the deterioration of the organization because predictability of interaction becomes increasingly difficult to maintain. Overdetermination of response, however, may also threaten the organization if established routines become increasingly inappropriate as circumstances change.[38] Unfortunately, acceptance of a certain range of deviation in order to encourage "positive" (that is, survival-enhancing) innovations may also threaten the organization. Innovation necessarily undermines established routines, violates expectations, and threatens personal security. The existence of a gap between an organizational "explanatory" structure and the demands of the environment *may* prompt innovation, but inadequacy neither guarantees that innovation *will occur* nor guarantees that it *will improve* the situation if it does. Moreover, if an organization is well adapted to existing conditions, its capacity to adjust to a shift in environmental demands may thereby be diminished. If it possesses the capacity to innovate to meet the challenge of change, it will tend to be less well adapted to existing conditions. *Adaptation* to and *adaptability* refer to two different and somewhat competitive organizational capabilities.*

Nevertheless, all organizations, even highly determined and stable ones, do change, though not all changes are deliberate, nor do they all enhance the probabilities of survival. The basic source of change, and the major target of organizational efforts at control, is simple behavioral drift. From an explanatory perspective, the problem is simply that "nobody ever gets anything right." No matter how comprehensive and continuous the controls of socialization and policing, some deviation from the established rules and norms always occurs. Drift grows more severe in the absence of precise standards of behavior and unambiguous feedback. When performance criteria become more diffuse, as they tend to do at the higher levels of an organization,

---

*This is essentially a "neo-Darwinist" analogy. A species that is well adapted to a particular environmental niche commonly lacks the resources to cope with the elimination of that niche. A less well-adapted species may possess within its population certain "deviants" who might be able to cope with the change. A successfully adapted species may carry the germ of its eventual failure.

a consensus over a paradigmatic consensus becomes more important.[39]

Behavioral drift can also result from competing explanations contending for control of the behavior of individuals within an organization (cf. "formal" vs. "informal" organizations). In these circumstances, it is not simply a failure to get things right, so much as the members getting different messages concerning what is "right." The consequences, however, are essentially the same: a deterioration in the predictability of organizational routines.

Behavioral drift is not necessarily lamentable, however, at least not within limits and under certain conditions. University professors, for example, exhibit considerable drift, owing to the significant amounts of unstructured time in their jobs and the lack of clear criteria for evaluating success in their one activity that is fairly structured: teaching. Yet, flexible time schedules, even if much of the time is apparently "wasted," may be necessary for a research environment. Additionally, any attempt to impose a single, quantifiable standard of "good" teaching may outrage the complexity of the learning process (the tasks of research and teaching therefore require more ecologically adequate organizations). Behavioral drift can be tolerated because faculty members are not highly interdependent; the drift is atomized and the effects on the overall organization are limited. As interdependence of function increases, behavioral drift has more serious consequences. The deterioration of established routines under these circumstances contributes to "entropic" change—the breakdown of shared meaning.*

Change in complex, interdependent organizations needs to be monitored closely in order to contain the inevitable disruption. Deliberate innovation must involve a mutual shift in the structures of shared meaning, not merely a drift away from shared meaning into mutual meaninglessness. Organizations,

---

*The administration of a university, because of its higher level of interdependence, cannot tolerate a similar level of drift. Professors may be able to go their separate ways, but those responsible for scheduling classes, collecting fees, and paying bills had better function in a predictable, reliable fashion.

like explanations, may be modified in a controlled fashion through adjustments made in response to negative feedback.[40] The character of this feedback may suggest the need for moderate, cumulative modifications in directives and regulations. Incremental organizational change at this level is the functional equivalent of "normal science." Within this prevailing paradigmatic consensus, authoritative directives (explanatory hypotheses) are used to guide behavior (experimentation) producing results (the feedback), which are presumably used to guide necessary revisions of the original directives. Ideally, just as normal scientific research refines the theories we have of the world, normal organizational adjustments refine the effectiveness of an organization's functional and hierarchical structure. If such adjustments proceed in an orderly and systematic fashion, the structures of shared meaning upon which the organization is based, though continuously altered, never collapse.

Unfortunately, the reality of organizational operations seldom replicates this model of "normal" change. Unclear directives result in a drift of organizational experimentation, and the information generated by the experiments may often be ambiguous, thereby failing to provide adequate guidance for subsequent modification. Negative feedback, even if available in relatively unambiguous form, is often blocked for a variety of reasons such as the reluctance of subordinates to correct the misapprehensions of their superiors. The consequent tendency to overemphasize positive feedback reinforces, of course, the likelihood that the organization will continue on an operational path that may prove disastrous. Finally, the negative feedback generated may be of the sort not easily accommodated within the existing organizational structure.

Serious problems require, though they need not produce, more radical innovations. Negative feedback, if recognized, may reveal anomalies that call into question not only existing rules and regulations but also the structural "theories" underlying them. New structures may be required in order to accommodate the anomalies, resulting in a change of the organization, not merely in the organization. If incremental adjustments of directives and regulations are analogous to theory elaboration in

normal science, more fundamental shifts in structure and function approximate the more radical experience of theory construction, which lies somewhere between the incrementalism of
normal science and the "revolutionary" shifts involved in the
abandonment of one paradigmatic orientation for another.

An organizational "revolution" occurs when the organization
confronts the prospect of a collapse so serious as to call into
question the shared assumptions and values that constitute its
paradigmatic premises. Successful innovation in this crisis approximates Thomas Kuhn's somewhat ambiguous notion of
a scientific revolution.[41] The ambiguity in the cases of both
organizational and explanatory structures arises in large part
from the same source: change is a continuous not a dichoto-
mous (e.g., normal science vs. scientific revolution) concept.
Although we may analytically distinguish among three or four
levels of change in organizations (directives, rules and regulations, structure and function, and premises) or explanations (hypotheses, laws, theories, and paradigms), in fact each
level appears to blend into the next. Organizational revolutions, moreover, like their political and scientific analogs, do
not sweep away the entire past. Some central premise may be
abandoned, but other assumptions and values may remain relatively untouched.

Dramatic alteration of an organization's paradigmatic assumptions, although necessarily disruptive, differs from entropic
dissolution because of the effort made to direct the shift.
The organization may be radically renovated, but the change is
from one structure of shared meaning to another as opposed
to a steady deterioration into a behavioral sink or an outright
collapse.

Economic firms adjusting to the relatively precise feedback
on profit and loss illustrate how increasingly radical innovations
may be incorporated in an effort to enhance performance. Stag-
nating or declining profits may initially stimulate alterations in
the particular directives and regulations governing operations at
the productive frontier in an attempt to enhance efficiency.
Continuing losses encourage more dramatic reforms, such as
the divestment of unprofitable divisions (or selling profitable
ones to raise needed capital), which alter the functional and

hierarchical structure of the firm. Imminent bankruptcy approximates the threat of explanatory collapse. Under such conditions, the enterprise may just be abandoned. Alternatively, a paradigmatic revolution may be attempted, as when the workers purchase and manage the troubled firm. Such a syndicalist experiment represents a major shift away from the premises and values that underlie most economic organizations in advanced capitalist societies. There is, of course, no guarantee that even such a dramatic innovation can stave off the collapse of an obsolete firm.

Conclusion: The Metaphorical Construction of Reality

Metaphors are more than mere word games; actually, many of our conceptual systems, and the consequent ways in which we deal with the world, are metaphorically structured.[42] Many of these metaphorical constructions of reality are so deeply embedded in our thought processes we fail to recognize them for what they are and thus miss what they obscure, as well. The choice we face in thinking about the world is often between metaphors rather than between metaphor and the direct representation of reality.

One contribution of our systematic exploration of the metaphor that organizations are explanations is simply to make explicit what often goes unnoticed. Even if the explanatory metaphor remained unconvincing, some value would come from the heightened awareness of other organizational metaphors (machine, organic, dramatic, etc.). A new metaphor, moreover, can produce a shift in attitudes, emphasizing what other metaphorical constructs neglect.[43] Specifically, the explanatory metaphor for organization discourages the tendency to hypostatize organizations into concrete entities, emphasizes their nature as verbal and nonverbal behavioral arrangements for coping with the world, and highlights the interpenetration of power and explanation.

The explanatory metaphor, however, is more than simply another useful perspective; a good case can be made for its superiority. Other organizational metaphors seem to multiply entities unnecessarily, in part because one develops in response to the inability of another to address the experience of organization in an adequate fashion (e.g., the organic response to the machine metaphor). While it would be presumptuous to claim completeness, the explanatory metaphor seems capable of incorporating many of the worthwhile concerns of other organizational metaphors.

Metaphors attempt to illustrate the relatively unfamiliar with the more familiar. The appeal of the machine and organic metaphors rests on the relative familiarity we have with the totality of a machine or a body, whereas our grasp of the totality of large-scale organizations is tenuous at best. A case can also be made here for the superiority of the explanatory metaphor. We all have, to be sure, some direct contact with both machines and bodies, but most of us only dimly understand their inner workings. Our experience with explanation is much more direct, for we all make and act in accordance with these verbal constructs. What Turbayne says of language in general can be extended to explanation in particular, for language is mostly explanatory in intent:

Many more know better how to use a language than how to use a machine. It has, indeed, grown so familiar that we are blinded by excess of light. Again, however, we can use it without knowing the rules of its grammar. There are experts here too. Accordingly, from the standpoint of familiarity with laws or rules, the choice may be difficult [between the machine and linguistic metaphors], but from the standpoint of familiarity with use, the choice is easy.[44]

Finally, in our attempt to work out some of the analogs between explanations and organizations we have begun to move from simple metaphor toward the development of a systematic model. Close investigation of the machine and organic metaphors seems unlikely to reveal more than superficial entailments, for organizations are behavioral, not physical or biological, constructs. The explanatory metaphor, therefore, draws more directly upon the actual character of the experience of the participants in an organization. The conclusions of methodological and epistemological analyses of the character of social knowledge and explanation will probably yield further analogs for organizational operations. In this way, we may begin to systematize our understanding of organizations through comparison with the most fundamental of all human activities: explanation.

COUNTERPOINT TO CHAPTER 5
Science, Bureaucracy, and Violence

IF A SOCIAL PROBLEM ever falls completely within a sphere of bureaucratic domination, insofar as standards of rationalized control unmitigated by any other values pervade the political process, then all hell, literally, can break loose. Richard Rubenstein argues that in Nazi Germany only after the Jewish problem was given over to a bureaucratic solution

was it possible to contemplate the extermination of millions. A machinery was set up that was devoid of both love and hatred. It was only possible to overcome the moral barrier that had in the past prevented the systematic riddance of surplus populations when the project was taken out of the hands of bullies and hoodlums and delegated to bureaucrats.[1]

The forces that contributed to the bureaucratization of slaughter in the death camps—secularization, disenchantment of the world, and rationalization—are also related to the development of modern science, especially in its positivist, manipulative form. Indeed, as we have argued, positivist science and Weberian bureaucracy are dominated by analogous procedural controls. Connections, therefore, exist among science, bureaucracy, and the ultimate horror of the twentieth century. The nature of their consanguinity might be illuminated by exploring the functions of religion in the control of violence, for religious institutions were significantly undermined by these processes of secularization, disenchantment, and rationalization.

René Girard, in a brilliant and disturbing study, peels back the palimpsest of religious ritual to reveal the violence—the sacred violence—at its core.[2] His analysis is too rich to summarize fully, but certain particulars may be drawn upon to illustrate the connections among science, bureaucracy, and violence.

The fundamental threat to human communities, Girard plausibly argues, is an outbreak of reciprocal violence—a violence that destroys all distinctions and recognizes no bounds, contributing to an awesome cycle of retribution and revenge. Most modern societies seem relatively immune to this cycle, owing to the effectiveness of their judicial organizations. As Girard observes,

The system does not suppress vengeance; rather, it effectively limits it to a single act of reprisal, enacted by a sovereign authority specializing in this particular function. The decisions of the judiciary are invariably presented as the final word on vengeance.[3]

Premodern communities generally lack this highly articulated system of control; however, they gain some protection through religious rituals "in which sacrificial rites divert the spirit of revenge into other channels."[4] The sacrificial violence embodied in these rituals commemorates an aboriginal act of violence that ended a "sacrificial crisis," that is, a period of reciprocal violence. At that time, the crisis-torn community divested all of its enmity upon an arbitrarily chosen surrogate, who by his death reunified the community. In retrospect, such a miraculous result would appear to be the consequence of divine intervention; consequently, the despised surrogate for the community's mutual blood lust is endowed with a sacred aura. Subsequently, established religious rituals substitute a sacrificial victim in the hope of being able to reconstitute the community continuously.

Religious prohibitions also serve to protect the community. The sacrificial crisis results from and contributes to the breakdown of distinctions—the "degrees" upon which order and shared meaning depend. Reciprocal violence produces a truly vicious equality among all the participants. This "monstrous doubling," Girard observes, lies at the heart of many of our violent myths, as in the rivalry between Achilles and Agamemnon or among Oedipus, Creon, and Tiresias. Wherever a violent rivalry can occur, religion promulgates a prohibition (the last seven of the Ten Commandments aptly illustrate this). Religious sanctification props up a structure of shared meaning based upon distinctions and limits. Girard concludes:

Religion, then, is far from "useless." It humanizes violence; it protects man from his own violence by taking it out of his hands, transforming it into a transcendent and ever-present danger to be kept in check by the appropriate rites appropriately observed and by a modest and prudent demeanor.[5]

More modern societies largely dispense with religious protection for, after all, they are defended by the judicial system. Yet Girard raises a sobering prospect:

As soon as the essential quality of transcendence—religious, humanistic, or whatever—is lost, there are no longer any terms by which to define the legitimate form of violence and to recognize it among the multitude of illicit forms. The definition of legitimate and illegitimate forms then becomes a matter of mere opinion, with each man free to reach his own decision. In other words, the question is thrown to the winds.[6]

The disenchantment, secularization, and rationalization of the world—the processes from which science has grown and to which it mightily contributes—corrode the transcendental justifications for the judicial distinction between acceptable and unacceptable coercion. The nihilism of the modern age infects all institutions of shared meaning and raises the threat of another sacrificial crisis.

The complicity of science in a contemporary sacrificial crisis extends beyond its contribution to the dissolution of the sacred. Science, at least for the past century, has maintained an ideological commitment to noncommitment. Such a stance leads to a remarkable capacity to exploit categorical instability. No categorization, no explanation, is adequate; all must be open to challenge, to revision, to abandonment. Modern science, not Trotsky, has ushered in the permanent revolution, a continuous structuring, restructuring, and destructuring of the world. This ability has contributed to remarkable advances in the prediction and control of certain phenomena, as well as to the dissolution of differences as the scientific perspective spreads throughout society. Girard notes, "The very essence of modern society might be said to be its ability to sustain the possibility for new discoveries in the midst of an ever-worsening sacrificial crisis—not, to be sure, without many signs of anxiety and stress."[7]

In his discussion of the public reactions to recombinant-DNA research, Lewis Thomas admits, "Classical mythology is peopled with mixed beings—part man, part animal or plant—and most of them are associated with tragic stories. Recombinant-DNA is a reminder of bad dreams."[8] These fears are not merely dreams, however, for the horror of a collapsing order is not immaterial, and myths, as Girard convincingly demonstrates, are rooted in experience. "A dynamic force seems to be drawing first Western society, then the rest of the world, toward a state of relative indifferentiation never before known on earth, a strange kind of nonculture or anticulture we call modern."[9] A major factor in this force is the innovating ideology of science.

The innovative drive of science therefore contributes to the threat of continual categorical disintegration, a major component of a sacrificial crisis. At the same time, the forces intimately associated with the rise of modern, or at least positivist, science dissolve the authority of those institutions—religious and judicial—designed to protect the community from outbreaks of reciprocal violence. What survives, if these processes remain dominant, are the organizations that have most closely patterned their operations on the model of positivist procedural controls and manipulative goals: Weberian bureaucracy. And, as the Holocaust suggests, there may be no *inherent* limits on what these organizations will do. The critics of positivism, then, may have real reason to fear the sovereignty of technique and calculability in social relations. Shared meaning is required for any social arrangement, and, in the absence of other bases, it will be generated through coercion and manipulation.

6

LEADERSHIP AND THE INNOVATION OF MEANING

The *creator* they hate most: he breaks tablets and old values. He is a breaker, they call him law-breaker. For the good are unable to create; they are always the beginning of the end: they crucify him who writes new values on new tablets; they sacrifice the future to *themselves*—they crucify all man's future.

You run *ahead*? Are you doing it as a shepherd? Or as an exception? A third case would be the fugitive.

NIETZSCHE

The Innovator as Hero

CRITICS OF POPULAR CULTURE periodically lament the demise of the heroic leader and the triumph of the banal. In our age, the celebrity and the superstar serve as pallid substitutes for those of truly heroic stature, presumably a sign of decadent times. But this nostalgia for the hero is misleading; indeed, we might be better advised to support the position that no age *ever* welcomes a hero. Although exaggerated, this conclusion reflects a clearer recognition of the nature of the heroic.

Joseph Campbell, in his classic study of heroism, identifies characteristics common to many heroic myths that together form something of a heroic cycle.[1] The hero usually emerges in a corrupt or enslaved community. He leaves or is exiled from his homeland and wanders alone (or with a small band of faithful) in the wilderness where he faces and overcomes tests of his courage and wisdom. The struggles of his wanderings purify and transfigure him, and, ultimately, he returns to his homeland bearing a message of salvation. Yet his erstwhile people do not always embrace him and his message; they are just as likely to crucify him. The hero may bring salvation, but he also carries the incubus of change. The true hero innovates new meanings that necessarily disrupt the comfortable assumptions and established behaviors of the community.

The popular craving for the heroic, then, must be qualified. People may intuit that some change is needed but may not desire to have the established rhythms of their lives upset, their cherished beliefs condemned, or the very basis of their self-definitions called into question. The hero, as Nietzsche notes, can be frighteningly perverse:

He shall be greatest who can be loneliest, the most concealed, the most deviant, the human being beyond good and evil, the master of his virtues, he that is overrich in will.[2]

The hero as deviant rejects the traditional ways. He stands beyond conventionally defined good and evil, because he creates new standards. The great hero and the great criminal are barely distinguishable—they are both enemies of the people.*

The hero differs from the criminal, however, in that his deviancy points the way to a fruitful adaptation, at least for those with "ears to hear and eyes to see." His role as savior is inseparable from both the innovation he brings and the qualities of the disciples he attracts. His deviancy must, in some sense, be recognized as a better way. The followers, to accept salvation, must themselves possess certain qualities that reciprocate those of the hero. Lacking heroic stature, they nonetheless sense the sickness around them, even though they may not be able to give their feelings of unease a cognitive shape or define a coping response.

The hero's ultimate quest involves more than the triumph over his trials through the innovation of new responses (meanings). In order to save his people, the innovations he devises must be made relevant to their needs and aspirations. Thus, the challenge of heroic *leadership* consists of the double task of innovation and institutionalization. The leader as hero must be capable of creating new meanings to replace those that have become obsolete. The hero as leader must be able to integrate his people into these new systems of shared meaning. Not all heroes are leaders, nor all leaders heroes. Different contexts call for (although they do not necessarily call forth) certain types of leaders. To understand the context appropriate for heroic leadership, let us turn first to a consideration of the nature and functions of other forms of leadership.

---

*The romantic aura surrounding certain criminals may originate from a recognition of this similarity.

Nature and Functions
of Leadership

Leaders need followers. This truistic observation forms the core of the debate over the role of leadership. "Great" personalities—those who stand emphatically apart from their fellow human beings—attract considerable attention, whether from historians, political analysts, or the popular press. We easily slip into the mode of seeing the course of human events in the light cast by these luminaries, who seem to possess such great capacity to initiate good or evil.

Leaders, however, amount to nothing without followers. The crisp directives of an executive depend upon the disciplined response of organizational minions for their impact. The mesmerizing diatribes of Adolf Hitler become the paranoid rantings of an asylum inmate in the absence of an adulating (and gullible?) throng. Leaders, to lead, must evoke "appropriate" responses from their presumptive followers. Successful evocation makes leaders appear to be their own cause; that is, they seem to create supportive emotions and actions that would not have been demonstrated without their presence. Behind the appearance of self-causality, however, is the question of whether leaders merely respond to and organize deeply felt motives and meanings that the followers already possess, or whether they actually create them.

Viewing the leader as the initiator clearly favors a voluntaristic, "great man," approach to political history, whereas considering the leader as reflector suggests a more deterministic interpretation of the role of leadership. In the latter case, political events are understood as the products of underlying social and economic forces, with leaders essentially viewed as interchangeable, epiphenomenal exploiters of these preexisting conditions. Consequently, masses or classes responding to fundamental contradictions in their systems of shared meaning make history, not their leaders, whose appearance of being at the head of historical movements is of no greater significance than the froth on a wave.*

Whatever the relative merits of the contending interpretations of voluntarism versus determinism, certainly leaders must have some resources, and followers must be motivated to respond to the inducements made possible by these resources (the voluntarist interpretation emphasizes the leaders' resources, while the determinist stresses the role of the followers' motivations and their latent resources). As James MacGregor Burns observes, "Even the most fearsome of power devices, such as imprisonment or torture or denial of food or water, may not affect the behavior of a masochist or a martyr."[3] Burns adds, however, that good leadership is not the simple exercise of "naked power" overcoming resistance. Rather, he argues that good leadership addresses the "wants and needs, the aspirations and expectations—of both leaders and followers."[4] His implication appears to be that the motivations sparking the followers should be "positive" in nature. A tyrant, for Burns, is not a leader, for he directs solely through fear and domination.

Burns's distinction, though normatively compelling, cannot be analytically sustained. Even the most fearsome leaders, like Tchaka, the nineteenth-century king of the Zulus whose mere gesture meant death, or Stalin and Hitler, who sent millions to their doom, did not relate to their followers only on the basis of fear. Moreover, the relation between the most beloved leaders and their followers is unlikely to be altogether free from fear (especially fear of rejection). Obviously, the components of a leader/follower relation may be used as a ground for comparison and evaluation. The differences between Christ and Tchaka are not trivial, but to use such judgments as defining characteristics of leadership *per se* seems unnecessarily arbitrary and tendentious, particularly given the inevitable mix of positive and

---

*A determinist need not hold that anyone could perform leadership functions; rather, he could hold that no one person is uniquely capable and that success depends upon fundamental factors, not leadership initiative.

negative sanctions—of love, fear, respect, and simple calculation—suffusing all leader/follower relations.

Burns correctly argues, however, that the mere control of
power resources does not create a leader. These resources must
be related to the needs and motivations of the followers. But the
definition of leadership does not depend upon the "quality" of
these motives. It depends upon the role played by a particular
individual in sustaining or transforming systems of shared meaning.* The introduction of leadership into systems of shared
meaning necessarily entails directiveness and hierarchy, even in
the case where the leader is an ephemeral phenomenon. Specifically, then, leaders perform an explanatory function for
their followers who, in turn, exemplify these explanations in
their responses. The relation of leaders to followers is one of
explanatory subsumption.

Bargaining interactions among individuals to establish
mutually agreed-upon expectations need not involve any leadership. Relative power positions alone also do not determine
explanatory subsumption. Rather, the presence of leadership
is a continuous function of outcomes. In any interactional
arrangement, a leader's definition of appropriate meaning
disproportionately structures response. How leaders actually
accomplish this structuring, whether by rewards, punishments,
persuasion, or institutional authority, is incidental to the definition of leadership, although not to evaluations of its quality or
desirability.

Just as explanations may differ in development and structure,
so also may styles of leadership. Thus, pure democratic leadership (insofar as this is not a contradiction) may be compared
with inductive generalization. Democratic leaders try to sum up
the desires of their followers in their articulation of a general
policy. In the absence of unanimity, these democratic leaders
may follow some type of majority-decision rule which produces
policies analogous to probabilistic generalizations. Conversely,

---

*Using power simply to destroy is certainly not leadership, but most tyrants
have something more than simple destruction in mind.

pure authoritarian leaders pattern their style on the deductive model. The followers' responses are "rationally deduced" from the *a priori* declarations of the leader.*

Most leadership roles, of course, call for a combination of deductive and inductive "styles." A relatively deductive style contributes to a leader/follower relationship characterized by a high degree of directiveness in which the activities of the followers tend to be regimented rather than being left to their free discretion. Alternatively, a relatively inductive style increases the responsiveness of the leaders, making them more susceptible to influence from below. Even a deductively styled, directive ruler, however, must be open to some feedback in order to be effective, just as well-constructed explanations should provide for some means of testing and of provisional validation.

Generally, the explanatory function of leaders orients their followers in the world. More specific delineations of the possible contributions of leadership further illustrate this orienting, explanatory function. James Downton, for example, divides the tasks of leadership into two broad categories.[5] The first concerns the instrumental contributions of leaders:

1. *Goal Setting:* Leaders often define the purposes of political action.

2. *Communication:* Leaders tutor their followers, harmonizing their desires with the goals defined by the leaders. In performing this function, leaders often serve as "gatekeepers," organizing and validating the information received by followers. Through information control, the leaders attempt to channel the followers' behavior.

3. *Mobilization:* Once the goals of political action have been defined and communicated, leaders then confront the task of organizing the skills and resources of the followers toward their realization.

---

*A perhaps apocryphal story about Stalin illustrates pure deductive leadership. Asked to select the course of a railroad, Stalin drew a straight line across a map, and this was the course his engineers followed, regardless of obstacles.

Downton also recognizes that leadership often involves something more than pragmatic, instrumental coordination; leaders may also perform certain emotional and psychological functions. In these affective relations, the leaders again assume an essentially explanatory position with respect to their followers:

1. *Ego Support:* Leaders may be able to validate the followers' sense of self-worth. Discontent or even self-loathing may arise from a number of sources, including a perceived discrepancy between one's performance and aspirations, the belief that one's status is not appropriately recognized, or the tensions arising between one's drives and values (between id and superego for the Freudians). Successful leaders are capable of providing avenues for the realization of their followers' aspirations, "appropriate" recognition of their worth, and a rationalization for and a channeling of their drives (e.g., a leader could validate violent aggression against a pariah group).

2. *Inspiration:* Leaders can impart a purpose to life and particularly to the presence of struggle and suffering. Ultimately, all leaders must define, or at least support, a "theodicy," a justification of the evil the followers endure in the relationship.

The various facets, both instrumental and expressive, of the explanatory role of leadership, suggest a connection between leaders and the articulation of a formal ideology. Admittedly, considerable ambiguity surrounds the concept of ideology. Some analysts treat ideology as equivalent to dogmatic, essentially false creeds or crude rationalizations of self-interest, while others equate ideology with any set of values and beliefs held in common and used to structure responses to the world.[6] Some ideologies, to be sure, are dogmatic, and all partake in some way in the shared meanings of a community. The concept, however, may be usefully restricted to those explicit efforts to formulate a reasonably coherent set of sociopolitical beliefs and values used to guide political action.

Some ideologies represent the dominant values in a community, while others help to define the position and needs of deviant groups. Not all people hold to a developed ideology, for it requires a certain degree of reflection and self-consciousness, but politically active individuals who strive to follow a course of action related to consciously developed principles possess at least the rudiments of an ideology. Ideologies are commonly associated with groups advocating significant change, because they must justify something new, whereas the defenders of the established order can usually depend upon the tacit, and essentially automatic, support of much of the population.

An ideology potentially assists leaders in carrying out their explanatory functions in a number of ways:

1. An ideology explicitly explains the nature of "reality" and orders the social cosmos. For this reason, an ideology often appeals to intellectuals seeking the "truth" and to the alienated searching for an explanation of their sense of frustration and isolation.

2. An ideology provides a framework of values and identities for a community of the faithful. Sometimes described as secular religions (or are religions sacred ideologies?), an ideology provides a source of security and identity for its believers.

3. An ideology endows a particular structure of relations with legitimacy. All political value systems must grapple with the existence of social evil in the forms of scarcity, uncertainty, powerlessness, and human perversity.[7] By validating a particular distribution of power and value, an ideology, directly or implicitly, condemns other systems of rule.

4. An ideology orders the goals of political action, establishing a hierarchy of significance, and thereby aids choice.

5. Finally, an ideology attempts to supply some of the inspiration that motivates people to action. This portion of an ideological system, sometimes called the exoteric or mass component (as opposed to the esoteric or élite component), often incorporates broad slogans that promise a brave new world of peace and plenty (e.g., Workers of the world unite! You have nothing to lose but your chains! Peace, Bread, and Freedom! All power to the people! etc.).[8]

Leaders make the world meaningful by structuring the responses of their followers. A formally articulated ideology can assist in this general and multifaceted explanatory function, but such explicit intellectualization, though potentially useful under certain circumstances, is not a necessary correlate of leadership.* Leaders may guide follower response in ways more direct even if less well conceptualized. The utility of ideological formulations partly depends upon the essential goals of the leaders, whether they aim to *sustain* or to *transform* the dominant systems of shared meaning, and the nature of the relations they establish with their followers, whether *transactional*, *catalytic*, or *charismatic*.

Given a tacit consensus on basic distributional questions, sustaining leaders generally maintain follower response through the manipulation of tangible rewards and deprivations. They organize a transactional relation with their followers in which explicit patterns of reasonably concrete exchange develop. Some transactions may be positive in that the followers commit themselves to certain behaviors in the expectation of some reward (wealth, status, influence, etc.), whereas others might be essentially negative insofar as compliance avoids the imposition of some sanction (loss of a job, imprisonment, etc.).

Burns suggests that transactional leader/follower relations are usually transitory:

Their [the leader's and the followers'] purposes are related, at least to the extent that the purposes stand within the bargaining process and can be advanced by maintaining that process. But beyond this the relationship does not go. The bargainers have no enduring purpose that holds them together, hence they may go their separate ways. A leadership act took place, but it was not one that binds leader and follower in a mutual and continuing pursuit of a higher purpose.[9]

Some transactions, probably more often between relative equals than between leaders and followers, may be transitory in character. Burns seems to underestimate, however, the importance of the covert context within which the transactions of particularly

---

*Although ideologies may serve to reinforce the explanatory capabilities of leaders, the development of an explicit ideology runs certain risks, as well. For example, (1) an ideology's purported explanations may be seen as irrelevant to the problems at hand; (2) promises contained in an ideology may inflate followers' expectations beyond the capabilities of the leader to fulfill them; (3) an inclusive ideology may politicize all areas of life, eliminating privacy; (4) rigid, absolutist ideologies limit the possibilities for compromise (ideologies, though, need not be rigid); and (5) exclusionist ideologies may heighten conflict by excluding key groups from the community of believers.

sustaining leadership take place. Consider, for example, the imperative coordination of workers within an industrial organization. The relation of the foreman to the workers on the assembly line is essentially directed at maintaining certain forms and levels of performance. These actions, in turn, help to support a complex organization and, ultimately, a distribution of power. Superficially, it may appear that the workers and the foreman are related on no other basis than that of an immediate exchange of performance for wages. Yet, as Burns implies, the exchange would not proceed smoothly without a tacit acceptance on the part of all parties of the structural context of the relationship.

In accepting the coordinating directives of the foreman, the workers not only recognize a hierarchy of authority but also a pattern of ownership. They may think of nothing more than putting in their forty hours and drawing their pay, but their failure to consider alternative organizational relations helps to sustain established patterns of interaction.

Transactional relations need not be associated solely with sustaining leaders. Exchanges may also be used to alter response, that is, transform meaning. Even the leadership of a bureaucratic organization must be prepared to adapt to changing circumstances. A bureaucratic entrepreneur will manipulate the exchange process in an effort to generate more adequate routines. Transactional transformation, we might suppose, frequently occurs when an organization faces external challenges.

When the participants themselves begin to question and reject the authority of the sustaining leadership or, more significantly, the underlying distribution of value and power, transactional relations alone may not be sufficient to sustain previously secure habits of obedience. Under these altered circumstances, explicit ideological formulations, developed by all the contending parties, may be called upon to justify maintaining or abandoning existing values and routines.

Ideologies are associated with either catalytic or charismatic leader/follower relationships. These two resemble each other and are sometimes confused, but each involves a different tie between leaders and followers. In both, the leader often seems to personify the followers' world view, giving direction and value to their collective existence. In a catalytic relation, though, the leader does so by representing (that is, *re-presenting*) the beliefs of the followers. The leader articulates the values and attitudes of the followers and in so doing gives them greater definition and order so that they might serve as better guides to action. Through such representation and articulation, such leaders inspire their followers into coordinated action in order to accomplish the goals they already desire, at least in some inchoate manner.[10]

The overt articulation of latent values may serve either to sustain or transform the dominant system of shared meaning. Sustaining leaders, confronted with the failure of transactional inducements, may be able to rally support for the flagging system by providing an explicit justification for the existing distribution of power and value. The challengers intent upon transformation, by giving voice to underlying discontents and aspirations, may be able to catalyze actions that restructure the macro-order of shared meaning.

The essentially inspirational content of catalytic leader/follower relations can lead to their being mistaken for "charismatic" leadership. Highly emotional and personally directed outpourings of energy and devotion often seem to characterize both. In a catalytic relation, however, the leaders depend upon preexisting values and orientations for their authority, whereas the reverse holds in truly charismatic relations. Catalytic leaders do not introduce new meanings to their followers so much as they organize and institutionalize ones already possessed. No matter how significant the alteration in the dominant systems of shared meaning, catalyzing leaders essentially reflect and effect the attitudes of their followers.

In a true charismatic relationship, in contrast, the leaders function more as "independent variables"; they do not simply catalyze change in the dominant structures of shared meaning by making manifest what was latent, but they can actually inculcate new meanings in their followers. Burns notes that such a transformation "becomes *moral* in that it raises the level of human conduct and ethical aspiration of both the leader and the led, and thus has a transforming effect on both."[11] We might add the Nietzschean caveat that the transforming charismatic leader may actually alter the definition of morality.

Though currently beset by vagaries of both definition and application, charisma most aptly identifies the relation between great religious leaders—Christ, Moses, Mohammed—and their more avid followers. In these extraordinary cases, the disciples believed the objects of their devotion to be set apart from ordinary humans by a "gift of grace" implying divinity or at least privileged access to the Godhead.[12] In more secular terms, the followers develop an intense faith in the ability of the leader to identify the correct course of action (i.e., define meaning).

Charismatic leader/follower relations, unlike the catalytic, can directly affect the meanings incorporated in the responses of the led, as opposed to merely reflecting and synthesizing them. The followers believe the leader "to be uniquely capable of cognitively structuring or restructuring the world."[13] Through their personal authority, charismatic leaders endow new patterns of response with legitimacy. At some point, these personally validated meanings must be routinized; that is, they must come to be held for their own sake and not simply because of the status conferred upon them by the charismatic leader. Without this routinization, or institutionalization, the incorporated meanings will tend to wither with the passing of the charismatic leader.

Charismatic leader/follower relations tend to be unstable, for the faith of the followers must be continuously renewed by repeated demonstrations of the leader's gift of grace. Until these relations are routinized in some way, both the position and the message of the leader may decay. The successful charismatic leader, then, must ultimately establish these personalized meanings on a transactional or an inspirational basis and eliminate the personalized loyalties of charismatic relations. The final test of successful charismatic relations may be that they wither away while the meanings originally so engendered survive. Charismatic relations, for this reason, provide a weak foundation for sustaining systems of shared meaning over the long term.

Many of the leaders of the newly independent Asian and African countries during the 1950s and 1960s were depicted as charismatic, while in retrospect they seem more aptly described as leaders who catalyzed their followers into acting on their beliefs. Nationalists such as Sukarno of Indonesia and Nkrumah of Ghana were initially able to engender considerable enthusiasm among large numbers of people of their countries, because they personally articulated widely shared strivings for national independence and personal dignity. In some sense, they did, indeed, personify the nation. Their stature depended upon the salience of these particular values and desires. After political independence was secured, these values declined in significance. The nation became the arena within which competition developed, and the primary challenge was to define and maintain internal institutional forms.

Sukarno and Nkrumah catalyzed the sentiments of millions of their countrymen and helped to effect a significant transformation of the dominant political structure. Neither, though, made a successful transition from transforming to sustaining leadership, in part because of the limited resources available to them to establish and maintain transactional relations.* Both tried to revive their faltering leadership positions through new ideological appeals to both domestic variations of socialism and the threat of neocolonialism to their newly won independence. Neither socialism nor neocolonialism proved to have the initial catalyzing power of the original desire for national independence and dignity. They lacked the charisma to introduce new values to their followers, and their declining catalytic appeal, combined with inadequate transactional resources, contributed to their ouster in the mid-1960s.

The categories of sustaining and transforming leadership goals, as well as the alternatives of transactional, catalytic, and charismatic relations, are ideal types (see diagram). A leader may perform both roles at different times, or even at the same time with different subjects. Followers commit themselves to leaders for a variety of reasons, and not all followers necessarily relate to the leader in the same way. Formalized leader/follower relations in a bureaucracy, for example, may usually be essentially transactional in nature, and most authority holders will adopt sustaining leadership roles. An organizational ideologue, however, may try to catalyze latent energies and values of the membership. Some officials may even be able to develop charismatic relations with some of their subordinates. Certainly some of the great military leaders, from Alexander to Patton, appear to have inspired loyalties that transcended routinized transactions.

*Each regime was also marred by considerable corruption and inefficiency, further eroding their transactional capabilities.

LEADER/FOLLOWER RELATIONS

GOALS		Transactional	Catalytic	Charismatic
	Sustaining	Manager	Conservative Ideologist	Charismatic Conserver (Pharaoh?)
	Transforming	Entrepreneur	Transforming Ideologist	Charismatic Innovator (Classic Hero)

Alternatively, the dynamic and powerful leadership often associated with revolutionary movements may at first appear to be predominantly transformational, but revolutionary leaders must also sustain certain meanings within their organizations once they have attracted support. They may draw upon transactional relations to do so. All successful movements, after all, attract those seeking their personal advantage as well as a common ideal, and these motives may be manipulated by the revolutionary leader.

A revolutionary leader may find it easier to catalyze the latent aspirations of his potential supporters, or to manipulate rewards and punishments, than actually to engender new values in them. When Gandhi advocated Indian independence, for example, he articulated the desires of vast segments of the population. When he tried to remove the pariah status of the "Untouchables" or instigate his vision of social development, he strove to transform the micromeanings of his followers as well as the dominant structures of shared meaning. His success in mobilizing people for the struggle for independence was significantly greater than his efforts to inculcate new values.

Transformations involving the innovation of new responses constitute the most demanding task of leadership, and the more significant the innovation sought, the greater the challenge to leadership. First, the leaders themselves must generate new meanings, and then they must effect this transformation among their presumptive followers. Success in the stage of innovation, as we noted earlier, does not guarantee success in the latter stage of institutionalization.

Transforming Leadership: Innovation, Deviance, and Creativity

One of the least beneficial bequests of the Romantic era is the strong positive connotation of the notion of "creativity." The creative act, originally associated with the Divine movement above the waters and, later, by the Romantics with the artist, has been appropriated to describe everything from the behavior of children to one of the preconditions for scientific progress. Certainly, to be considered creative is a good thing in our culture. It may be, though, that we have the judgmental sequence reversed: An innovation or new accomplishment is not good because it is creative; rather it is declared creative because it is judged to be good.[14]

Creativity, then, is socially validated innovation, with innovation defined as a patterned divergence from an established behavioral norm (i.e., haphazard drift is not innovative).[15] From this perspective, innovation should be considered a neutral term: If we believe that a particular innovation is valuable or useful for some purpose we possess, we validate it as being creative. If we give the innovation a negative evaluation, we condemn it as perverse or deviant. Creativity and perversion are both innovative; the difference between them reflects a social judgment, and, of course, such judgments may be in error or may change over time (as illustrated by changing fashions in the arts).

Human beings cannot avoid either attempting to impose coherence and order upon experience or innovating divergent and therefore unpredictable responses.[16] The former drive arises from the need for shared meaning in order to ensure smooth social interaction. The latter emerges from a number of factors, perhaps the most fundamental of which is the nature of the brain, which contemporary evidence suggests is best conceived as a stochastic rather than a simple, causally determinant system.[17]

In some way, deviance appears to be built into the human brain. Daniel Dennett, in an insightful essay, develops a model of a mechanism that helps to account for this phenomenon.*[18] Dennett notes that the "law of effect" (reinforced actions tend to be repeated) seems to have considerable explanatory power in the area of learning, even though behaviorist use of the principle accounts only for learning through direct experience. Unfortunately, even monkeys, much more human beings, seem capable of selecting "an adaptive course of action without benefit of prior external feedback and reinforcement."[19] Dennett suggests that such learning could be accounted for through an extension of the law of effect by positing an "inner" environment "conceived as an input-output box for providing feedback for events in the brain."[20] A creature possessing such an internalized process would be capable of selectively reinforcing *potential* behavior before incorporating it into *overt* response. As Dennett remarks, "The advantage provided by such a benign inner environment has been elegantly expressed in a phrase of Karl Popper's: it 'permits our hypothesis to die in our stead'."†[21]

True innovation must be underdetermined self-design. It "must tread the fine line between the idiocy of pre-programmed tropism on one hand and the idiocy of an over-plastic domination of fortuitous impingements on the other."[22] To walk this line, Dennett argues that:

the new design is determined by the combination of the old design and contributions (from either the inside or the outside or both) that are themselves *arbitrary*, that is undesigned or *fortuitous*. But if the contribution of arbitrary elements is to yield a better than chance probability of the new design being an improvement over the old design, the old design must have the capacity to reject arbitrary contributions on the basis of design features—information—already present. In other words, there must be a *selection* from fortuitous contributions, based upon the old design. If the arbitrary or undesigned contribution comes from within, what we have is a nondeterministic automaton.[23]

---

*Dennett's hypothesis, while not definitively established, appears compatible with both experimental evidence and introspection. Compare D. N. Perkins, *The Mind's Best Work* (Cambridge: Harvard University Press, 1981).

†If a creature randomly generated such a capacity, it would have a selective advantage over its less gifted competitors for a particular environmental niche.

Innovation, as opposed to the repetition of previously reinforced behaviors (habit or tradition), is the product of a process
of "generate and test." In this process, the alternative potential
behaviors generated are undesigned or underdesigned, and the
testing (in the internal environment) and selection of a manifest
response is based upon prior experience and established characteristics, such as "hard-wired" genetic proclivities. Dennett
suggests that the generator of which we are aware may be highly
selective, but this selectivity itself can be explained by a prior
generate-and-test process, and so on. A completely randomized
generator (if it exists, for some selectivity may be a genetic trait)
probably functions only at the preconscious level, unless we
scramble our brains.

We need not assume that all people are equally capable of
generating, selecting, and incorporating innovative behavior in
their manifest responses. Extrapolating from Dennett's argument, generators and selectors may be more or less constricted.
Simplifying these distinctions of degree to either/or compari-
sons, we may distinguish two basic dichotomies:

Unconstricted vs. Constricted Generators. Some people may
be able to generate a wide array of divergent potential behaviors
from which to select and incorporate a manifest response. In
others, the overt generator itself may be highly selective, presenting few alternatives that vary little in their range.

Unconstricted vs. Constricted Selectors. Selection, according
to Dennett, depends upon prior design. Again, some people may
be more capable of selecting a divergent response from among
the potential alternatives presented by the generator. Alternatively, a constricted selector will tend to choose the alternative
that most closely resembles strongly rooted behavior patterns. In
mentalist terms, the unconstricted selector may be characterized
as having a high toleration for ambiguity, intellectual flexibility,
and a capacity to accept negative feedback on established
behaviors. The constricted selector, in contrast, possesses
a low toleration for ambiguity, intellectual rigidity, and a tendency to block negative feedback concerning established behavior patterns.

These two dichotomies may be combined to suggest four different mind types with respect to the potential for innovative behavior (see diagram, page 180):

I. *Unconstricted Generator/Unconstricted Selector.* This mind has the capacity for generating alternative potential behaviors that deviate significantly from previously established responses. In addition, it has the capacity to accept negative feedback on current behavior and to incorporate a divergent alternative in manifest response. This is the mind type of a potential innovator.

II. *Constricted Generator/Unconstricted Selector.* Some minds may possess the capacity to accept and incorporate divergent responses, but their own internal generators may be unable to present them with a significant range of alternatives from which to choose. This type of mind would be receptive to exogenous innovations.

III. *Unconstricted Generator/Constricted Selector.* Some minds might be able to generate divergent alternatives but refuse to consider any except those that conform closely with previously established response. This mind type characterizes the "repressed" personality.

IV. *Constricted Generator/Constricted Selector.* Highly selective generators might present only alternatives that closely approximate previous responses from which only the most similar alternative will be selected for incorporation in overt behavior. Such a mind type might be that of the true conservative.

The potential innovator, of course, need not select the most deviant alternative to any and all situations; rather, he *could* do so if, on the basis of negative feedback to currently established patterns of behavior, he judges it appropriate to do so. Nor will the innovative response necessarily constitute an "improvement." The innovator could innovate himself out of existence.

Innovative responses to shared environments threaten smooth interaction, resulting in tremendous resources being invested to channel the range of response as narrowly as possible, at least in critical areas. Social controls function to structure

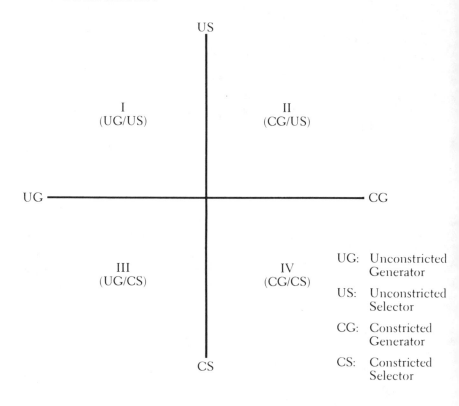

Four Mind Types. These four ideal mind types can be represented as the four cells of intersecting continua. Such a representation allows us to conceive of any population being distributed along these two continua, rather than assuming that they are all pure types of one form or another. We could hypothesize that a population would not be equally distributed among the four cells. Because of the need for a considerable degree of order and the consequent resources invested in social control, a population should be heavily skewed toward cells III and IV. As social institutions decay and fall into disrepute, many might shift into II. We could reasonably presume that the numbers in cell I would always be relatively small.

both generators (by inculcating prior constricted generate-and-test routines) and selectors. "The central concern of humanity," Peckham observes, "is and must be with the stabilization of responses, that is, the stabilization of the conventions of appropriate response."[24]

The basic means of controlling response, as all social scientists know, are socialization and policing. Socialization works to structure prior design so as to ensure that only a narrow range of possible alternatives will be seriously considered. Yet, socialization is always more or less inconsistent and inadequate (see Chapter 3) and policing—external restraints on response—attempts to fill in the gaps created by "breakdowns" in the socialization process. Policing, however, can be evaded, for resources are never sufficient to cover all the possible areas of breakdown. Lapses and contradictions in the socialization process, combined with the possibility of evading policing, contribute to social conditions conducive to innovation or, at least, drift. The weaker the mechanisms of social control, the wider will be the delta of deviance.

Gaps always exist between conventional responses and the demands of any particular situation; if the gap widens significantly, survival will be threatened. Paradoxically, then, "humanity is self defeating, for the condition of its existence, stabilization by policing [and socialization] is antithetical to that existence."[25] Innovations can both threaten and enhance chances for survival. Usually, a life-enhancing innovation will be validated as creative, but this is not always the case, nor is the judgment always universally shared or correct. Unfortunately, we often discover whether an innovation improves life chances only after the fact.

Nonetheless, since we need innovation as well as stability, we should recognize some of the conditions that seem likely to favor an innovative generate-and-select process. These conditions, though, produce perversity as well as creativity, an inevitable cost of social transformation. Peckham, in his studies of the nineteenth-century Romantics (a creative and often perverse group), identifies certain factors that encourage deliberate innovation[26]:

Explanatory Collapse

We cannot deliberately set out to innovate a new pattern of response until we first reject responses available in our culture. If we accept one or another of the available meanings, then our selectors, in Dennett's terms, will tend to incorporate from among whatever potential responses we might generate those most in conformance with our accepted values. Only if we find the available meanings questionable will we be willing and even able to consider truly innovative alternatives from among the potential behaviors we generate.

The few early Romantics, for example, around the turn of the eighteenth century endured an explanatory collapse due to their perception of the failure of Enlightenment beliefs and values as demonstrated in the Reign of Terror. They were unable to return to a belief in a Christian theodicy, the other major source of meaning and value available in the culture of the time; thus, they felt forced to innovate a new ground of meaning. In order to *cultivate* a similar experience (as opposed to waiting for the "fortuitous" catastrophe), we must adopt an antiexplanatory attitude; that is, we must reject the necessary authenticity and adequacy of any and all explanations. This Nietzschean goal of a continuous revaluation of all values can be, as his personal biography suggests, a rather demanding task master.

Alienation

To challenge the current explanations is not sufficient. Once these meanings have been rejected, we must be able to withstand the social and psychological pressure to reimpose some order, to reembrace the rejected meanings. Alienation, in this sense, simply implies separation from the cultural directives that reflect the abandoned explanations and the people that embody them in their behavior.

Three interrelated factors contribute to successful alienation: social protection, psychic insulation, and the ability to endure long periods of problem exposure. High rates of interaction (social penetration), and the psychic subordination they imply, tend to reinforce conventional patterns of response and thereby to channel behavior along expected paths and to undercut the capacity to endure problem exposure. We might recognize this type of alienation not only with the Romantic artist isolated in his garret but also to some extent with innovative scientists, scholars, and businessmen, all of whom try to separate themselves to some extent from conventional interactions that reinforce conformity.

Randomization and Search Behavior

Confronted with a problem and having rejected the available solutions, we engage in search behavior (the generative side of Dennett's model). Peckham suggests that "the greater the randomization of behavior, the greater the statistical probability for innovation of a new and fruitful mode or pattern of behavior."[27] In Dennett's view, only *potential* behaviors need to be randomized; that is, we do not actually have to manifest random responses so much as produce a randomly generated array of potential behavioral alternatives.

Randomization must be considered a matter of degree (cf., constricted generators); indeed, search behavior may be under the control of certain hueristic procedures found to be productive in the past (i.e., learning how to learn better). These procedures may also be considered the product of a generate-and-test process, and they, too, could be abandoned and new ones innovated.

In any case, expansion of the range of potential responses considered increases the likelihood of innovation, in terms of patterned deviation from a norm, whatever its presumed impact, beneficial or otherwise. Isolation from normal social intercourse not only insulates us from the many pressures for conformity but also provides a "space" within which we can engage in randomization away from the "noise" of conventionality. Innovative behavior increases at the higher cultural levels of a society— whether in the arts, science, or business. Not coincidently, higher cultural roles tend to provide spaces such as the studio, laboratory, study, or inner sanctum for such search behavior.

Randomization, however, demands more than an insulated setting. The ability to resist the rush to impose some order must also be deliberately cultivated.* We might speculate that the ability to endure the tension created by an unsolved problem and so allow time to generate a range of alternative solutions may be a genetic, hard-wired proclivity. Clearly, people differ in their toleration of ambiguity, and this may be partially inherited, as well as mediated by cultural directives.

Cultural Vandalism

Significant innovation, then, depends on two factors: first, the capacity to generate a range of potential behaviors and, second, the ability to break away from previously established proclivities and select a divergent response from among the potential alternatives. If the capacity to either generate or select is constricted, so also will be the degree of innovation. Once we have successfully generated an alternative response we deem less inadequate than those conventionally available, we must then engage in cultural vandalism. The more significant our innovation, the more disruptive it will prove for the existing systems of shared meaning. "One of the first great scientific discoveries, Galileo's," Peckham wryly notes, "was clearly labeled for what it was, a crime."[28]

The mere existence of innovative behavior need not imply its necessary promulgation throughout society. Many innovations go no further than the innovator's private world or a closed circle of intimates (e.g., the initial stages of artistic or scientific innovation or, for that matter, sexual perversion). Others may

---

*In one of his more provocative books, *Man's Rage For Chaos: Biology, Behavior, and the Arts* (New York: Schocken, 1965), Peckham argues that exposure to the arts of the higher cultural levels may contribute to the cultivation of such a capability: "Art is the exposure to the tensions and problems of a false world so that man may endure exposing himself to the tensions and problems of the real world" (p. 314). Art, especially at the higher cultural levels, presents problems and discontinuities of perception that defy easy resolution, for they generally challenge preexisting approaches to art. Art, moreover, is generally contemplated under conditions of isolation and thereby allows for the postponement of the imposition of meaning and encourages search behavior.

be intended for the public domain but may never acquire any significant support or may even provoke open hostility (e.g., the response to certain revolutionary or utopian proposals). Some innovations may percolate throughout a community by means of imitation, or contagion, without the benefit of any organized efforts at communication and institutionalization. Innovating *leadership* is not really evident in any of these instances. Innovative, transforming leaders must not only generate new meanings/responses but must also play a pivotal role in having these innovations incorporated in the shared meanings of a community.* This process of institutionalization is the second stage of innovative, transforming leadership.

Transforming Leadership: The Institutionalization of Innovation

An innovating leader does not simply transform the dominant structure of shared meaning in a community. A catalytic transformer may also foster such change on the macro-level. Innovating leaders themselves have changed, and they introduce new meanings to their followers. This type of transformation requires restructuring the basic patterns of response of the led, but innovating leaders cannot work such a transformation in a vacuum. Their presumptive followers must also be prepared in some way to accept the message.

In order for such a conversion of meaning to occur, the followers must also experience something of an explanatory collapse. They, too, must be alienated from the prevailing response

---

*We assume for the purposes of our discussion that the same person is both innovator and leader. The two roles could be separated.

expectations, even though they may continue to conform outwardly. Ritualistic conformance, while indicative of explanatory collapse, nevertheless supports the established order. Reformist activities, although possibly effecting a modest amount of change, are, by their nature, limited and restricted to relatively noncritical areas of social interaction. Although a ritualistic conformer may be poised for a more significant transformation (perhaps lacking only courage or imagination) and the reformer may actually bring about a modest alteration in shared meanings, significant transformation involves two more extreme responses to alienation: revolution or withdrawal.[29]

In a revolution, the personal transformation is projected outward to the whole community, whereas in withdrawal, rather than working for the redefinition of the shared meanings of the rest of the community, the objective becomes to break off contact with it. The paradigmatic example of the former, of course, is a revolutionary movement, while the latter may be seen in some utopian communes. Although both constitute radical responses to the dominant meanings of a culture, and thus often appear similar to those who continue to identify with the status quo, revolution and withdrawal are, in fact, opposite responses to the experience of explanatory collapse. Nevertheless, both withdrawal and revolution represent significant transformations. Leaders who effect either response depend upon followers who possess certain characteristics.[30]

First, those who are primed for transformation must be threatened by the explanatory collapse they have experienced. Conceivably, although they might believe that the available meanings in their culture fail to account for certain perceived anomalies, they may not view this failure as having much import for their lives. Moderate discontent would incline potential followers to ritualism or efforts at modest reform but not to the rigors of either revolution or withdrawal. As people grow more threatened by the failures of existing explanations, they will become less tolerant of the compromises necessary for either outward conformance or reform. They will tend to be more receptive to messages that promise some threat-reducing alteration of circumstances. The degree of threat perception, then, affects the openness of people to innovative messages.

Second, the extent to which the threatened feel isolated in their plight reinforces the tendency toward a more moderate response. If, however, they see others as sharing the same disposition, they will be inclined to a more radical response. One of the critical tasks of any transforming leader is to overcome the sense of separateness that understandably accompanies the initial loss of faith in the prevailing explanations of a community. By recognizing the existence of others who share their experience, the threatened will be better able to consider the possibility of a new basis of shared meaning to be accomplished either by the transformation of the whole community through the introduction of revolutionary innovations or by the withdrawal of like-minded people from it.

Third, overcoming the sense of isolation contributes to a growing sense of invulnerability from reprisals of significance, further encouraging a radical response. Certainly, a fear that the forces of the establishment will crush any dissent would work to discourage a major revolutionary challenge. Even the "passive" radicalism of withdrawal is repressed by many regimes.

Finally, those most susceptible to radical appeals possess a low need to be reintegrated into the dominant order. A repressed person might be attracted to a movement that justifies his surrender to impulse, at least under some conditions (e.g., attacks on some enemy), but most likely the need for order will eventually win out. Perhaps many revolutions die because of the predominance of order-prone personalities (e.g., Stalin). Similarly, the reformer and the ritualist conformer do not really wish to cut themselves free from the established community, an attitude that moderates their response. Those who withdraw must accept a complete severing of ties. The revolutionary moves to an even further extreme, not only rejecting the possibility of reintegration but also working toward the radical restructuring of the existing community.

Since revolutionaries engage in direct attacks upon the prevailing systems of shared meaning, as opposed to simply withdrawing from them, we could presume that their sense of invulnerability must be proportionally higher and their need to be reintegrated somewhat lower than those inclined to a more passive radicalism. In addition, the radical activist may have higher energy and anger levels and have the ability to sustain these feelings of anger, whereas those who withdraw may mainly feel sadness and disappointment.

To develop a tempting analogy: innovating leaders generate, and followers test and select. The value of this analogy depends upon our recognition of the highly selective nature of the "generator." Transforming leaders who essentially catalyze their followers' latent values and orientations are more constricted generators than the leaders who develop truly innovative alternatives. Whether the innovative message will be acted upon depends upon its content. The followers must see the substance of the innovative message as addressing the causes of their discontent. Every culture produces "saviors" who are dismissed by even the dispossessed.

The successful innovative transformer provides answers for those who lack the imagination to produce their own alternatives, even though they have lost faith in the available meanings in their culture ("mind type" II). More marginally, the innovating leader might help the repressed accept some of their impulses ("mind type" III). Such followers are undependable, for they can betray the transformation both by the potentially consuming and uncontrollable nature of their released passions and by their underlying tendency to revert to an order-prone form. Finally, all transforming leaders help overcome the paralysis of fear caused by a sense of isolation.

Innovating transformers, in contrast to their catalyzing counterparts, adopt a more independent status vis-à-vis their followers, for they actually effect a change in the followers as opposed to synthesizing previously established, if unarticulated, beliefs and values. Yet, even leaders who instigate a major social innovation cannot be considered uncaused causes, for they can only transform those ready for transformation. This raises the question whether the transforming leader can contribute to the followers' experience of explanatory collapse which seems to be a prior condition for the acceptance of an innovative message.

Karl Marx, whose theories certainly reflect the position that an explanatory collapse must develop from changes in fundamental forces beyond the reach of the will of the innovating leader, could not resist trying to contribute to worker disenchantment. John McMurtry notes that the brutality of Marx's invective was in part the result of his desire to break down the "servility of the very mind structure" characterizing those captured by the "forms of consciousness" supporting the existing relations of production.[31] Marx recognized that his innovative message would be meaningless to the proletariat (that is, it would fail to structure their response) unless they first rejected the prevailing explanations or ideologies. He apparently hoped that his denunciations would contribute to this end, even while he developed a theory that posited that changes in the underlying productive forces were necessary to bring about a recognition of the inadequacy of the dominant productive relations as well as the justifications that support them.

Marx's efforts suggest a possible answer to the problem of the relation between the innovating leader and the precondition of explanatory collapse. The followers must experience the collapse for themselves by encountering serious anomalies for which the prevailing social explanations, or ideologies, cannot account. The innovating leader may contribute to their recognition by synthesizing the discontinuous experience of these anomalies into a coherent interpretation of cultural collapse. Consequently, before they can institutionalize their innovations, the leaders may first need to catalyze discontent.

Once discontent has been catalyzed and the innovative alternatives accepted by the followers, the movement must be sustained. The successful innovator, then, may need to draw upon all leader/follower relations—charisma, inspiration, rewards, and punishments—and must himself change from a transforming to a sustaining leader. The general directives of the social innovator must be prepared for through the processes of catalytic inspiration and, perhaps, sustained through potentially sordid and compromising political transactions.

Revolutionary innovations, as Jon Gunnemann suggests, are the social equivalents of paradigm shifts in a scientific field of inquiry.[32] No reason exists for presuming them to be any more frequent. Similarly, the true innovating leader, a Copernicus of politics, is as rare as scientific genius.

COUNTERPOINT TO CHAPTER 6
Pornography and Innovation

> In the end this transformation of Eros [by the Church] into a devil wound up as a comedy: Gradually the "devil" Eros became more interesting to men than all the angels and saints, thanks to the whispering and the secret-mongering of the Church in all erotic matters: this has had the effect, right into our own time, of making the *love story* the only real interest shared by *all* circles—in an exaggeration which would have been incomprehensible in antiquity and which will yet be laughed at someday.
>
> NIETZSCHE

CONDITIONS ENCOURAGING INNOVATION need not produce only results judged to be creative. One consequence of an innovative culture, for example, may be the production of pornography. Examinations of the sources and role of pornography often inspire a considerable amount of conflict, but when the debates about community standards, redeeming social value, and the exploitation of women subside, one point remains clear: The definition of what constitutes pornography is "controlled by the interests of the definer."[1]

In most cases, the dominant interest is to demonstrate some form of political mastery. The forces of stability demonstrate their mastery through the strict socialization and policing of behavior.[2] On the other hand, those intellectuals who defend pornography (or, at least, the rights of pornographers) do so not because they necessarily value such material. They also generally wish to condemn it but for their own reasons: in order to demonstrate their mastery as the "final judge in verbal and related nonverbal behavior, such as the nonverbal arts."[3]

One approach to the definition of pornography emphasizes the capacity of these materials to produce genital stimulation in the perceiver. However, there are few phenomena to which someone or another cannot have a sexual response. Moreover, the reverse is also true: what may prove powerfully stimulating to one person may not have any effect on another or, indeed, in the same person at a different time. Morse Peckham, in his analysis of the nature of pornography, chooses to ignore perceiver response altogether and develops a definition based upon its content: "Pornography is the presentation in verbal or visual signs of human sexual organs in a condition of stimulation."[4] This definition remains, admittedly, somewhat ambiguous, but it does allow him to address the relation of pornography to art and its place in our culture while it avoids peripheral political issues. Often other participants in the debate discuss only the appropriate goals and mechanisms of social control and do not consider the relation of pornography to wider cultural currents.

Analyses of the relation of art to pornography are generally tendentious and circular: If the perceiver decides that the work is pornographic, he refuses to validate it by categorizing it as art. Alternatively, if he wishes to validate the work, he will deny that it is pornographic or assert that the artistic elements constitute redeeming social value. Peckham suggests that the explanation for this behavior lies in the overestimation of sexuality in our culture which prevents the observer from engaging in an artistic response to works with a powerful sexual content.[5] Rather, "he resolves the tension between artistic form and sexual content by asserting that there are no other interests [other than pornographic] and even that the work is not art."[6]

Art consists of objects produced (or selected, as when a person places a piece of driftwood on the mantel "to serve as the occasion for playing the art perceiver's role."[7] A work of art presents a viewer with a perceptual problem, the solution to which can be postponed indefinitely because the problem does not require action. The contemplation of art objects, whether a book, painting, concert, or whatever, commonly occurs under conditions of psychic insulation. Finally, the semantic content of the work offers material capable of engaging the perceiver's interest.[8]

Now pornography most certainly is contemplated under conditions of psychic insulation, thanks largely to policing (both external and internalized) associated with sexual matters. The content, too, is capable of arousing one's interest (so to speak), so much so that it creates problems for some perceivers. The perceptual problem generated by any art work develops from the formal discontinuities injected by the artist (see the counterpoint to Chapter 2). As works are produced at the higher cultural levels, these discontinuities usually become more pronounced and, thus, the perceptual problem increases.

Pornography is often denied the status of art because of its repetitiousness. Monotony and a high degree of accessibility, however, are a function of the cultural level at which most, but not all, pornographic art is produced. They are not distinguishing characteristics of pornography but of lower cultural levels.[9] Pornographic material can be found in works produced at the highest cultural level, including Molly Bloom's soliloquy at the end of James Joyce's *Ulysses* and several striking scenes in Thomas Pynchon's *Gravity's Rainbow*. Peckham concludes:

Since pornographic art is in its formal function indistinguishable from art in the full stylistic and cultural range of the European culture area, since there is no uniqueness in the formal aspect of pornographic art, there is nothing to be said about it that cannot be said about non-pornographic art.[10]

If artistic interests are essentially reflected in the contemplation of the formal aspects of pornographic art, what are the interests behind the contemplation of its semantic content? Commonly, answers to this question sense a problem but miss the point. Those, for example, who assert that the sole semantic function behind the production and consumption of pornography is the degradation and exploitation of women either have not seen much pornography or do not consider sadomasochistic relations with males in bondage or homosexual relations pornographic. I suspect they are less concerned with understanding the functions of pornography than with demonstrating mastery and exercising social control.

Peckham, in contrast, argues that the semantic content of pornography can serve a number of functions, though not necessarily for all people. Sexual activity, like any other aspect of human behavior, can be conceived as a role which must be learned by those who wish to engage in the activity. Sexual role performance in our culture is rather poorly transmitted, at least by authorized agents of socialization (especially in comparison with important roles such as automobile driver). One possible function of pornography is educational. A person can use pornographic materials for "self reinforcement of genital response to sexual role cues."[11] To put it more bluntly, it helps teach a person what is supposed to turn him (or her) on. More outrageously, Peckham suggests that pornography, like a liberal education, provides an inventory of one's culture. Pornography, he says,

is virtually the only means currently available in the culture for showing what interests may be engaged in playing the sexual role, and presenting those interests in the form of exemplary verbal and nonverbal mediating signs of role factors. As with a liberal education it provides the individual with an opportunity to make an inventory of factors in the sexual role and modes of genital response so that he may discover what really appeals to him.[12]

Like a liberal education, pornography may provide the resources with which a person can overcome the boredom with routine that necessarily sets in with the extended performance of any role.

Pornography also provides the pleasures of simplification and relief from tensions that accompany performance of the sexual role.[13] Principally, it eliminates concern for the other person—a major source of sexual dysfunction. The appeal of masturbation, perhaps the most innocent and, ironically, the most shameful of all human pleasures, largely rests on this tension relief. The contemplation of pornography can even be disinterested, eliminating the demands for any type of genital activity.

Sadomasochism reflects a deeper interest of human beings: the will to power and its obverse, the will to submission.[14] In such relationships, the object upon which the sadist imposes his will has been rendered totally powerless. The user of sadomasochistic material is submitting to the ultimate human fantasy —the dream of totally successful adaptation, either through unhindered aggression or through unresisting submission.

Peckham suggests that pornography might perform one final function, at least for a few individuals, of providing a means of cultural transcendence.[15] Pornography, indeed all sexual behavior, is an area subject to considerable policing. This fact, combined with the overvaluation of sexual matters in our culture and the inadequacy of the directions for role performance, means that considerable personal energy is exhausted simply through role anxiety and evasion.[16] Tremendous resources might be liberated for the innovation of new responses to the demands of the environment if a person could manage to free himself from sexual concerns and evasions.

Increased personal energy resources, of course, are only a necessary condition for innovation; one must also have experienced explanatory collapse and go on to innovate a new response. Yet, unless a person is freed from absorption in the trivial, the subsequent stages of innovation are unlikely to be reached. The best way to achieve such freedom is to exhaust the interest. Pornography grants sexual interests "a gratification that simply wears them out," producing genuine boredom and releasing the individual from the bondage of the trivial.[17]

The potential link between pornography and individual innovation suggests aspects of another relationship between pornography and the wider culture. Peckham notes that the rise of pornography in the European cultural area correlates with the increasing tempo of technical and social innovation over the last five hundred years.[18] The existence of a powerful pornographic tradition in Japan gives further credence to a possible link between pornography and innovation in a culture. Only Japan, with its capacity to incorporate and adapt innovations from outside its culture, matches the capacity of the European cultural system to generate innovations internally.[19] Pornography, Peckham suggests, reveals the forces of which a culture is most proud:

When one examines the full range of European and American pornography from the late fourteenth century to the present, one is struck by an irresistible fact: it has been as steadily innovative as science itself....[20]

Pornography, then, may not be an incidental and avoidable perversion; rather, it appears to reflect the central innovative thrust of our culture.

7

FREEDOM AND ORDER IN THE CONSTRUCTION OF SELF AND SOCIETY

That my life has no aim is evident even from the accidental nature of its origin; that *I can posit an aim for myself* is another matter. But a state has no aim; we alone give it this aim or that.

NIETZSCHE

Individuals and Society

D IVERSE QUESTIONS of political value often reflect various facets of the same central problem: the appropriate relations among individuals and between them and the society in which they find themselves. "Society," that tempting and convenient reification, can be used to categorize any sustained interaction among two or more individuals. Sustained interaction depends upon a foundation of shared meaning. Debates over values, then, concern the appropriate structure of systems of shared meaning.

Traditionally, a division has developed over the character of the relations between individuals and their systems of shared meaning. One view, to paraphrase Rienhold Niebuhr's well-known book, might be encapsulated as "moral man and immoral meaning."[1] Individuals, from this perspective, are considered primary and their systems of shared meaning are merely their collective artifice. This artifice, however, is flawed, for it commonly consists of outmoded constraints that impinge upon and cripple the capacity of individuals to find self-fulfillment. More emphatically, evil in the world results from perversions in the social arrangements that shackle the presumably innate capacity of human beings to behave benevolently toward one another. If we tend to such a position, several value orientations seem to follow:

1. Individual freedom will be stressed in opposition to order and authority, which only impose distorting restrictions that must be transcended for self-actualization to occur.

2. A belief in the essential equality of human beings will tend to prevail over arguments protecting differences, for social distinctions will be considered the insupportable consequence of essentially arbitrary social arrangements.

3. Attitudes toward the possibility and desirability of change will be positive, progressive, and potentially revolutionary. Underlying any specific program for social renovation will be the quality of hope—hope that improvement is indeed possible. The belief that human beings are essentially moral entities whose potential is constrained by obsolete conventions of shared meaning helps to fuel the engine of social change.

Alternatively, the relations between human beings and their social arrangements can be conceived of in opposite terms: "immoral man and moral society." Human beings are inherently flawed, whether by original sin, the continuation of atavistic impulse, or whatever. The social constraints implied by systems of shared meaning, although perhaps imperfect, exist to channel individual impulse to support at least a chance for collective survival and civilization. Without such constraints, humans, with their insatiable and egotistic passions, would fall upon one another in a war of each against all and soon would descend into a condition of mutual meaninglessness. From this position, it is but a small step to consider individuals, insofar as they are civil at all, as the products of existing social ties and relations and dependent upon them for whatever humanity they possess. Without these systems of shared meaning, we would all be feral. This essentially organic conception of the relations between individuals and society leads to substantially different value orientations:

1. Freedom, defined as the minimization of social constraints, will be rejected. After all, if human beings are innately inclined toward chaos, they can hardly be left to their own devices. Order, authoritatively structured and imposed, will replace freedom as the primary value.

2. Essential differences among human beings will be stressed at the expense of their presumed similarities. Justice, in terms of treating different individuals differently, will be deemed essential to the proper functioning of the established social arrangements.

3. Change, therefore, will be viewed with suspicion, especially the changes that weaken social strictures and widen opportunities for individual degeneracy. Underlying this basically conservative resistance to any proposal that might prove to be

disruptive to the established order is a profound skepticism about the possibility for true progress. As Plato noted in the *Republic*, if the existing arrangements are the best possible under the circumstances, then any change must necessarily be for the worse.[2]

Though undoubtedly overstated, these contending themes reflect some fundamental aspects of human experience as evidenced by their stubborn recurrence in Western political philosophy. Nonetheless, the inability to resolve satisfactorily the tensions between the two positions suggests that the major terms of the dispute might be fruitfully reformulated.

Perhaps it is misleading, first of all, to consider human beings or their social arrangements as being *inherently* moral or immoral. "There are no moral phenomena at all," Nietzsche observes, "but only a moral interpretation of phenomena."[3] When we judge something to be moral or immoral, we do not discover essences; rather, "we know only numerous, individualized, and thus unequal actions, which we equate by omitting the unequal...."[4] At any point, this strategy of categorization can be undermined by calling attention to previously ignored differences. All judgments of morality of individuals or the systems of shared meaning in which they are enmeshed are, therefore, unstable.

If morality cannot be discovered or revealed as a system of absolute truth but only interpreted, human beings must be seen as the creators of morality and responsible for the consequences of their judgments.

Verily, men give themselves all their good and evil. Verily, they did not take it, they did not find it, nor did it come to them as a voice from heaven. Only man placed values in things to preserve himself—he alone created a meaning for things, a human meaning.[5]

Our responsibility, tragically, is somewhat divorced from our ability to control. The systems of shared morality which we create and sustain by our actions often confront us as apparent givens. In this sense we do "discover" morality; that is, we discover other people's expectations as to how we ought to behave, or, perhaps more accurately, we have these expectations thrust upon us. Unless we declare total independence from all communities of meaning (an improbable undertaking, except maybe through insanity), we depend upon certain interactional arrangements for our survival, and these tend to be buttressed by moral opinion. Our need for predictable interactions forms the behavioral basis of moral judgments. "To confirm the great principle with which civilization begins: any custom is better than no custom."[6] This need for order produces a "morality of constraints."

The element of artifice in these constraints, their essential arbitrariness, their inevitable inadequacy as unerring guides to all choice situations present and future, anticipated and unanticipated, and the alienation often caused by their imposition combine to contribute to their instability. All human creations are flawed, and moral precepts are not exempt. Consequently, customary constraints can always be condemned as immoral, although often the judgment implicitly made is one of inadequacy. The drive to abandon those constraints that appear outmoded contributes to the "morality of liberation."

The debate over the respective morality of human beings and their systems of shared meaning recurs continually because of the human origins of human morality. The categorical nature of all moral postulates makes it impossible to stabilize any notion of inherent good or evil. Nor can we derive such comfort from a "moderate" position that human beings are a mixture of good and evil impulses. If such categories are conventional and unstable, they cannot identify essential traits of human beings unless this "essential" nature is seen as altering along with the moral climate. Many of the attributes so facilely assigned to human "nature"—good vs. evil, egoism vs. altruism, aggressiveness vs. benevolence—necessarily suffer from categorical instability, a fate which affects any analysis of the meaning of the political values of freedom and order, justice and equality.*

Another problem underlies the debate over whether human beings should be subordinated to or liberated from the constraints imposed by systems of shared meaning. Often formulations of the liberation/constraint controversy seem to imply that

---

*Somewhat paradoxically, the instability of all systems of categorization suggests one human trait that may be "inherent"—inadequacy. Even if humans are essentially inadequate, this does not seem to justify the conclusion that they are innately inclined to evil.

either, but not both, the individual or the social arrangement based upon shared meaning is a real and coherent entity, while the other is merely the consequence of the working of the real partner in the relationship. Those who lean toward a morality of liberation tend to see the individual as fundamental with society being the dependent product of individual interrelationships. Since social constraints are secondary and derivative, they can and should be dispensed with when they impair the fulfillment of the dominant partner—the individual. Some pessimists like Thomas Hobbes, however, may accept the primacy of the individual and the artificiality of social and political arrangements but still believe that individual fulfillment, indeed survival, depends upon the maintenance of certain imposed constraints.

Commonly, however, those who favor a morality of constraint tend to see the "individual" (in this context properly placed in quotes) as only a social product. Without the network of interactional associations, individual self-identities could never form. When confronted with such divergent views, we are often tempted to concede a degree of validity to each position. Adopting this stance, both individuals and society might be seen as real and conjunctive, or they might both be seen as fictive and disjunctive. We adopt the latter perspective.

Defining society as any sustained interaction among two or more organisms avoids the tendency toward reification, but it hardly suffices to exhaust the character of human experiences of interaction. Norbert Elias captures more of the qualitative aspects of human interactional arrangements with his term "figuration," defined as "a structure of mutually oriented and dependent people."[7] He believes that this conceptualization

expresses what we call "society" more clearly and unambiguously than the existing tools of sociology, as neither an abstraction of attributes existing without a society, nor a "system" or "totality" beyond individuals, but a network of interdependencies formed by individuals.[8]

Society, then, is the product of both mutuality and individual behavior, rather than being either the embodiment of a transcendent mutuality or merely the additive consequences of atomized behaviors. Societal figurations are both constructed and transcendent, both fictive and "objective." As the fictive result of fallible human behavior, social figurations can never be wholly coherent or completely conjunctive. Individual responses incompatible with the prevailing figurations of shared meaning continuously intrude, in a more or less serious fashion, to disrupt mutuality. Insofar as we think of society as being well integrated, we must either ignore or consider extraneous the breakdowns that mar mutual expectations. The experience of incoherency and conflict, however, seems to possess as good a claim to transcendence as the networks of interdependencies upon which we rely. The possibility of transcendent incoherence, in fact, lies at the center of the experience of existential absurdity, wherein we confront each other and the natural world in a condition of meaninglessness, unable to respond.

The individual as a behavioral entity also is incoherent. Although as a physical organism, the individual possesses a fairly stable definition, no such coherence pertains with respect to social behaviors from which the sense of self or persona is constructed. A persona, rather, "is the selective, deceptive, and coherent semiotic interpretation of the behavioral individual by the individual himself or by someone else."[9]

Our self-images or personas, then, may be viewed as typifications, albeit ones of considerable complexity. As with our typifications of others, our self-typifications are explanatory constructs through which we try to subsume observed behavior. Self-typification possesses one major advantage over the typifications we construct of others: we have direct access to our covert motives and meanings, assuming that we are not laboring under serious self-deceptions, and this access explains why we never see ourselves quite as others see us. In order to develop a coherent self-typification or persona, we must ignore disjunctive elements of our behavior. In this sense, then, the persona, like society, is fictive.

Fictive coherence (that is, an integrity achieved only through selectivity) serves to stabilize behavior. Just as the successful categorization of a previously unencountered perception "tells" us how to respond to it, our self-categorization serves to structure our behavior in the series of relatively unrelated experiences that comprise our daily existence. Just as it would be difficult to deal effectively with the world if each perception had to be treated as an entirely new experience, unrelated to anything else and requiring the creation of a complete fabric of meaning before a particular response could be generated, so too would it be difficult to function if we had to inquire who we "are" at each juncture of experience. Questions of self-identity can obsess people to the extent that their effective involvement in the world is impaired.

Unfortunately, the strategy of stabilization through categorization, whether of the world or of our responses to it, can also become pathogenic. Since the subjects of categorization are never identical ("Every concept originates through our equating what is unequal"[10]) and are in constant flux, there will always be a gap between our behavior and our image of it. We are constantly tempted to conclude that our categories, because of their apparent coherence, are more real than the disjunctive experiences being categorized. This urge to the absolute, Nietzsche cautions, leads to placing "that which comes at the end... namely, the 'highest concepts,' which means the most general, the emptiest concepts, the last smoke of evaporating reality, in the beginning, *as* the beginning."[11] Though Nietzsche here was concerned with the concept of "God" being used as a first cause, today it appears that the "self" often holds the position of "highest concept." Solipsism seems to be a major contemporary strategy for stabilizing actions in the world.

Stabilization through categorization contributes to our survival and smooth interaction with the world as long as the differences ignored by the imposed categorization are not so great as to threaten seriously the adequacy of our responses, and our categories remain open to revision. The persona, like other explanatory constructs, may be modified by feedback.[12] A person, though, may block negative feedback here as in other areas, stubbornly resist any revision of self-image, and maintain a fictive consistency regardless of the consequences.

Rigid personas become a particular problem when we confront contexts that differ significantly from our prior experiences and expectations. A well-adjusted person, under these circumstances, might be one who can easily pick up and slip into and out of a variety of "masks" and perform a variety of social roles.[13] Multiple contexts call for multiple selves. Such persona flexibility is not likely to be indefinitely elastic. Even if we do not have a rigidly defined self-image, our repertoire of selves is still limited, and we may still encounter situations for which our array of masks has not provided an adequate response.

Type-transcending behavior, on the part of others or, for that matter, ourselves, probably raises the most significant challenge to the stability of our personas. Adjustment to plural worlds may be possible as long as we have been able to establish some reasonably accurate expectations concerning the responses of those with whom we interact in each world (i.e., plural systems of shared meaning). If these others respond in unanticipated ways, shared meanings erode, and our own fictive persona will become more difficult to maintain. If we recognize that we confront radically new circumstances for which we are unprepared, we must innovate new behaviors or risk extinction. These new and unprecedented responses, in turn, undermine the imposed coherence of our previously established persona(s). The stability of our persona may also be undermined when we are forced to recognize the inconsistencies in our behavior that we attempt to ignore by imposing a fictive coherence upon our experiences.

All of us, therefore, face something of a dilemma when creating our "selves." On the one hand, a stable persona (or established repertoire of personas) contributes to the predictability of our behavior. Yet, the inherent limitations of our self-categorization must also be recognized so that self-innovation is possible, at least under some circumstances. Too much flexibility, however, could lead to the dissolution of any sense of personal coherence as well as reduce the chances for smooth social interaction.

Although our personas arise out of an act of self-categorization, we may, nonetheless, feel somewhat alienated from our own creation. Self-typifications are continuous with other meanings in the world; that is, they are embodied in response. As with other meanings, we may feel that even as we respond to our own behavior in certain ways, these typical responses do not represent our "true" selves. Instead, they may be seen as forced upon us. Insofar as we feel alienated from our own persona, any manner of response modification may well be judged to reveal a "truer" self.

Self-alienation occurs because we cannot easily escape the webs of shared meaning in this matter any more than in others. Just as we learn "appropriate" responses to other aspects of our shared experiences, that is, we learn to respond in mutually expected ways, our self-typifications will also be affected by other people's typifications of us. Their expectations and, indeed, power impact upon our behavior, and we may incorporate aspects of these expectations into our own self-image without fully identifying with them. Their expectations can become a part of our behavior while still remaining apart from us. Moreover, previously accepted self-definitions can be called into question. Such identity crises contribute to the development of alienation where none was previously present and may result in the search for a new identity, particularly if certain restraints of shared meaning are relaxed or altered.*14

We are never, to be sure, perfect mirrors of each other's expectations. Such expectations are multiple, especially in our complex, somewhat compartmentalized systems of social arrangements, and this plurality always affords some opportunity for choice and manipulation (see the discussion of freedom, below). Other people's typifications of us need not be wholly consistent with one another, making it impossible for us to reflect them perfectly even if we so desired. Also, like other aspects of the socialization process, these expectations will be more or less imperfectly transmitted, contributing to a certain amount of "persona drift." Finally, we "may internalize different realities without identifying with them."†15 Instead, an *apparent* self will be overtly demonstrated for manipulative purposes, while we covertly define our selves in a different way.

---

*The question remains, of course, whether this transformation produces a "truer" self, particularly if the restraints relaxed are deemed oppressive in nature (a judgment that may be disputed). "True" can imply an absolute standard of individual integrity which I do not believe can be finally stabilized. "Truer" may also be considered to be synonymous with "better," a judgment based upon an evaluation of a particular system of shared meaning according to more or less defensible standards of justice, not a transcendent notion of a "true individual." Such determinations are discussed in the remainder of the chapter and in the counterpoint.

†"Reality" here refers to other people's expectations about who we are as demonstrated in our behavior. These expectations are external to us and not entirely subject to our control.

The tendency to ascribe almost atomistic coherence to the individual persona appears to be a cultural artifact. As Nietzsche notes, "The individual himself is still the most recent creation."[16] The extreme individuation of the persona developed along with, and indeed required, increasing controls being placed on impulse from the Middle Ages onward. Elias suggests that

The firmer, more comprehensive, and uniform restraint of the affects characteristic of this civilizational shift, together with the increased internal compulsions that, more implacably than before, prevent all spontaneous impulses from manifesting themselves directly and motorically in action, without the intervention of control mechanisms— these are what is experienced as the capsule, the invisible wall dividing the "inner world" of the individual from the "external world" or, in different versions, the subject of cognition from its object, the "ego" from the "other," the "individual" from "society."[17]

Ironically, the common view of the individual who is set against society arises, therefore, from the increasingly effective imposition and internalization of social controls:

The notion of individuals deciding, acting, and existing in absolute independence of one another is an artificial product of men which is characteristic of a particular stage in the development of their self-perception.

This self-perception in terms of one's own isolation, of the invisible wall dividing one's own "inner" self from all people and things "outside," takes on for a large number of people in the course of the modern age the same immediate force of conviction of the movement of the sun around an earth situated at the center of the cosmos possessed in the Middle Ages.[18]

Our contemporary notion of an individuated persona, as well as the content assigned to that persona, reflects the systems of shared meaning in which we find ourselves. Despite the powerful image of individualized atomization, the relation between the individual and other people is more complex and interdependent:

The image of man as a "closed personality" is here replaced by the image of man as an "open personality" who possesses a greater or lesser degree of relative (but never absolute or total) autonomy vis-à-vis other people and who is, in fact, fundamentally oriented and dependent on other people throughout his life.[19]

If individual personas are the self-constructs of people dwelling within, and taking shape from, humanly generated systems of shared meaning, neither self nor society can be plausibly construed as absolutely transcendent. Notions of freedom (the morality of liberation) and order (the morality of constraint) should reflect some recognition of their dependence upon the character of particular existential situations.

Freedom and Order

"Freedom," intone the lyrics of a song popular a number of years ago, "is just another word for nothin' left to lose."[20] We could do worse for a definition. Freedom commonly connotes the ability to act without constraint.* Whatever we cling to constrains our actions, channeling them to protect the possession (whether personally or materially embodied). "Possess not, that you shall not be possessed," for any valued possession leaves us open to coercion.[21]

Freedom defined as "nothin' left to lose" also draws attention to some of the ambiguities of the concept, for surely most of us would not actually seek out and joyfully embrace the loss of all we value simply to be free. One of the most powerful constraints on our behavior is love: Love directs our responses away from self-consideration, and threats to the beloved may be more powerfully coercive than threats to our own persons. If to be free involves the elimination of all ties of affection, undoubtedly most of us would not view it as an unqualified good.

Viewing freedom as the absence of constraint, furthermore, begs the question as to what should count as a constraint. If we set the individual against society in terms of a coherent, compartmentalized self confronting a set of arbitrary social ar-

---

*This is, of course, a notion of "negative" freedom. Various concepts of "positive" freedom are not considered here and often seem more appropriately subsumed under ideas of justice.

rangements that exist "out there" beyond an invisible barrier dividing "inside" from "outside," the answer seems simple enough. Constraints would be any force external to the individual that shapes behavior along directions that would not otherwise have been chosen. Freedom is the self-chosen vector; constraints limit freedom by altering individual inertia.

This mechanistic idea of freedom incorporates some valuable insights, for external constraints certainly may limit freedom. The problem, moreover, is shown to be one of being more or less free, rather than one of being free or unfree. Yet, even on its own terms, certain problems remain with this definition. For example, should we consider such inducements as rewards, affections, or moral beliefs as constituting external constraints on freedom, since they clearly can affect a person's choices?

One possible solution would be to posit that only "negative" constraints should be viewed as truly limiting freedom, for they actually harm the value position of the individual. Positive inducements—moral, material, or affectational—presumably do not harm a person's value position and may even improve it. But on whose judgment does the distinction between positive and negative inducements rest? Most certainly, it would have to be the individual's own evaluation that carries the most weight. But from where do the criteria used to make such an evaluation come? Consideration of this question raises a second difficulty with constraint theories of freedom, that of the role of internalized standards and restraints.

The dichotomy between the internal self and the external world begins to crumble with the admission of the possibility of manipulation. Crude, overt forms of manipulation, such as obviously distorted propaganda, do not pose a serious problem for they might be reasonably considered forms of external constraint. Thus, a lie constrains my ability to gather the information needed to act according to my interests. Difficulties begin to arise when we consider the origins of these interests, specifically, whether they might have been manipulated into existence. The most powerful form of tyranny, after all, is self-imposed; the most effective form of policing is self-policing. If these powerful tools of control are at least partly a reflection of systems of shared meaning, how then can we delineate the exact boundaries of our selves?

Our sense of self-identity, as we suggested earlier, possesses only a fictive coherence, selected from the components of a randomly assembled behavioral inventory, supported by the expectations embodied in the systems of shared meaning in which we find ourselves. By and large, we do not choose these shared meanings. Our parents, our economic class, our language/ culture group, even our peer groups are more the result of accident than deliberate choice. By the time we have constructed a "self" coherent enough to begin to select among potential interests and alternatives that we encounter, we will already be enmeshed in powerfully sustained systems of mutual expectation that channel the basic dispositions of our personas. Tremendous effort and trauma may be required to alter our personas significantly. How we see ourselves is at least partly the result of the ways others see us, especially when these expectations are supported by routinized constraints.* How, then, can we get free of our socially constructed selves?

For some, like B. F. Skinner, the answer is simple: We cannot. Freedom is a chimera, and the possibility of free choice is an illusion.[22] The sooner we recognize and accept this reality, the sooner we will be able to structure systems of shared meaning so as to end their more haphazard influences and produce more orderly results. It may still be desirable, from the point of view of the behavioral engineers, to engender the illusion of freedom into people's behavioral inventory so as to create a perfect order willingly embraced.

This Skinnerian model of the relationship between behaving individuals and their social environment assumes an unequivocal connection between an external stimulus and a response. Attenuating this connection, then, may open up the possibility for freedom. If, as Daniel Dennett supposes, the intervening organism is capable of generating alternative potential behaviors in response to a stimulus situation, the ultimate re-

---

*This perspective on the development of individuals in a context of mutual expectations appears compatible with structural notions of power that attempt to define the "field" within which individual relations occur. See Steven Lukes, *Power: A Radical View* (London: Macmillan, 1974).

sponse selected will no longer be absolutely dependent on the external stimulus.[23] If the precise external stimulus, moreover, cannot be effectively isolated, people may respond differently when they are placed in the same stimulus field.

Consequently, the "educational" stimulus and the "learning" response vary somewhat independently of one another, and "man is, in this sense, free, whether he likes it or not, and on the whole he doesn't like it very much, since that freedom is a constant threat to social stability and interferes, often savagely enough, with the smoothness of predictive behavior."[24] This threat of unpredictability prompts the imposition of external and internalized controls in order to restrict the range of behaviors actually incorporated in overt response. In fact, *all* forms of predictable behavior may be indicative of the absence of freedom and evidence for an external power structure. Although some internalized constraints might not reflect the subtle controls of the systems of shared meaning in which we are raised, the problem remains as to how these "legitimate" constraints may be distinguished. At least with externally imposed, overt restrictions, we know the score; with internalized ones, we often do not even know we are in the game.

Perhaps the only safe position for the person who desires freedom, then, is to question all constraints, external and internalized, no matter how plausible or personally beneficial. In this way, we move inexorably toward the radical romantic vision of the great crime being a sign of freedom. It is not sufficient that we outrage others to demonstrate our freedom from their manipulative intents; we must also outrage ourselves in order to be free of the constraints that we no longer recognize as such. "The creation of freedom for oneself, and a sacred 'No' even to duty" seems demanded, as Nietzsche observes.[25] Those who wish to be free "must find illusion and caprice even in the most sacred, that freedom from his love may become his prey."[26] Even a carefully measured outrage would not, however, demonstrate freedom from subtle social constraints, for any considered act, even a crime, reflects some rules of reason. Ultimately, along with Doestoevski's "underground man," we must reject even reason and exemplify our freedom in the totally gratuitous act.

Such an extreme conception of freedom, to be sure, does not seem to have much to recommend it. It stands in total antithesis to any semblance of order and, consequently, of shared meaning. Strictly speaking, freedom so construed cannot even be considered a *political* value. It represents antipolitics—not the effort to control shared meaning but to sever oneself from it altogether. Insofar as the constructed self reflects these shared meanings as well, then it, too, must be cut away. What remains? Frithjof Bergmann correctly suggests nothing at all (except the randomizing organism); the self dwindles away.[27] A radical conception of freedom as the absence of constraint, combined with a recognition of the social impact on the construction of the individual persona, leads, it would seem, to the dissolution of shared meaning, society, and self.

Bergmann, like most of us, rejects these implications. He believes, to the contrary, that if we identify with that upon which we depend, we may nevertheless still be free.[28] Only if we are alienated from the systems of shared meaning can we reasonably consider them to be a form of constraint that takes away our freedom. In order to identify with anything, however, we must possess an identity that is self-constituted and not manipulated into existence. If we assume such a self-constituted identity, freedom consists of "acting out" our identities, a matching of our outer lives with our genuine values and interests.[29]

Bergmann's idea of *being free*, if valid, resolves a number of common difficulties associated with the idea of freedom. First, unlike the radical rejection of all constraint, in Bergmann's view we can be free and have order, too. The key to this happy solution, of course, lies in our identification with those patterns of response that make our actions mutually predictable. Even determinism does not appear to contradict his conception of freedom, if we accept the causes of our actions as reflections of our genuine selves.[30] Any way of overcoming the separation of self and systems of shared meaning would seem sufficient to constitute the state of being free. Consequently, not only may we become free through political action, that is, by gaining control of our systems of shared meaning and shaping them in accordance with our identities, but we also could be free in a state of organic identification with the systems of shared meaning.

Obviously critical to Bergmann's notion of freedom is the reality of, indeed the possibility for, self-constitutiveness. If our identities are not, in some meaningful sense, "our own," we cannot be free. Paradoxically, then, freedom depends upon a persona, or identity, admittedly fictive in nature, that nonetheless can be plausibly considered genuine. Freedom requires constraints that are not only self-imposed but which are also, in some sense, self-generated and not manipulated into existence.*

We are what we are interested in, and our personas consist of what we *think* these interests to be.[31] Who we think we are and who we actually are resemble, but need not be equivalent to, each other. Our interests channel our behavior, but we may not always recognize just what all these interests are.† We might expect a considerable correspondence between our acknowledged and actual interests, at least insofar as we will not often believe that we possess an interest in radical opposition to those that actually direct our responses. Rather, the interests we construe into our personas will be selected from among all the interests reflected in our behavior; that is, in our self-image, we may fail to recognize actual interests of greater or lesser significance.‡

---

*Manipulation here includes not only deliberate deceits but also the subtle reinforcements that are used to create habitual responses.

†The distinction between what we think our interests to be and what they actually are resembles Dennett's distincion between beliefs and opinions. In our terms, opinions constitute our personas, whereas beliefs comprise our actual behavioral inventory. We always act on our beliefs but not always on our opinions. See "How to Change Your Mind" in *Brainstorms*, pp. 300–9.

‡The relation between recognized and actual interests resembles the problem of false consciousness. Insofar as "false" consciousness is taken to mean that a deep, unacknowledged motive underlies the consciously admitted one (e.g., as with the Freudian notion of repressed impulse), the concept is compatible with the distinction between recognized and actual interests. If, however, false consciousness refers to the absence of genuine interests that *would* develop *if* people found themselves liberated from certain shackles of shared meaning, then the two ideas differ. In this latter instance, we would be concerned more with potential, not actual, interests. The former interpretation of repressed interests appears to be a special case of our argument, for not all unacknowledged interests are, strictly speaking, repressed.

A genuine identity can be constructed out of the interests that emerge independently of the imposed channels of external control and the haphazardly developed constraints of the accidents of experience. Oddly enough, Nietzsche, conventionally dismissed as a negator, suggests how such freely "created" interests might come about if we become like a child:

The child is innocence and forgetting, a new beginning, a game, a self-propelled wheel, a first movement, a sacred "Yes." For the game of creation, my brothers, a sacred "Yes" is needed: the spirit now wills his own will, and he who has been lost to the world now conquers his own world.[32]

The need to will our own will neatly epitomizes the paradox of developing a genuine self.

Taking a lead from Nietzsche's vision of the child as "yea-sayer," we might approach the goal of self-definition, of willing our own will, through play or understructured experimentation. Children play without deliberation, and from this play, their interests develop. Play provides a means through which potential interests can be rehearsed; many are tried, and a few are chosen.[33] We can "play" more self-consciously by deliberately exploiting the potential randomness of experience in order to develop self-generated interests. In this way we do not simply let it happen; we try to make it happen. Playing frees us from the controls imposed by other people's games and allows us to encounter alternatives that might not otherwise be engendered.* The interests finally selected will reflect in some way our prior learning and experience, though not in any necessarily predictable fashion, and new interests can always replace old.†

Children seem to play naturally, until stifled by imposed rules. As Nietzsche (and, ironically, Christ) admonishes us, we must become like children in order to enter into the kingdom of

---

*I choose to emphasize the randomizing element in "play" as opposed to "games." Games may bracket the "real" world and suspend normal time, but only by imposing a functionally equivalent, though more limited, structure. The relative absence of structure is the essential characteristic of true play.

†Playing as a rehearsal of interests is a version of Dennett's generate-and-select model of underdesigned human learning.

the genuine self. To play deliberately demands that the inertia of established interests be overcome—no easy task. Yet avenues of unstructured or understructured experimentation are available, even to adults. An appropriately designed liberal education provides one.[34] Professional education programs, in contrast, channel students and their interests along predetermined paths. A well-exploited liberal education does not structure behavior in the same manner. Instead, it introduces the students to the resources of their culture. By deliberately undertaking to study an assortment of essentially unrelated areas, ones that may even undercut one another, a liberal education allows for the rehearsal of an array of intellectual interests. Although only a few of the alternatives so encountered may be immediately selected for further exploration, exposure to the others provides for an "interest pool" that may be drawn upon as the need arises in the future. Consequently, a liberal education at one point may be a resource for self-innovation at some later time.

Other opportunities for play may arise from the segmented, multiroled social configurations in which we find ourselves. As Peter Berger and Thomas Luckmann note, "identity is a phenomenon that emerges from the dialectic between the individual and society."[35] Established expectations of social interaction can confront us with an apparent objectivity that molds our response. Even rebellion need not liberate us from similar controls if we still conform with someone else's role expectations. The opportunities provided in modern society to move from role to role, to wear a variety of masks, suggest an alternative to either simple conformance or reactive rebellion. We can play at who we wish to be, and, ultimately, we may choose to become that at which we initially only played.

Through the process of play, we may be able to develop interests that neither rest determinantly on externally imposed social arrangements nor derive absolutely from previously established characteristics. In this way, interests more truly our own may be established or altered and a more genuine self constituted. *Being free*, accepting Bergmann's position, involves acting in accordance with our genuine interests, ones that are not so much discovered as they are created through play, which may be considered *acting freely*.

The condition of acting freely, though, can neither be absolutely achieved nor unequivocably embraced. Both the available opportunities and the capacity for play limit the possibilities for self-constitutiveness. A newborn infant seems essentially (but not deliberately) playful in much of its interaction with the surrounding environment. Yet, even at the beginning, much of its activity and energy is channeled by the urgent demands for survival. These demands begin to impose an order on the behavior of the infant that often takes precedence over the playful exploration of sensation.

Similarly, the adult world affords only limited opportunities for play, as apparent necessities structure response in various, and often alienating, ways. People also seem to vary in their capacity for play even when the opportunity presents itself. This would be no problem if their established identities already reflected self-constituted qualities, but we must admit the possibility of stable self-alienation maintained through psychological rigidity and social constraint.

The extent to which existing social arrangements nurture the realization of a state of being relatively free involves at least two considerations. First, there must be "spaces" or opportunities for play or acting freely. Second, a wide variety of identities and interests must be tolerated and expressed, so that once people have developed genuine interests they may be free. Certainly, the realization of either of these conditions is a matter of degree. Indeed, some limitation on freedom construed in this way may still be necessary and even desirable.

The element of play, first of all, introduces unpredictability into the development of the self. This unpredictability, to be sure, is not that of the totally gratuitous act; rather, it more closely resembles the process of innovation; play may be considered a form of self-innovation. Survival depends upon the capacity for judicious innovation, but not all innovations necessarily enhance the likelihood of survival. All innovations do, however, disrupt established routines that make smooth interaction possible, regardless of whether they are praised as creative or condemned as perverse. Consequently, the need for innovation must be balanced by the need for predictability. Similarly, the desirability of play must be judged against the need for some rules of the game.

Spaces for play are commonly isolated in time (e.g., child-hood) or space (e.g., the university as set apart from the "real" world). To create and maintain these spaces calls for a commitment of considerable resources to activities that produce no obvious return. Thus, the social invention of a prolonged child-hood removes children from economically productive roles, and a liberal education does not seem to train a person to *do* anything. A society with little or no disposable economic surplus can ill afford to provide many such spaces. Under conditions of severe scarcity, only aristocrats are allowed to play.

Even assuming a considerable toleration of unpredictability and the availability of a significant surplus to devote to the provision of spaces of play, we may still be unwilling or even unable to accept all the consequences of acting freely. When we set out to play, there is no telling what interests we might develop. This problem goes beyond simple unpredictability, for, after all, some surprises may be pleasant.* There exists, in addition, the question of the range of interests that can be tolerated within any set of social arrangements. As Bergmann admits, a genuine self, like a genuine innovation, may be perverse. There is no generic difference between an interest in theft and one in poetry, except that the latter may be easier to tolerate. All social arrangements, even the most open, must control certain forms of self-expression, no matter how genuine.† The inevitable scarcity of resources, moreover, suggests that even some acceptable interests may go unfulfilled, because people lack the means to express them.

Being free and social order, though not absolute antinomies, exhibit certain essential tensions. Order characterizes the relations in which those involved are able to form stable and accurate expectations about each other's behavior, *regardless* of the basis for this stability and accuracy. Order, then, demands a

---

*I am suggesting, therefore, that in our need for order, we do not desire many pleasant surprises either.

†We could adopt a quasi-Thomist position and hope that all humans at play will tend to the good or, alternatively, if they adopt perverse interests, these are, by definition, not genuine. The latter position strikes me as a frivolous solution by definition to a serious quandary. The former position seems belied by the evidence.

restricted range of response, and response can be restricted through a variety of means including coercion. Order relates directly to the concept of shared meaning (mutually expected response); when people share meanings, they necessarily form stable and accurate expectations.

Freedom, however, subverts shared meaning at two points. First, all innovations can disrupt shared meaning since they introduce something new into the relation. Since the development of a genuine self through play is a form of self-innovation, it necessarily injects a degree of unpredictability into relations based upon previously expressed interests. Second, the innovated interests may be incompatible with established shared meanings.

Innovations, of course, may be more or less radical departures from previous interests. Engaging in play injects a certain amount of randomness, a certain widening of response, into our behavior. The play, itself, may affect social arenas of varying significance, and the interests ultimately selected and incorporated from among those rehearsed may be more or less deviant. People who experience a considerable amount of self-alienation are, if they rehearse a variety of potential interests, probably more likely to adopt ones that differ significantly from those that previously existed. Discontent, identity crisis, and personal innovation follow along together.*

Eventually, a person with changed interests may be integrated into realigned patterns of shared meaning, even though the playfulness and the shift of interests may have been initially disruptive. Some people, though, may develop genuine interests that others find difficult to integrate into their expectations under any circumstances. The divergent interests, therefore, will most likely be labeled deviant or criminal and will be subject to various forms of external control or suppression. The difference between a creative and a criminal interest is a matter of evaluation by the affected parties.[36]

Despite the potential incompatibility between people de-

---

*Thus, innovation at the micro-level of self-identity recapitulates the experience of explanatory collapse, alienation, and randomization that characterizes cultural innovation (see Chapter 6).

veloping genuine interests (acting freely) and order as predictable interaction, the two may coexist in the same interactional arrangement, albeit somewhat uneasily. If the arenas for play can be effectively isolated, the toleration of diversity expanded, the suppression of radically deviant interests be swift and effective, and genuine identities, once established, remain relatively stable, then most people, most of the time, may be able to act in accordance with their genuine interests but still remain within the limits placed on playfulness and deviance. Whether such a happy combination of freedom and order can be established and maintained indefinitely is, of course, another matter.*

Order, both as it *appears* to be and as it *is*, may, in any case, be its own worst rival. The idea of shared meaning as mutually expected response should not obscure the possibility that people may share and *not* share at the same time. This problem extends beyond the existence of certain incompatibilities in an otherwise integrated relationship; rather, it involves the possibility for deception that exists in every *apparently* ordered relation.

When our behavior reflects shared meaning, we act in accordance with mutually understood and accepted protocols. We may, however, also be governed by another set of protocols unknown, or ignored, by others with whom we interact. For example, we may lie. Consequently, we should distinguish between behavior actually governed by a set of mutually recognized protocols and the behavior apparently so governed but really under the control of other protocols. The former may be called *action* and the latter *performance*.[37]

A successful performance is one taken by others to be an action. Those who engage in a performance must be familiar with the relevant protocols, and, thus, they do share some meanings with those whom they set out to deceive. Some performances may be harmless enough, depending on the actual

---

*Nietzsche comments: "It is not unthinkable that a society might attain such a *consciousness of power* that it could allow itself the noblest luxury possible to it—letting those who harm it go *unpunished*. 'What are my parasites to me?' it might say. 'May they live and prosper; I am strong enough for that!'" See the *Genealogy of Morals*, trans. and ed. Walter Kaufmann (New York: Vintage, 1969), Second Essay, section 10, p. 72.

protocols governing the performers' actions. For example, we might consider a "white lie" told to save someone from needless suffering to be relatively harmless and even beneficial.*

Other performances need not be so benign, for they could disguise actions intended to devastate the systems of shared meaning which they appear to uphold. Erving Goffman observes that the most dangerous person is the one who appears to be harmless, for he may be clever at disguising his murderous intent; the most dangerous place is the one that appears to be innocent, for it may be perfectly sabotaged.[38] The appearance of order, therefore, may merely conceal terrors unrecognized until too late.

Order truly established and genuinely reflective of covert motives and meanings also carries the infection of disorder. Order depends upon mutually expected response. We establish and maintain certain responses because they are presumed to be adequate in meeting the demands of the environment. Yet the world always threatens to slip away from our efforts to respond to it. A rigid and maladapted social order resembles a mistaken explanation: To use it as a guide to action contributes to the unsettling surprise of failure.

Conclusion

Freedom and order are not simply externally imposed values used to judge the quality of a particular social arrangement; rather, they are dialectically related existential necessities intrinsic to any established relationship. From our perspective, they recapitulate at the micro-level of self, the macro-dilemmas of innovation and stability. No system of shared meaning can definitively determine fully adequate response; thus, the potential need for innovation must be accepted. Similarly, the need

---

*The potentially innocuous nature of performance is illustrated in the theater. An audience thoroughly engrossed by a masterful performance treats it, in effect, as action. Once the curtain drops, of course, they recognize it as performance; the real actions were those of dramatic acting governed by a different set of protocols from those exhibited in the performance.

for a predictable self to ensure smooth social interaction with others must be balanced against not only the possibility of self-alienation but also the constant threat of mutual inadequacy to environmental demands.

Unfortunately, neither social innovation nor self-innovation guarantees enhanced adequacy of response. Moreover, the relative need for freedom and order fluctuates according to the dynamics of these environmental demands. A turbulent context demands innovation, which under settled conditions could prove more destructive than constructive.

Freedom and order, then, do not appear to be inherently valuable. Their value is relative to the shifting demands of an existential situation and their consequences evaluated in accordance with other standards such as justice. Like innovation and stability, freedom and order are both necessary and hazardous. Without one or the other, the political quest for shared meaning would fail; with both it might, for a time, succeed.

COUNTERPOINT TO CHAPTER 7

Explanatory Instability in the Evaluation of Social Arrangements

FREEDOM AND ORDER, from the perspective of the fictive character of both self and society, are not absolute values, but closer to "existential necessities," whose desirability must be evaluated according to other human purposes. Most fundamental would be their contribution to survival of the individual and (or) the social relationship. Survival, to reiterate a point made in an earlier chapter, is not posited as the ultimate value, but merely the necessary condition to achieve most other human objectives. The quality of the conditions of survival may lead a person to choose oblivion (or, perhaps, salvation) to a continual temporal existence. Moreover, the survival of a particular individual may clash with that of another or with the maintenance of a system of shared meaning, forcing some allocation or choice. Finally, a significant range of conditions may reasonably guarantee survival; questions of value choice need not involve extreme consequences. Judgments under these circumstances require more positive criteria, such as embodied in principles of justice and equality.

Justice and equality, as Aristotle indicated in defining justice as treating equals equally, are closely identified.[1] Both address the same problem: the appropriate treatment to be meted out to different participants in a social arrangement. The question begged, of course, concerns the grounds for determining just who is equal to whom. Those who stress equality argue for the essential similarity of human beings, while those who emphasize justice strive to identify essential differences.*

Principles of equality/justice tend to compete with one another, and all suffer from a consequent instability. None seems to serve as a foundation for a definitive consensus, even within the same general political community. James Fishkin provides an incisive analysis of the incompleteness and instability of several of these principles. He suggests that the major bases for establishing a legitimate distribution of resources, such as majority rule, utilitarianism, or absolute rights principles, if applied without qualification, "legitimate acts of government imposing severe deprivations when those deprivations were entirely avoidable."[2] Fishkin admits, however, that his alternative, that serious harms cannot be justified when they can be avoided by modifying the principles, does not provide any concrete guidance in "a) cases where *every* alternative imposes severe deprivations, and b) cases where *no* alternative imposes severe deprivations."[3]

Similarly, Ralf Dahrendorf declares that if principles of equality are pushed too far they may eliminate what they set out to accomplish:

To the extent to which equality has come to occupy the actions of those who make decisions as well as the minds of those who think about them, we have lost sight of the differences which alone give the greatest life chances to the greatest number; and to the extent to which political thought and action have thus been foreshortened, society itself has become rigidly unable to effect the changes necessary in order to create the colorful world in which a hundred flowers bloom on the same fertile soil. For a society in which all are equal in all respects is also one devoid of realistic hope and thus of incentives for progress.[4]

It would be tempting to attribute the incompleteness of any principle of equality/justice to human frailty and leave it at that.

---

*It might be argued that justice is the fundamental concept, and that principles of equality are simply one approach to the problem of justice. While I have no objection to this position, I prefer to emphasize the contrast between principles that stress similarities and those that stress differences.

Such a facile conclusion, though, leaves the dynamics of this failure largely unexplored. Essentially, the instability afflicting all principles of equality/justice appears to be related to the general dilemma of categorical instability and the consequent deterioration that afflicts all systems of shared meaning.

Debates over alternative standards of equality/justice are, in a sense, epistemological in nature, for they address the appropriate grounds of our knowledge of, and our consequent response to, those with whom we are engaged. In some general sense, we know and respond to the world according to our categorizations of it. These categories may be more or less systematically related to empirical feedback but, even so, our perceptions are already organized by our categories. Without some categorical conventions, we would have to treat each sensation that gains our attention as discrete from all others, requiring its own uniquely construed, unprecedented response. We might be able to engage the world in such a disconnected fashion, but we could not move very far or very fast.

Principles of equality/justice attempt to define the appropriate categorical bases for responding to different individuals. Debates over equality concern the extent to which people who, though clearly different in many respects, should be placed in the same category and, therefore, accorded the same treatment. Alternatively, disputes about justice involve the extent to which people who, though similar in some respects, should be placed in different categories and therefore treated differently.

To be considered equal in a behaviorally relevant sense does not imply any concession of inherent identity; rather, those placed in the same category are treated *as if* they are identical in all relevant aspects. Similarly, to categorize and respond to people differently need not imply an absolute contrast; rather, people are treated *as if* they are dissimilar, at least in all relevant aspects. Any strategy of categorization that emphasizes one aspect implies the other. Once we have established the grounds for treating people similarly, we have also defined the basis for differential treatment, and vice versa. Principles of equality/justice, when viewed as alternative categorical strategies, do not differ in "methodological" character.

All categories are potentially unstable, especially those at a relatively high level of abstraction, for they can be undermined by drawing attention to elements for which the category does not adequately account. Similarly, principles of equality/justice can be subverted by challenging the judgment of which attributes of different people should be considered relevant or similar. Disputes over the appropriate treatment to be given to different people arise out of the application of different conventions of categorization. Such disagreement can be partly attributable to the characteristic contradictions and inadequacies of the socialization process.

Even assuming that the elimination of such vagaries of the learning process were possible or even desirable, we may still doubt that human beings will ever be able to establish absolute and stable principles of equality/justice. Certainly Fishkin's argument that several major principles, if applied without qualification, could legitimate tyranny suggests the need for continuous compromise and revision.

This process of revision might proceed in a fashion analogous with other categorical systems where explanations guide behavior that produces feedback used to correct the governing explanation or categorization. Such a process could be pursued more or less consciously and systematically. Principles of equality/justice, given their generally high level of abstraction, provide guidance for behavior only after their implications have been specified. In the course of such exemplification, differences of interpretation easily arise, depending on the strength of the relevant procedural controls. Moreover, as is commonly the case with social feedback, the results of following any particular principle may be ambiguous or contradictory. Circumstances may develop where the results of following a particular principle appear to be inconsistent with its formal objectives. Dahrendorf suggests, for example, that the principle of equal participation in the political process may lead to such self-contradictory results:

If the political society is organized in such a way that all groups are represented everywhere, and representatives are in fact delegates, then decisions become virtually impossible, and participation loses all meaning. All that is left is a right to be present at endless debates, but no longer a chance to do things, to effect changes, however modest they, or the contribution of the individual citizen to them, may be.[5]

Ambiguity of result, admittedly, may allow the adherents of a particular principle to cling to it regardless of the evidence of internal contradictions. Ambiguity, however, also encourages the multiplication of alternative interpretations and leads, inevitably, to the emergence of competing "paradigms" of "equality/justice." Even those principles apparently untroubled by significant internal contradictions may still be challenged by alternatives arising from different assessments of the same murky consequences.

Theories of equality/justice suffer from an additional source of instability other than those that could affect empirical explanations. Unlike the categorical schemes generated by natural scientists, categories of equality/justice devised by social philosophers lie wholly within communities of shared meaning. Natural scientists use their categories to refer to the world of natural signs, a world that, in some sense, lies beyond their systems of shared meaning. Categories of equality/justice cannot break outside the closed circle of humanly constituted signs.* The characteristics that we use to establish distinctions are essentially cultural artifacts. Inalienable rights, legitimate procedures, and structural principles only exist and are specified within communities of shared meaning. Even Fishkin's notion of tyranny depends upon the social construction of an idea of severe deprivation.†

The development of an accepted standard of equality/justice hinges upon the success of the political process. The success of

---

*We might suggest a theory of equality that mandates equal treatment on the basis of biological existence, but such a theory would find it difficult to distinguish between humans and other animals (cf. the abortion controversy).

†Fishkin elaborates a definition of deprivation based upon the violation of private-regarding interests, essentially involving the defeat of a "personal life plan." A life plan can be decisively defeated if it has not been developed with a minimum degree of autonomy and if the person suffers reversals for which he cannot be fully compensated. None of this makes much sense unless one assumes intentional social creatures dwelling within communities of shared meaning.

politics in establishing shared meaning short of the recourse to force or bribery depends, in turn, upon the political process functioning in accordance with some commonly accepted standards of equality and justice. This apparent paradox is eased once we recognize the dialectical nature of temporal processes. Whatever we may think of the results, it is possible for tyranny to eventually become legitimate in the eyes of many of its subjects.

An action may be said to be in accord with principles of equality/justice when, as Carl Friedrich argues, "it involves a comparative evaluation of the persons affected by the action, and when that comparison accords with the values and beliefs of the political community."[6] Since beliefs and values are never completely coherent or stable, the perceptions of the nature of equality/justice will not only differ from community to community but also within the same community over time, as well as between dominant and subordinate groups within the community. Perfect justice can only be achieved in a completely stable and coherent community.

The claims of this relativist, categorical account of equality/ justice might still be countered by the assertion that certain principles are common to all conceptions of equality/justice. Among the presumed universals commonly mentioned are[7]:

1. Treating equals equally.
2. Applying community standards generally.
3. Establishing the truth of the case.
4. Requiring only what is possible.

Each of these universals is empty until filled by the community of shared meaning within which it is applied. Just who is to be considered equal to whom and what standards apply to the whole community are precisely the types of issues that can be resolved only within the political community. The criterion of "truth" appears to raise empirical issues that transcend the boundaries of any particular community, but here too the implications of such facts can be established only within the community of shared meaning. Factual questions involve issues of relevance. How problems of relevance are to be decided will be affected by cultural values. The judgment of what may appear to

Western, secularized eyes to be an ordinary and innocent event may be quite different in a culture imbued with a belief in the supernatural. A brush on the shoulder may cause violent reprisals if the person touched believes he has just been cursed with impotence.

Similarly, the definition of impossibility seldom resolves into a clear either/or proposition. The demands of equality/justice usually admit to a considerable range of difficulty. At what point does the merely difficult become impossible? Perhaps extreme cases are fairly easy to resolve, but a vast judgmental area remains where questions of possibility can be answered only within communities of meaning. Again, a belief in the efficacy of magic, for example, adds a whole dimension of possibility absent from most secular world views.

The categorical instability and cultural relativity of principles of equality/justice should, nonetheless, not be viewed as leading to a nihilistic recapitulation of Thrasymachus's view that justice is nothing more than what is in the interest of the stronger party. First, power is seldom so concentrated that the stronger party can simply dictate its value position and have it embraced. Second, the stronger party's position may not be coherent, allowing for different conceptions of equality/justice to emerge. Third, the values characterizing any social arrangement, although a product of human action, emerge over time and confront any particular individual or faction at any given time with a considerable degree of intractability. The strong, in short, cannot *act* as they please and still be in accord with community values. Finally, as Friedrich indicates, although presumed universals do little to provide a basis for cultural transcendence, they do suggest that those living *within* a community of meaning may well be called upon to justify the distinctions they make in accordance with the principles of that community.[8]

Principles of equality/justice, then, are forms of explanation and, though not free from a degree of indeterminability, neither are they entirely arbitrary. Those who argue for some particular principle have not so much discovered transcendent truth as they are trying to make a contribution to the political process. We create our explanations of equality/justice, and we must live with the consequences of our creations. Only we can determine whether the consequences are acceptable.

The politics of explanation "is the ineluctable condition, the defining attribute of human behavior."[9] It sets us apart from the other animals and contributes to both our triumphs and our anguish. "To grasp the centrality of explanation," "and to accept the indeterminability of explanation and therefore of behavior is to enter Golgotha. And Golgotha is the place of skulls and crucifixion."[10]

8 ⏱

THE ENTROPY OF MEANING AND THE FUTURE OF POLITICS

They felt unable to cope with the simplest undertakings; in this new world they no longer possessed their former guides, their regulating, unconscious, and infallible drives: they were reduced to thinking, inferring, reckoning, coordinating cause and effect, these unfortunate creatures; they were reduced to their "consciousness," their weakest and most fallible organ.

As the will to truth thus gains self-consciousness —there can be no doubt of that—morality will gradually *perish* now: this is the great spectacle in a hundred acts reserved for the next two centuries in Europe— the most terrible, the most questionable, and perhaps the most hopeful of all spectacles.

NIETZSCHE

Introduction

POLITICS SEEMS such a fragile means of creating systems of shared meaning. How much more efficacious, for example, appear the instincts of the social insects. Admiration for the order of the anthill, as Melvin Lasky wryly notes, "crawls through all of Western thought."[1] The deliberate effort to structure complex interactions confronts us with a difficult, often overwhelming challenge. Our past attempts to create order and stabilize shared meaning sometimes seem, like the entropic processes in the physical world, to threaten us with greater chaos. As the organic solidarity of tradition and transcendental faith erodes, we find ourselves "on a darkling plane/ Swept with confused alarms of struggle and flight,/ Where ignorant armies clash by night."[2]

Nietzsche sensed where the nihilism of the nineteenth century led: As the moral myths of previous centuries lost their power to regulate response, "most terrible, most questionable" acts would occur. Even he might have been astonished, though, at the extent to which the loss of moral solidarity contributed to the routinization of slaughter. The mindless massacres of World War I could conform with his rather jaundiced estimation of the emerging German nationalism.[3] Yet, how could he, or anyone of his time, imagine an international system where security is measured in megadeaths?

These terrible spectacles may be accompanied by a measure of hope, however, for they result from our becoming conscious of the will to truth as a problem. Only now can we begin to strip away our illusions concerning the origins of morality or, more broadly, shared meaning. Supposedly absolute, infallible, and self-evident systems of belief can now be recognized as human creations propped up by myth. Remove these props, and nothing but consciousness, our "weakest and most fallible organ," remains to establish common values and orientations. Politics as the deliberate effort to control systems of shared meaning is a product of human reason. The desire for control is a manifestation of the will to truth.

Reason, unbounded by the illusions arbitrarily imposed by tradition, easily falls prey to the greatest illusion that it needs no limits at all—as the horrors of our century amply attest. New limits, though, are not to be discovered or revealed; rather, they must be devised and implemented through the political process. Perhaps the promise of the twentieth century consists of the opportunity for us to assume, for the first time, full responsibility for the consequences of our actions through the political process.

Through politics, however, we may merely devise and impose a new set of illusions that succeed in stifling their own source. Human beings seldom enthusiastically embrace responsibility for their actions nor, especially, for the principles guiding them. We find it so tempting to attribute the source of such principles and the causes of our acts to some transcendent being or realm, whether God, Platonic forms, immutable historical laws, or any of the other theologies and teleologies which we have so profusely multiplied. If this proclivity holds true once again, the salutary shock of nihilism will be muted or lost altogether, and we will embrace illusions like those from which we have so recently emerged, albeit with devastating results. Indeed, perhaps self-deception is the only way that we can impose limits on our acts.

Certainly the need for controls, for limits, has been well demonstrated by the horrors perpetrated through the political process over the last decades, as well as being increasingly evident in the contradictions and crises exhibited by our modern cultural system. The political process must either develop these limits itself, or they may well be imposed by a combination of catastrophe and collapse. Limits emerging from the political process need not, however, support the continuation of politics; rather, they may foreclose politics through the imposition of new absolutes. To speculate upon the possible future of politics, we first need to epitomize the modern cultural context and its emerging contradictions. We can then address how these contradictions might be eased through an alternative system of shared meaning, and how this new system might arise as a consequence of yet another illusion of Truth not created but discovered.

Modern Culture Epitomized

Modern societies have risen on a promise of escape, a belief in the power of reason to transcend the bonds imposed by the physical limitations of a fragile planet. This modern faith in the inevitability of progress is increasingly challenged by those who warn that the apogee of culture's accomplishments occurs just before its necessary and often precipitous plunge.

The "thermodynamic critique" develops a particularly powerful argument: specifically, modern economic and social organizations ignore, at their peril, the Second Law of Thermodynamics, the entropy law.[4] Essentially, the entropy law states that, although mass/energy can never be created or destroyed, only transformed, this transformation moves in one direction only—from usable to unusable forms.* While the extension of the entropy law into other realms of meaning may be more metaphorical than scientific, we could argue that modern cultural forms, that is, systems of shared meaning, also demonstrate this movement from order to disorder. Modern meanings appear to be breaking down, and political efforts to prop them up seem to generate even more disorder.

To speak of modern culture, however, is to entertain something of a double fiction. Cultural directives themselves are

---

*When we burn a gallon of oil, no mass/energy is lost, but part of it is converted into unusable forms such as waste heat and petrochemical pollution.

fictions about the nature of the real. To generalize about these directives, to detect a coherence about them, or to subsume them in an intellectual framework, extends the fictive enterprise to another level. Nevertheless, any identification and discussion of the scope of the modern cultural crisis require that some order be imposed upon the currently dominant systems of shared meaning, even though this presents a degree of coherence that does not, in fact, exist.

All explanations are abstractions, and the greater the degree of abstraction, the more contrary data will tend to be ignored. Certain aspects of advanced industrial societies may be plausibly identified as dominant and contrasted with those characteristics that appear to epitomize premodern systems. In doing so, however, contradictory values and meanings existing alongside the presumably preeminent meaning are necessarily slighted. Indeed, these subcultural or countercultural directives may well be the source of a culture's transformation. Certainly, the strange ways of the modernized, as Marion Levy cautions, have not been around long enough to establish their viability.[5] A brief contrast with certain premodern characteristics, although also an idealization, serves to emphasize the strangeness of modern meanings.[6]

Material Conditions

Premodern societies tend to be tied closely to nature, as demonstrated by the dominance of subsistence agriculture in the productive process. The productive cycle depends heavily upon natural forces largely outside the physical control of human beings. The technology of production is not highly developed, and it only slowly improves over time. Human or animal power provides the primary source of energy. The burden placed upon natural resources and the ecosystem tends to be relatively light, except in those instances where population growth leads to the exhaustion of agricultural potential (severe population pressure, however, is often the result of the partial penetration of certain modern technologies). Owing to the limited application of energy and technology, output per capita tends to be fairly low.

The material level of living for the vast majority of the population is bare subsistence.

In contrast, modern economic relations are separated from the natural sphere by technologies designed to give control over the environment, or at least to minimize the consequences of those natural forces still beyond direct manipulation. Industrial and "post-industrial" occupations (in service and knowledge industries) comprise the major areas of economic activity. Continuous research sustains the development of new technologies of production. Energy comes primarily from fossil fuels or other more esoteric sources. Productive relations tend to be highly centralized. Continual expansion of the demand for natural resources and the residual products of modern production and living patterns place a great burden upon the natural environment. The combination of nonanimal energy and high technology produces increased output per capita, which results in material levels of living considerably above subsistence for the vast majority.

Cognitive Orientations to Nature

The dependence of nonmodern societies on forces beyond their control produces an essentially fatalistic outlook. Little incentive for problem solving exists, and the fundamental attitude toward the surrounding world tends to be self-adaptive rather than context adaptive. Fatalism, and the consequent stress on the adaptation to circumstances, is generally complemented by religious theodicies which give at least some meaning to the presence of suffering and death. Often the sacred infuses the entire natural world, and magic offers a promise of control beyond normal human capabilities. The relatively narrow margin between susbsistence and nonexistence discourages innovation, for the consequences of failure are too great; far wiser to rely upon those methods that have proven sufficient under most circumstances in the past.

Modern culture, however, encourages an activist, interventionist orientation toward the problems posed by the natural environment. A rational, pragmatic, problem-solving mentality —a "can-do" attitude—supports this stance. The general confidence in the ability of modern science and technology to surmount almost any obstacle encourages a spirit of optimism. Sacred theodicies decline in persuasiveness as people place greater faith in themselves and their works than in supernatural forces. The natural world, concurrently, undergoes the corrosive scrutiny of scientific analysis and loses its capacity for inspiring awe. The cushion provided by substantial material surplus encourages innovation—risks are taken, in part because the cost of failure no longer appears to be fatal.

Social Relations

Interpersonal contacts in nonmodern societies tend to be limited in number and relatively diffuse and totalistic in nature. The family, multigenerational and horizontally extended, fulfills most of the primary nurturing needs (food, clothing, shelter, education, employment, old-age care) of human beings. People's social functions undergo little differentiation and are largely determined by birth rather than achievement. Social arrangements develop a considerable degree of organic solidarity.

Interpersonal relations in modern societies are multitudinous in number and specific in nature. The family, even the nuclear family, declines in importance, as large-scale organizations take over more of its nurturing functions. The individual, consequently, spends less time in primary social groups and more in diverse bureaucratic settings. Social functions undergo considerable role differentiation and compartmentalization, and social position grows more dependent upon performance. As social arrangements become more complex and compartmentalized, people confront a variety of behavioral norms and reference groups, which encourages a certain degree of value plurality and relativism. Social relations, moreover, are often seen from an instrumental perspective, as devices to facilitate the accomplishment of individual goals.

Pace of Change

A final point of contrast between modern and nonmodern societies concerns the pace of change: technological, social, and personal. The relatively passive, nonmodern society tends to be static unless disrupted from the outside. The low rate of innovation means that technological change, and its attendant effects on social relations, is minimal. The acceptance of "tried and true" methods encourages reliance upon established traditions, and the value of the experience of the elderly increases. Determination of social position by ascription restricts occupational mobility, and, along with strong attachment to the land and the importance of the primary group ties, it discourages geographic and psychological mobility as well (i.e., the ability to imagine oneself in a significantly different psychosocial setting).

As a society modernizes, the pace of change quickens. The assertive attitude toward the natural environment helps to stimulate technological intervention which, in turn, affects the entire pattern of social relations. The prevailing mood of optimism further reinforces the desire to find new and better ways of gaining a material advantage. As technological knowledge expands, the talents of the most recently trained acquire a premium value. Relative youth begins to take precedence over the experience of age in many professions, as the elderly often lack the flexibility to adjust to rapidly changing social and occupational demands. Previously established norms decline in persuasiveness as social patterns alter, and rule formation becomes the product of explicit and presumably rational decision making. The emphasis placed on expert knowledge and technocratic performance expands the avenues of occupational mobility. The loosening of primary ties and the absence of strong psychological linkages to a particular place reinforce geographical mobility. These factors, combined with the multiple roles and diverse settings to which people must learn to adapt, encourage a certain psychological mobility as well.

The notion of modernity also implies a considerable faith in the probability (even inevitability) of continual progress, largely conceived as the aforementioned traits becoming progressively more pronounced. Modern societies, therefore, grow increasingly removed from nature, and their technological and productive capabilities become more powerful. The role of technocratic rationality in decision making continues to expand (the "decline" of ideology). Primary groups diminish in importance, and the forces of bureaucratization and compartmentalization in social relations become more pervasive. The pace of change—technological and social—intensifies, and shared norms of behavior become more ephemeral.

The Incoherencies of Modern Culture in Crisis

Over the past decades we seem to have encountered a rising curve of unpleasant surprises with regard to our modern ways of living. "Good" things (e.g., the automobile, pesticides, nuclear power) are turning out to be bad, and bad things (e.g., the long-term consequences of nuclear war, the insidious effects of pollution) are even worse than initially feared. Indeed, the prophets of doom foresee the progressive degeneration of modern social arrangements into a state of entropic nihilism. Even if we reject the harshest conclusions of the Cassandras, ample evidence of incoherence does suggest the need to alter the dominant directives of modern culture.

Incoherency I: Material Growth and Thermodynamic Limits

The most debated, and perhaps the most fundamental, incoherence of modernity involves the addiction of modern economic arrangements to the continual expansion of material production and consumption. The finite capacity of the earth cannot support indefinitely the exponential growth in industrial output, population, and pollution. The best known embodiment of this position is found in *The Limits to Growth* which reported the results of a computer simulation of the presumed relations among five major elements of the world economic system: industrial output, pollution, population, nonrenewable resources, and renewable resources.[7] The study concluded that no plausible amount or combination of resource discovery, recycling, and pollution control could significantly delay a systemic collapse brought on by the continued growth in industrial output and pollution. Only a cessation of growth in both population and production could postpone or prevent such a collapse.

The world of *The Limits to Growth* has been both attacked and refined.[8] We need not depend upon a computer simulation, however, to recognize the crisis latent in any excessive dependence upon a finite resource base. The past is replete with extinct societies (and species) that have declined and disappeared as they depleted an essentail resource reserve, whether through overgrazing, exhaustion of the soil, or deforestation. The material incoherencies of the modern age, though unprecedented in scope, are hardly unique.

More recent critics of the modern materialist addiction base their doubts less on computer simulations than on a new economic paradigm that William Ophuls refers to as thermodynamic economics:

The laws of thermodynamics tell us that we cannot get something for nothing. The matter and energy (which are thermodynamically interchangeable) from which we derive economic benefit have to come from somewhere, and the inevitable residuals remaining after we have obtained the benefits have to go somewhere. Unless the thermodynamic cost of obtaining the energy and disposing of the residuals is less than the benefits of the use to which the energy is put, the system as a whole loses. Thus, a "thermodynamic economy" based directly on an accounting of energy or entropy has become essential, otherwise social decisions based on traditional economic critieria will continue to compromise the system through so-called externalities or side-effects that create more entropy—that is, increased disorder or reduced energetic potential—in the system as a whole.[9]

The rapid depletion of the "stored energy" of nonrenewable resources, from this perspective, contributes enormously to the progressive degradation wrought by an incoherent economic structure. As the easily recovered sources of usable stored energy are exhausted, the economic system, to sustain its growth, must progressively exploit less accessible and impoverished resources, leading not only to increased energy expenditure per unit produced, but also to ever greater amounts of pollution. Shale oil and coal gasification projects aptly illustrate this trend toward both increased cost and pollution. The ultimate consequence of exploiting these resources to sustain modern economic arrangements is simply to spread ever greater chaos.

The thermodynamic irrationality of growth-obsessed exploitation of the material base of production can be illustrated by activities such as the soil depletion caused by contemporary agricultural methods, the ways in which patterns of urban living create vast "energy sinks," and, finally, the "investments" devoted to the military, the most entropic of all resource expenditures. All these characteristics interrelate and reinforce one another, and all, from the perspective of thermodynamic economics, hasten the spiral decline into economic disorder.

Optimists, of course, look to technological innovation as a way to postpone or reverse entropic decline, and technological optimism is one of the basic predilections of the modern age. Such advance, to be sure, has been steady over the past several centuries and helped to invalidate the original doomsday projections of Thomas Malthus. Yet such progress has not been continuous over a longer time span, and frequently technological innovations that initially appear to resolve certain economic dilemmas eventually only reinforce the spread of entropic decay. For example, many devices to save labor (a largely renewable resource) do so at the expense of a more rapid depletion of nonrenewable energy resources. It would be foolish to assume that the incoherencies of the modern production/consumption cycle will necessarily be solved by this literal *deus ex machina*. Indeed, the continuation of technological innovation itself may engender significant incoherencies.

Incoherency II: Technological Innovation and Its Limits

The modern socioeconomic system and its processes depend upon a sophisticated technological infrastructure, a foundation that is, in the words of one critic, both the unique excellence and the tragic flaw of the age.[10] The effects of technology often contribute to the problem, and to rely upon ever more technology to correct the distortions of earlier innovations places the system on a treadmill that may be difficult to maintain indefinitely. Instances of the contradictions of the technological treadmill abound, but two may suffice to suggest that modern technosystems are already falling behind in their efforts to keep pace.

The first technological treadmill involves the challenge of feeding the world's population. Population growth itself results in part from improved technologies of sanitation and disease prevention. In order to fill the multiplying number of mouths, more food must be produced from each acre under cultivation. One major means of improving agricultural productivity has been through the expanding use of chemical pesticides. The production and use of the approximately 35,000 existing pesticides, however, is fraught with hazards. Increasing evidence suggests that even those exposed to small amounts suffer increased risks of cancer.[11] The possible choice between food shortages and cancer hardly attests to the coherence of the modern agricultural production cycle. Moreover, extensive use of these pesticides may contribute to the progressive degradation of the soil by killing the microorganisms that maintain fertility.[12] Finally, modern methods of farming, including mechanization and chemical fertilization as well as chemical pesticides, consume enormous amounts of nonrenewable energy sources.

The area of energy production provides another critical case of the treadmill effect. Modern life-styles require tremendous amounts of energy. An early source of nonanimal energy— wood—proved insufficient to fuel the industrial revolution; technologies were then devised to exploit fossil fuels. These technologies, in turn, encouraged the development of other energy-consuming technologies, resulting in growing pressure being placed upon the readily available reserves of these fuels. Recognition of the limits of fossil-fuel supplies stimulated the development of alternative energy sources—most significantly, nuclear power. Apart from the risks of power-plant accidents, thermal pollution, nuclear proliferation, and the theft or sabotage of nuclear fuels, reactors produce waste that remains radioactive for millenia. No safe way of disposing of this waste has yet been devised. Even if nuclear engineers were to solve this problem, we still wonder what political organization will monitor this technology for several thousand years. As Alvin Weinburg, former director of the Oak Ridge National Laboratory observes:

In a sense, what started out as a technological fix for the energy-environment impasse—clean, inexhaustible, and fairly cheap nuclear power—involves social fixes as well: the creation of a permanent cadre or priesthood of responsible technologists who will guard the reactors and the wastes so as to insure their continual safety over millenia.[13]

The treadmill effect, on the assumption that we can maintain the pace required to resolve the problems created by prior fixes, complicates a second limit on technological innovation: the ability to anticipate the side effects of new technologies. The more rapidly the treadmill turns—the faster innovations are introduced—the more difficult it becomes to identify correctly and compensate for undesirable consequences. As Ophuls notes, under these conditions "time will be one of our scarcest resources."[14] Given the complexity and interdependence of the modern technostructure, an undesirable effect that goes unrecognized and uncorrected may ultimately be devastating.

The cost of research and development, additionally, appears to be steadily rising. The inventions of previous centuries came relatively cheaply, but now billions must be invested in an organized effort to keep pace. At the same time, however, declining material growth rates increase the intensity of the competition for available resources. Technological innovations, therefore, may encounter more than the limitations of the human imagination. At some point, the world economy may simply be unable to afford either research or the costs of implementation.[15]

In any event, the ability of even the most committed research-and-development–oriented society to maintain the continued expansion of scientific and technical knowledge might eventually be exhausted. Economist Kenneth Boulding argues that an "entropy trap" may afflict these research efforts as well, for at some point, the "stock of knowledge will be so large that the whole effort of the knowledge industry will have to be devoted to transmitting it from one generation to the next."[16] Even if we do not reach this ultimate limit, the ever-increasing costs of maintenance and transmission may reduce the amount of resources available for research.

The problems involved in supporting research and development indicate that the success of any technological fix depends upon political dynamics and questions of power as much as upon the intrinsic merit of any proposal or activity. The very process of defining the nature of the problem and selecting a technology to deal with it involves political considerations (as the debate over "hard" and "soft" energy paths illustrates), and the implementation of a fix certainly involves nontechnical factors. In the absence of a basic shift in the dominant systems of shared meaning, the definition, assessment, financing, and implementation of a fix will be shaped by essentially the same political forces that contributed to the problem in the first place.

Incoherency III: The Social Limits to Growth

Despite the incoherencies of the technostructure, modern society might be able to overcome material shortages through technological advance.* Such a triumph, though, would only worsen a second socioeconomic problem: As people's material position improves, more of their resources and energies tend to be devoted to the sector constrained by absolute scarcity. The problem of absolute scarcity, as we described it in Chapter 3, arises when the supply of a particular resource is either naturally (e.g., prime resort land) or socially (e.g., positions in hierarchies) fixed or subject to deterioration in value due to congestion and overcrowding (e.g., the value of a liberal arts diploma).[17]

---

*Some scientists and futurologists have suggested that space colonization may offer a solution to our material problems of energy, population, and pollution. Such a megafix, though, would be beset by all the political and economic problems noted above. Assuming, however, that these were overcome does not mean that the second law of thermodynamics would be transcended. Rather, some specific material limits of the planet would be supplemented by other resources available elsewhere in space. The problem of expanding disorder would remain. For example, the proposal to orbit solar collectors and beam more energy down to earth than naturally occurs so as to maintain high growth rates and energy consumption ignores the problems of thermal pollution.

The more an economy succeeds in expanding a population's level of material well-being, the more it encourages a shift in competition to the sector where the value supplies cannot be increased through improvements in productivity and where the competition is, therefore, zero sum. One's position can be maintained only by barring others and can be improved only at another's expense. Ironically, then, continual expansion of material production in order to avoid zero-sum conflict over material goods only encourages zero-sum conflicts over these absolutely scarce "positional" resources.

In the absence of any extra-economic value base for legitimately allocating positional goods, expanding material affluence may merely contribute to heightened discontent. The political process could well be characterized by increasingly intense distributional conflicts, and the state may inevitably become more involved in the regulation and collective provisions of these resources.

Contemporary state organizations also exhibit symptoms of strain. In part, these arise from crises in the economic arena. We must consider whether modern governmental organizations will be able to manage the "little demons" of inflation, recession, and resource shortages, as well as increased conflicts over positional goods. Even if these demons are cast out for a time, they may well return with others still more savage—famine, ecocollapse, and world war—that would most surely destroy the presently constituted political order. Disregarding the effects of other incoherencies, certain intrinsic contradictions increasingly afflict modern political organizations, including the inertia produced by organizational size and complexity and the crisis of legitimacy.

Incoherency IV: Bureaucratic Domination and the Innovation/Stability Dilemma

Bureaucratic organizations dominate modern societies, a paramountcy interconnected with the imperative of technological gigantism and the tendencies toward collectivism. Given the scale and interdependence of contemporary social and economic arrangements, bureaucratic organizations, with their capacity to manipulate skills and information, appear essential to the coordination of these relations. At the same time, however, they possess only a limited ability to adapt to changing circumstances. Modern societies may neither be able to survive without bureaucratic organizations nor, perhaps, adapt with them.

Organizational inertia should not be mistaken for simple lethargy. Bureaucratic organizations must devote considerable energy and resources toward sustaining the existing pattern of relations (See Chapter 5). All forms of change, behavioral drift as well as deliberate innovation, upset the predictability of any ongoing interaction, and the complex, interdependent relations of a bureaucratic organization are disturbed more than most. The more complex the relationships, the greater the effort that must be expended to maintain them through the determination of response. Since predictable response can never be assumed, the control of response becomes a central, indeed overriding, concern of even simple organizations like the family, even though this dominant concern may contribute to rigidity.

Rigidity, in this context, may be defined as resistance to necessary change. All innovations interject something new into ongoing relations, upsetting established routines and possibly threatening both psychological and positional security. Organizations tend to resist innovation; the more significant the proposed change, the greater will be the resistance. Since not all innovations, to be sure, necessarily improve organizational adequacy, resistance to change cannot be automatically condemned. An organization well adapted to the demands of a relatively stable environment does well to reject most proposed alterations in its affairs.

The stability/innovation dilemma increases as the demands of the environment progressively slip away from established organizational explanations and routines. The greater the "gap" between demands and operations, the greater will be the necessity for some kind of innovation. The greater the gap, unfortunately, the more significant and disruptive innovation must be. Bureaucratic organizations tend to resist precisely such radical proposals given the positional, economic, and psychological vested interests of their members.

Not all organizations currently confront a crisis of maladaptation. Material shortages, technological failures, and positional conflicts, however, may combine to present modern political organizations with just such a challenge. Many contemporary bureaucracies, from the modern corporation to the welfare state, depend upon an expansionary economy and the technostructure upon which it is based. If such material growth ceases, or, even worse, if a long-term material decline sets in, these organizations will require radical renovation. But radical renovation is precisely what these organizations resist most strongly. The alternative may be collapse.

Incoherency V: Individual Interests and the Legitimacy Crisis

Whatever the outcome of the organizational dilemma of inertia and innovation, modern organizations confront another incoherency—a multifaceted legitimacy crisis. The emphasis placed upon individual self-interest, combined with the pluralization and relativization of social values, erodes the basis for a community of shared morality. With the decline of communal norms, institutional legitimacy comes to depend upon the ability to fulfill material expectations. These expectations, though, may well be frustrated both by the limits to the expansion of material goods and by the condition of absolute scarcity afflicting the positional sector. Failure to meet economic expectations may leave modern organizations with little more than the threat of coercion as a means of ensuring obedience. Ironically, then, the emphasis on the primacy of the individual's material needs and values may lead, under conditions of severe scarcity, to his diminishment and repression. The sources of this irony go beyond the simple dependence of modern institutions on a materialistically based legitimacy.

First, the fundamental premise of laissez-faire morality, that each person pursuing his or her own private desires will produce the optimal social result, still suffuses many of the sociopolitical assumptions of advanced Western societies, especially the

United States. The successful pursuit of individual self-interest, as Fred Hirsch observes, always depends upon certain key persons continuing to adhere to some notion of the common good (e.g., judges and other law-enforcement officials or anyone else who has to mediate between conflicting individual interests).[18] Yet the laissez-faire ethic, in both politics and economics, tends to erode any notion of the social good, thereby undercutting the very condition that provides for its reasonable success. Moreover, in times of growing material scarcity, no commonly accepted ethic for justly distributing the burdens will be available, which further heightens the intensity of zero or negative-sum conflicts and reinforces the rise of coercive social arrangements.

Individualism contributes to another social problem which Garrett Hardin terms the "tragedy of the commons."[19] A commons exists whenever an environment is collectively used; the tragedy develops when only the benefits, not the full costs of the use, accrue to the individuals exploiting the commons. The separation of individual benefits from social costs encourages each user, in the absence of some type of restraint, to exploit the commons until it collapses. Indeed, to do otherwise would be irrational as long as any other user refuses to limit his activities as well.

Hardin draws his metaphor from the historical tendency to overgraze common pastureland to the point of exhaustion. The implications may appear to be relatively remote, until we realize how much of the world's commons is abused in just this fashion. The clearest examples involve air and water pollution, but the population problem, Hardin believes, may also result in part from a commons mentality. The right to decide whether to have additional children rests primarily with the individual, but the modern welfare state assumes a large part of the responsibility for caring for these offspring.

The tragedy, moreover, cannot be confined to the internal functions of national economies. Pollution, as the well-worn but accurate observation expresses it, respects no national boundaries. The behavior of the members of the world community toward the international commons displays many of the same tendencies as those of actors within nation-states. Overfishing and the pollution of the oceans result from states and corporations pursuing self-regarding interests at the expense of the global commons. Even interstate military competition and the enormous (and highly entropic) annual investment in armaments may be manifestations of the same mentality. Each state believes it must invest in defense as long as a single country exists that might take advantage of the disarmed world.

Policies that could well produce the global irrationalities of ecocatastrophe, economic collapse, and world war are seen as rational from the perspective of the individual decision maker. Institutions infected by a commons mentality may suffer from a pattern of exploitation that can ultimately destroy the very values, from personal wealth to national security, that individuals (or groups) selfishly pursue. This failure, in turn, undermines the legitimacy of those institutions valued in terms of their success in fulfilling such interests.

Alternatively, self-regarding exploitation of the commons could be limited, but in the absence of an essentially universal ethic of restraint, such limits would have to be coercively imposed.* Such an alternative, however, would further alienate the fragile moral commitment of individuals to these institutional patterns. In any case, with respect to the global commons, organizations capable of applying such coercion do not even exist, blocked by the narrow interests of the entropic nation states.

Incoherency VI: Value Relativization and the Decline of Both the Individual and Shared Meaning

Value pluralization and relativization further unravel the social fabric. The contemporary commitment to the sanctity of individual preference, along with the impact of secularization and rationalization, encourages both the deterioration of faith in

---

*A universal ethic of restraint would not so much guarantee that all people perfectly internalize such norms to the extent that no external constraints would be required; rather, they would be, to paraphrase Garrett Hardin, mutual constraints, mutually agreed upon.

absolute value systems and the consequent rise of value relativism. The initial implication of this trend appears to be liberating, as old tyrannies are cast aside while the scientific spirit of inquiry supports the establishment of a more open society. Nonetheless, the spirit of toleration and the commitment to free inquiry are themselves values which in a context of nihilistic relativism and moral atomism no longer possess any intrinsic merit.[20] Ironically, when all is relative, value relativism itself may become insecure, and forms of tyranny may be seen as having no less merit than anything else. Ultimately, value relativism can erode all limits, a condition hardly conducive to self-fulfillment.*

Although the advance of secularization and rationalization, concomitant with both the rise of contemporary science and the growth of bureaucracy, corrodes established religious theodicies, the suffering and death these theodicies sought to explain and justify continue.[21] The frantic pursuit of material gratification and the exaggerated pride in the accomplishments of science and technology attempt to paper over the abyss with an ineffectual veneer of escapism or arrogance. Some have penetrated these illusions and concluded that the human condition is one of existential absurdity. This conclusion, not surprisingly, has not proven to be especially attractive, and millions in modern societies pursue a bizarre array of presumptive theodicies from fundamentalist religious revivals to mysticism, the occult, and satanism.

Modern societies have lost faith in a divine ground of meaning because of secularization, and organizational gigantism and the transitory, declining significance of primary relations further alienate person from person. The compartmentalized, segmented nature of contemporary social relations, dominated

---

*Similarly, Ralf Dahrendorf argues that life chances depend upon both options and ligatures (bonds and allegiances). These latter ties provide the necessary foundation from which meaningful choices are made. Dahrendorf believes that the elimination of all differences would also take away all incentive. See Ralf Dahrendorf, *Life Chances* (Chicago: University of Chicago Press, 1979), pp. 30–31. René Girard, somewhat analogously, argues that the elimination of all differences would contribute to the breakdown of social order which depends upon the existence of degrees and distinctions. See René Girard, *Violence and the Sacred* (Baltimore: Johns Hopkins University Press, 1977).

by the requisites of organizational rationality, reduces and rou-
tinizes human interactions. Even primary relations within the
family and among friends have grown depersonalized, partial,
and fleeting. The occupational demands of many large-scale
organizations bear some of the responsibility for the deterioration of these primary bonds of shared meaning, yet the systems
of shared meaning they offer as substitutes seem arid and incomplete in comparison. Even if human beings can survive,
they certainly cannot thrive in such an emotional vacuum.
Many people attempt to reforge the links of shared meaning
through psychoanalysis, encounter groups, and the wide variety
of other therapies available, but the emergence of a "therapeutic
society" provides mere palliatives for what appears to be
symptomatic of a more profound social disorder.

Finally, the pace of change, both technological and social,
imposes another price: human obsolescence. The slower rate of
change in nonmodern societies results in a premium being
placed on the wisdom of experience, and, consequently, a person's value tends to increase with age. In a context of rapid
change, this process reverses, and value declines with age. In a
culture that abjures the obsolete and does not wish to be re-
minded of death, the aging often find themselves cast onto the
social rubbish heap. This tendency to depreciate lives as we do
capital goods is not a happy consequence of social change.
Movement toward zero population growth and increased
longevity will raise the average age, further reinforcing the tensions between the requirements of modern social arrangements
and human needs.

Modern life imposes a condition of homelessness on human
beings:

The correlate of the migratory character of his experience of society
and of self has been what might be called a metaphysical loss of
"home." It goes without saying that this condition is psychologically
hard to bear. It has therefore engendered its own nostalgias—
nostalgias, that is, for a condition of "being at home" in society, with
oneself and, ultimately, in the universe.[22]

A sense of being "at home," then, requires some reasonably stable, valued ground of shared meaning, a requirement
threatened by the growing incoherencies of modern social

arrangements. Taken individually, perhaps, none of these incoherencies are either irresolvable or inevitable. Like modernization, however, these problems come together in a "package," and, like modernization itself, they belong to the world of "becoming" rather than "being." These incoherencies appear as if they are becoming progressively more severe, contributing to a growing culture crisis, that is, a crisis of shared meaning.

The dominant directives of modern culture appear increasingly inappropriate to the demands of the emerging situation; their contradictory tendencies are growing more difficult to resolve, and previously established bases for mutual interaction continue to deteriorate, which encourages the more frequent resort to overt and covert coercion to maintain some minimal degree of social cohesion. The expanded use of coercion, of course, signals the failure of politics to establish shared meaning in other ways.

Refusal to recognize and respond to the incoherencies of the contemporary culture crisis could well lead to a catastrophe on the scale forecast by the "limits to growth" simulation: overshoot and collapse. A variant form of this disaster might be a steady material decline coupled with widespread socioeconomic pathologies, a long and painful whimper rather than an apocalyptic bang.

The Politics of the Future:
The Re-Creation of Shared Meaning

The crises of modern systems of shared meaning contain within their contours indications of the substance of a possible solution. As the contradictions grow more severe, a compensatory turning away, either deliberate or forced, from the previously dominant cultural directives could begin to define an alternative system of shared meanings. Since these turnings would attempt to redress the pathologies inherent in modern culture, they may together form a reasonably identifiable counterculture.*

Pitirim Sorokin, in his monumental analysis of the socio-cultural development of the West, delineates the characteristics of a meaningfully integrated alternative to the discontents of modernity.[23] The modern age he typifies as a Sensate culture and the corrective as an Ideational culture. The advanced countries of the West currently experience the dislocations associated with the twilight of a Sensate era, a conclusion that fits well with our analysis of some of the incoherencies of modernity.

The first table (page 252) contrasts the essential characteristics Sorokin associates with the Ideational and Sensate cultures. A casual survey of the Sensate traits reveals that they provide a pithy summary of the values associated with modernity. Alternatively, the Ideational attitudes suggest plausible, though not inevitable, resolutions of some of the contemporary incoherencies.

William Ophuls, in a work written forty years after Sorokin's, identifies a number of characteristics of a "steady-state" system that echo Sorokin's analysis. These values are summarized in the second table (page 253). Taken together, Sorokin and Ophuls suggest a possible alternative to modernity.

De-Emphasis on Material Growth

The drive for continually expanding material output and the consequent depletion of nonrenewable resources and the destruction of the natural environment develop out of an acquisitive culture that stresses the ultimate value of pursuing essentially Sensate pleasures. An alternative culture must discount such pleasures, emphasizing instead common values which encourage a certain degree of material self-abnegation.†

---

*The term "counterculture" is used guardedly. I do not wish to imply that the so-called counterculture of the 1960s exemplifies a meaningful alternative, although it may be seen as a response to the dominant culture.

†De-emphasizing material growth is not equivalent to zero growth. Economist Kimon Valaskakis suggests the more plausible idea of a "conserver society" organized around the principle of zero *waste*. The goal, then, is to alter our proclivity to material indulgence. See Kimon Valaskakis, "The Conserver Society, " *The Futurist* XV (April 1981): 5–13.

Summary of the Primary and Secondary Traits of the Ideational and Sensate Mentalities

MAIN ELEMENTS	IDEATIONAL	SENSATE
Reality	Ultimate reality eternal and transcendental	Ultimate reality material and empirical
Main needs and ends	Spiritual	Richly sensate
Method of satisfaction	Mainly self-modification	Mainly modification of external milieu
Weltanschauung	Being; lasting value, indifference to transient values, imperturbability, relatively static	Becoming; transient values; full sense of life, joy and grief, dynamic, endless readjustment (progress, evolution)
Power and object of control	Self control, repression of the sensual man	Control of the sensate reality
Activity	Introvert	Extrovert
Self	Highly integrated, spiritual, dissolved in ultimate reality; sensate world an illusion; anti-materialistic	Highly integrated, dissolved in immediate physical reality; materializes all spiritual phenomena; cares for body; sensual liberty and egoism
Knowledge	Develops insight into spiritual phenomena and experiences; education and modification of inner life	Develops science of natural phenomena and technical invention. Emphasis on technology, medicine, sanitation—modification of man's physical actions
Nature of truth	Based on inner experience, mystical; concentrated meditation, intuition, revelation, prophecy	Based on observation, measurement, experimentation with exterior phenomena, mediated through senses; inductive logic
Moral systems	Absolute, transcendental, categoric imperatives; everlasting and unchanging	Relativistic, hedonistic, utilitarian, seeking maximum sensate happiness; morals of "enlightened" egoism
Aesthetic values	Subservient to main inner values, religious, nonsensate	Secular, created to increase joys and beauties of a rich sensate life
Social and practical values	Those which are lasting and lead to the ultimate reality; only such persons are leaders and only such events are positive; all else is valueless or nearly so, particularly wealth and material comfort; principle of sacrifice	Everything that gives joy of life to self and partly to others, especially wealth and comfort; prestige based on the above; physical might tends to become "rights"; principle of enlightened egoism

SOURCE: Pitirim Sorokin, *Social and Cultural Dynamics* (Boston: Porter Sargent, 1957),pp. 37–39.

Steady-State vs. Modern Cultural Values

STEADY-STATE ORIENTATIONS	MODERN ORIENTATIONS
Communalism	Rampant individualism
Authority (to protect the environment)	License (to abuse the environment)
Aristocratic competence (based on a set of "fit" values)	Egalitarian emphasis on individual wants
Community control of the commons	Individual initiative and laissez-faire
Stewardship	Exploitation
Modesty about limits	Faustian striving
Diversity and dispersion	Standardization and concentration
Holistic thinking	Reductionist thinking
Moral consensus on ends	Instrumental ethics of means

SOURCE: William Ophuls, *Ecology and the Politics of Scarcity* (San Francisco: W. H. Freeman, 1979), pp. 225–32.

Freedom, Sorokin suggests, depends upon the extent to which we can fulfill our desires.[24] Today we find ourselves surrounded by directives that serve to multiply our material desires and, in turn, reinforce the exploitation of our limited resources to meet these wants. Yet, without the imposition of some limits, these desires multiply indefinitely, further exacerbating the destructive impact on the environment and, ironically, leaving us perpetually unsatisfied. The de-emphasis and limitation of material needs would lessen the destructive consequences of human activities and perhaps lead to greater satisfaction.

Kenneth Boulding observes that the realization of a steady-state economy depends upon the ability to identify with a community which extends through both space and time.[25] Modern culture stresses flux, transience, and the ultimate obliteration of the individual in death—a bias that contributes to a tendency to discount the future in calculations of profit and loss. This attitude encourages a profligate pattern of resource use. Conversely, steady-state values most probably would attempt to engender an identification with posterity.

The problem of overpopulation may also be partially related to the modern Sensate mentality. One irony of the modern techniques of medicine and sanitation is that their partial implementation led to a tremendous surge in world population but with no concomitant increase in the material well-being of most people. Compounding the tragedy of the explosion in numbers, modern patterns of investment and trade emphasize cash as opposed to food crops and lead to capital intensive patterns of investment which worsen problems of both hunger and unemployment throughout the world.

New birth-control techniques alone appear insufficient to halt this growth unless accompanied by a redistribution of power and value, because these techniques simply allow people to choose how many children they wish to have—a number that may or may not slow the rate of population growth. Population control depends, in part, on the identification with the whole community, a community which, in turn, can be depended upon to provide a minimum degree of support, security, and dignity for its members. To provide such support, wealth and power would have to be significantly redistributed in many Third World countries.[26]

Numbers, however, constitute only half of the population equation. The population growth rates in advanced industrial states have declined, but the per-capita consumption has not. Many people of these societies limit the number of their offspring because the economic burden prevents them from realizing other material pleasures. What is saved, therefore, in terms of the lower rates of population growth is lost through increases in per-capita consumption. The population burden, then, results both from the numbers explosion in the Third World and the consumption explosion in the developed states.*

---

*A common criticism of any position advocating limits to material growth is that such a stabilization would forever lock the poorer segments of the population in their poverty. Superficially, this charge possesses some merit, yet this fades upon closer consideration. First, the extent to which the poor benefit from current patterns of growth is debatable and, in any case, if these patterns of growth eventually lead to a collapse of the world economy, the poor would most likely suffer the most. A precise recapitulation of the vastly wasteful development of the few wealthy nations by the many poor ones seems extraordinarily improbable. The growth fetish serves to deflect attention away from the real problem of redistribution—specifically, the redistribution of the remaining potential for sustainable material improvement to the poorer peoples of the world. No Sensate system of values is likely to support such a redistribution.

Values stressing identification with a community as it extends through time would provide a surer guarantee that personal decisions will reflect a sense of collective responsibility than would an ideology of self-interest. The de-emphasis of material acquisitiveness, moreover, would help to ensure that the positive effects of the limitations on numbers would not be negated by a subsequent rise in indulgent consumption.

The Decline of Technological Interventionism

Contemporary cultural directives stress the modification and manipulation of the external environment as the primary means of satisfying individual goals. This attitude encourages the development and use of large-scale technologies. Technological interventionism is ill-suited, however, to cope with the problems arising from the technological imperative itself. The only way a technologically dependent age can deal with the effects of technology is through still more technology. Rather than simply relying upon more of the same, a revision of the relations among humanity, technology, and the environment needs to be undertaken.

A culture embodying values stressing limits and the need to identify with a community extending through time may provide an alternative to technological intervention. By deprecating material satisfaction and stressing self-control, such a culture would reduce its dependence on its technological capacity and reinforce other ways of knowing and coping. This reorientation does not demand the abandonment of technology; rather, the pursuit of material means of control would decline in significance. As William Irwin Thompson notes, "Only the man who is free to do without technology... is in a position to master it."[27]

The technologies most compatible with this reorientation would tend to be decentralized in control and relatively small in scale. The need for rapid technological innovation would decline. A slower pace, in turn, would allow for a better understanding of the possible implications of any innovation and would enhance the ability to account for the qualitative costs as well as for the quantitative benefits of any proposed technological fix. Decentralization would mean that a technological failure would not have calamitous ramifications throughout the entire economy.

Finally, some adjustment should be made in the ways that scientific reductionism and technological rationality impoverish systems of shared meaning. In the modern era, predictability of response has been largely determined by the rhythms of the machine and the demands of "positivist" organizations. Rather than undulating to the sun and the seasons, people pace their lives to the beat of the clock and the movement of the assembly line. The creation of limits and the rise of new norms stressing the value of human relationships could well mitigate the harshness of the technological imperative. Human beings might then be revalued in terms of a standard that treats people as something more than congeries of materialistic forces. As a result, they would be less likely to find themselves subordinated to the needs of technostructure, which itself would be more comprehensible in scale.

The Resolution of the Legitimacy Crisis

The crisis and transubstantiation of modern culture would necessarily alter the content of political relations as well. Contemporary organizations rely upon continued material growth to moderate conflict, political relations tend to be infused with the spirit of technological optimism and interventionism, and large-scale bureaucracies epitomize the organizational gigantism that diminishes human beings. Denied material growth, beset with technological breakdowns, and confronted with widespread alienation of their citizenry, modern governmental institutions face a future of serious decay. Sorokin foresees that in the declining Sensate cultures, "governments will become more and more hoary, fraudulent, and tyrannical, giving bombs instead of bread; death instead of freedom; violence instead of law; destruction instead of creation. They will be increasingly short-lived, unstable, and subject to overthrow."[28] Both Sorokin, the idealist, and Nietzsche, the destroyer of dead values, see the same nihilistic collapse in the future of contemporary governmental institutions.

If such deterioration does not culminate in complete destruction, out of the ruins of modern systems of shared meaning a new political order may arise. No longer would dominance be predicated simply upon the control of material power resources. Rather, a new political class embodying values of humility and restraint might arise. Law and public policy, which in contemporary Sensate systems often serve simply to disguise the selfish goals of powerful special interests, would come to reflect a stronger commitment to a transcendent community interest.

Since conflicts over the distribution of material and positional resources are especially devastating in a Sensate system when growth ceases, transformed institutions would have to succeed in minimizing the importance of material possessions and positional advantage. This solution might involve, but it does not necessarily require, greater material equality. As material demands become secondary to nonmaterial satisfactions, political institutions would be evaluated on the basis of their success in establishing a sense of community solidarity, security, and mutuality.

Legitimacy ultimately depends on ruling in accordance with the prevailing values. The absence of any firm value consensus in contemporary societies means that legitimacy largely depends upon meeting the material wants of every individual. The alternative would aim to develop a community consensus on the purposes of collective action with which each person could identify. Social relations would be defined in terms of the person *cum* the community as opposed to atomized individuals versus an objectified society. Ultimately, shared meanings would be viewed as embodied in, sustained by, and transcendent of individual response. In this way the alienation between necessary community restraints and the individual's goals would be lessened.

Contemporary skepticism and moral relativism help to weaken the efficacy of traditional theodicies, but hedonism, utilitarianism, and a blind faith in technological progress have proven to be inadequate substitutes. As material conditions worsen, the pressure to find some source of comfort will grow ever more intense. More people will turn away from the empty promises of affluence and seek a community better able to succor them through times of trouble. The material crisis and spiritual paucity of the modern era, therefore, could lead to a situation ripe for the introduction and spread of a new system of shared belief in transcendent values. This faith would promise to provide the foundation for a new community of believers. Through such a community, person would be reunited with person in a quest for the enrichment of their common lives. The recreation of a valued community of shared meaning would bring human beings home.

The Future of Politics

The substance of a reasonably coherent cultural alternative to the crisis of modernity is easy enough to sketch, at least in these broad strokes, for its essential characteristics exist as a part of human historical experience. Even if we are unprepared to accept the "creative recurrence" implied in Sorokin's essentially cyclical interpretation of history, we can recognize that ours would not be the first culture to cope with scarcity by limiting material wants and emphasizing organic solidarity. Yet, accepting the plausibility of an alternative to the discontents of the modern age merely begs the question as to how it might come about: What will be the politics of this transition? How will these new systems of shared meaning be created?

One reply, though it really provides no answer, places faith in the contradictions themselves to generate the new order. Such a belief in the efficacy of objective contradictions might be termed dialectical idealism, for the new ideas, values and shared meanings would presumably arise automatically out of the failures of the established systems of shared meaning. In this view, the politics of transition will be essentially epiphenomenal in nature: Leaders may formulate and others may follow, but only because underlying conditions structure the responses of both. Politics would do nothing more than define the particulars of an emergent steady-state culture.

Yet, just as the Marxist materialists have been frustrated in their anticipation of inevitable revolution—at least thus far—the belief in the necessary ascension of a new system of shared meaning arising from the contradictions of modern social arrangements may prove equally illusory. Rather, some significant political initiative may be required to bring these new meanings to fruition. The contradictions we have identified prepare for, but do not produce, these new meanings. Without some deliberate intervention, no new order is likely to emerge.

One possible source for such initiative could conceivably be a religious revival. Certainly the emphasis on transcendent community values and the stress on nonmaterial goals commonly reflect some religious impulse. Sorokin defines the Ideational alternative to the entropic Sensate cultures in highly spiritualistic terms. Values, moreover, are literally meaningless until embodied in response, and the counter meanings to modernity might be organized through a triumphant church militant.

The possibilities for a "second reformation" in the United States, according to Jeremy Rifkin, pivot around the reinterpretation of the meaning of God's admonition to Adam to "be fruitful and multiply and fill the earth and subdue it; and have dominion over the fish of the sea and over the birds of the air and over every living thing that moves upon the earth." This charge seems to justify the subjugation and exploitation of the earth and its resources. The planet exists solely for human use. Recently, though, the idea of dominion has been reformulated in terms of stewardship. From this perspective, God created the world out of love, giving it purpose and order. "It follows, then, that sin is people's hubris in believing they can treat God's creations differently than God does; namely manipulate and exploit them for purposes other than what they were created for."[29] Rifkin believes that the doctrine of stewardship "turns the modern world view upside down."

For example, private ownership of resources, increased centralization of power, the elimination of diversity, greater reliance on science and technology, the refusal to set limits on production and consumption, the fragmentation of human labor into separate and autonomous spheres of operation, the reductionist approach to understanding life and the interrelationships among phenomena, and the concept of progress as a process of continually transforming the natural world into a more valuable and more ordered human-made environment have long been considered as valid pursuits and goals in the modern world. Every single one of these items and scores of others that make up the operating assumptions of the age of growth are inimical to the principles of ecology, a low-entropy economic framework, and, most importantly, the newly defined stewardship doctrine.

Stewardship requires that humankind respect and conserve the natural workings of God's order. The natural order works on principles of diversity, interdependence, and decentralization. Maintenance replaces the notion of progress, stewardship replaces ownership, and nurturing replaces engineering. Biological limits to both production and consumption are acknowledged, the principle of balanced distribution is accepted, and the concept of wholeness becomes the essential guideline for measuring all relationships and phenomena.[30]

If the biblical doctrine may be reinterpreted to support such an alternative system of shared meaning, perhaps the rebirth of religious fervor in the United States should be viewed as a progressive event. As Rifkin notes, a transforming political movement must have the confidence and drive to challenge the dominant order as well as the ideas and organization to create a new era. He suggests that the Charismatic movement may provide the challenge to the technorationality of modern culture, and the new evangelicals could supply the organization, "to carry out the two pronged process of conceptualization and implementation."[31]

Consequently, the conditions for political transformation may already be present. First, the multifaceted crisis in the modern systems of shared meaning generates millions of people available for mobilization. Second, the rebirth of faith provides an alternative to the waning confidence in materialistic attitudes and values. Third, the evangelical movement develops an alternative system of shared meanings presumably capable of alleviating the discontents and distress produced by the incoherencies of modern culture.

Such a scenario, though possible, does not seem probable. Whether the Judeo-Christian legacy, largely responsible for the separation of God from the material world to begin with and, in the first Reformation four centuries ago, a major contributor to the rise of the modern culture, can now be a source of a radical revision of values repudiating this tradition can certainly be doubted. On the contrary, as Rifkin himself admits, "the evangelical awakening could end up providing the essential cultural backdrop that a fascist movement in the United States would require to maintain control over the country during a period of long-range economic decline."[32]

The appeal to an absolute faith, even one that includes elements that apparently address the incoherencies of the modern world system, is a political move that would ultimately prove to be self-defeating. Such a strategy may initially effect significant changes in the systems of shared meaning, particularly if large numbers of people have rejected the available alternatives. As Nietzsche reminds us, "any meaning is better than none at all."[33] An absolutist faith, however, ultimately culminates in antipolitical politics. For true believers, once the faith has been embraced, all further questions and investigations cease. Indeed, they must cease, for they can only introduce error. They need no longer trouble themselves as to the content of appropriate response, for it is known, absolutely and unambiguously.

All quests for such certainty, however, are likely to prove futile. Our systems of shared meaning abstract from the world. Regardless of where we convince ourselves they originate, they remain human creations that fit only imperfectly the circumstances for which they were devised. Any effort to bring about a cessation of deliberation through the imposition of meaning thought to be absolutely and irrevocably true will most likely result in the constriction of response by other means. All our responses to the world rest on simplifications, and to cling to a simplification in the face of a recalcitrant reality tends to lead to conflict and coercion.

The error of absolute faith is one of hubris: an unwarranted, overweening belief that human constructions are capable of finality. The crisis of shared meaning which we now face results, in part, from such hubris; it would be folly merely to substitute another set of directives reflecting an equivalent degree of arrogance. The hubris of modern cultural directives arises from an absolute faith in the power of reason to subdue and control; we must avoid replacing it with an absolute faith in faith. Any transformation of the dominant world culture must be worked out in a spirit of humility and tentativeness that recognizes the limits not only to growth but also to our ability to discover final solutions.

As we struggle to forge new systems of shared meanings, what we aim for will not be what we finally achieve. To paraphrase Marx, we make our own meanings, but we do not make them just as we please. Not only must multiple meanings be conflated into a consensus, but our past creations confront and shape our current responses. We approach solutions only asymptotically, at best.

Human beings exist in a fallen state. The genesis myth has Adam and Eve eating of the Tree of Knowledge, but we might better call it the Tree of Consciousness. With the acquisition of consciousness, we lost the innocence of tropism and introduced the potential for flexibility and innovation as well as the possibility for error. From then on, we deliberately structured our systems of shared meaning through politics. We had no choice, for without politics we have nothing. With politics...we have a chance.

COUNTERPOINT TO CHAPTER 8

Ethical Action in the Absence of Moral Absolutes

> A new pride my ego taught me, and this I teach men: no longer to bury one's head in the sand of heavenly things, but to bear it freely, an earthly head, which creates a meaning for the earth.
>
> NIETZSCHE

WE CREATE MEANING by acting in the world, by pouring our energies into it. These meanings are sustained over space and time only if embodied in our repeated responses. But "we" are not isolated individuals, rather interacting ones, and our responses are shaped by other people's expectations, behavior, and, indeed, power. The consequences of our energic outpourings, and those of others, tend to be objectified and turn back upon us to shape further our actions. This objectification of our mutually expected response contributes to the impression of transcendence and permanence of shared meanings. In reality, these meanings have no existence apart from their embodiment in human response. In this sense, we are responsible for the meanings of the world.

Our responsibility is unavoidable. We must respond in some way, and whatever way we choose has some impact—either to maintain or alter systems of shared meaning. We cannot avoid this responsibility either through passive acceptance of what is or through subordination to any creed asserted to transcend human experience. Unfortunately, this existential need to act and the unavoidable responsibility for our actions offers us no guidance, beyond challenging us to avoid evasion.

In an exact sense, no criteria, no precise rules, no cookbook recipe for ethical behavior exist. All efforts to produce exactitude generate only illusions. The instability and inadequacy of all ethical critieria reflect their fundamentally explanatory nature. Like other explanations, ethical systems are verbal structures that slip and slide over the world, never fully able to freeze and fully capture it. Yet, we can only "know" the world through these structures, whether empirical or normative in nature.

If our behavior were tropic, we would have no problem with ethical choice. We would still construct our world out of the responses we make in it, but since these would be essentially automatic, they would not be problematic. As Nietzsche notes, though, our instincts are insufficient guides for the tasks we confront. We must explain, and control our conduct according to these explanations, if we are to act at all.

No principle—not "right reason," not "the sanctity of life," not "love"—can definitively establish a basis for ethical conduct. At best, they offer cautionary considerations that should affect how we construe a course of action in a particular context. Such principles must be interpreted and applied to a series of concrete circumstances that are never equivalent. For the vast proportion of our behavior, however, such concerns are moot. Our "rage" for order is so great that we absorb and accept the dominant directives of our culture without much question. To evaluate the ethical dimensions of every action would lead to paralysis. We, individually and collectively, lack the capability to reconsider and reconstitute all our shared meanings. We accept most of them on faith, perhaps unwarranted but unavoidable.

At some point, over some choices, we might consider what is the right or appropriate course of action. We cannot assume, however, that these decision points will be the most ethically significant; they may seem so, but this may be only because we have acknowledged a problem, not the other way around. We cannot be aware of the significance of a problem that goes unrecognized. Any particular criterion, at such a point, offers us precise guidance only to the extent to which we blind ourselves to the complexity of the confronted situation. The more we push a particular principle in a specific existential situation, the more unstable it is likely to become. Those who act vigorously in the world often do so with the assistance of imposed blinders, not because they have discovered more adequate guidelines.

The belief that human beings can ever be fully adequate is essentially a "comic" faith, for comedy "is the dramatization that man is adequate to the conditions of experience, that, if he uses his wits, he can triumph over them."[1] The acceptance of the inadequacy of human explanatory efforts is, then, a tragic perspective, for tragedy is the dramatization of the orientation that "man is inadequate to the conditions that life imposes upon us."[2] The tragic vision, however, is simply another comforting explanation, one that "reconciles us to life by persuading us to submit to it."[3] This illusion also must be transcended, but to what? What remains is a perspective that embraces the indeterminability of all guides to action. We must recognize our responsibility, accept our fallibility, and construct limits to channel our interactions. We must accept limits, because we have no basis for unrestrained action in the world because of explanatory fallibility. To paraphrase Nietzsche, any limit is better than none at all. But limits, too, are the product of our fallible capacities and cannot be embraced uncritically. There must be limits on the limits.

In his thoughtful book, *After Virtue*, Alasdair MacIntyre decries the nihilism of the modern era and calls for the construction of new moral communities capable of sustaining virtuous life. Justifiably skeptical of Nietzsche's radical individualism, he poses the choice as either Aristotle *or* Nietzsche.[4] Yet, what he selects from the Aristotelian tradition—a functional process-oriented concept of virtue, embodied in practices carried out by people who conceive of themselves not as atomized monads but as unified, mutually interdependent persons embedded in an encompassing moral tradition—appears compatible with what I choose to emphasize from Nietzsche—skepticism and perspectivism.*

Any principle, no matter how attractive, if unrestrained is, or will lead to, evil. MacIntyre observes, "when men and women identify what are in fact their partial and particular causes too easily and too completely with the cause of some universal principle, they usually behave worse than they would otherwise do."[5] Aristotle warns against excess, and the most dangerous excess is certitude (and is this far from the Christian sin of pride?). We are

---

*MacIntyre abandons Aristotle's "metaphysical biology," his culturally specific notion of the polis, and his limited view of tragedy as rooted in a flawed character rather than in the conflict between contending goods.

responsible for avoiding this excess in our creation and sustenance of ethical communities. We shall not have our dramatic
quandary resolved by the appearance of some *deus ex machina*.

What seems demanded of us is a cautious, continuous, skeptical politics involving the shared construction of shared constraints. Between certainty and chaos, between heaven and hell,
lies the realm of earthly values and earthly limits. This realm, if
it is to avoid betraying the quest for mutual meaning by in-
stitutionalizing particular meanings and temporary experiences
of value and adequacy, must be built on a process that maintains
the continuous critique, that does not stifle negative feedback.
Such a politics will be stressful, as the confrontation with and
recognition of inadequacy always is, but as Aristotle recognized
better than Nietzsche, we become fully human only through our
participation in this type of politics. Neither angels nor brutes
need politics, and so much the worse for them.

This sense of ethics and politics is, in some ways, fundamentally conservative, at least in a conserving culture. But what
about a world characterized by the arrogant, destructive violation of limits? It is one thing to advocate the necessary revision
or abandonment of outmoded custom, another to violate the
fabric of people's lives, to rend them from any sense of meaning
other than brute survival, to sunder shared relations, however
imperfect, that human beings have created, and place nothing
better in their stead. Concentrations of power must be suspected
wherever they develop, regardless of the pious declarations
that prop them up. Any system that raises a single principle
above all others must be challenged. Any cause that seeks to
limit the violence done to the limits that we have constructed
should be supported, while reserving the right to criticize its own
shortcomings.

All this must be done without any final promise of success,
without a faith in some final resolution, without a belief in ultimate salvation. Although this vision of ethical action offers no
definitive hope, neither does it counsel despair, for though no
system of the "Good" can ever be permanently established, evil,
too, is fallible and cannot endure.

CHAPTER NOTES

Chapter 1: Meaning and Politics

1. Morse Peckham, *Explanation and Power* (New York: Seabury, 1979), p. 16.

2. For a survey of how unsatisfactory philosophical explorations of the meaning of meaning have been, see William P. Alston, "Meaning," *The Encyclopedia of Philosophy*, vol. 5 (New York: Macmillan and the Free Press, 1967), pp. 233–41.

3. Peckham, pp. 34–35.

4. Ibid., p. 107. See also Hubert L. Dreyfus, *What Computers Can't Do*, rev. ed. (New York: Harper Colophon, 1979), pp. 159–62; also Daniel C. Dennett, *Brainstorms: Philosophical Essays on Mind and Psychology* (Montgomery, Vt.: Bradford Books, 1978), pp. 77–89; also Erich Harth, *Windows on the Mind: Reflections on the Physical Basis of Consciousness* (New York: William Morrow, 1982).

5. Cf. Peter L. Berger, *The Sacred Canopy: Elements of a Theory of Religion* (Garden City, N.J.: Doubleday, 1967), pp. 3–4. Berger labels these three moments of our social experience as externalization, objectivation, and internalization.

6. Richard Rorty, "Introduction: Pragmatism and Philosophy," in *The Consequences of Pragmatism* (Minneapolis: University of Minnesota Press, 1982), p. xlii.

7. Peckham, p. 35.

8. For an extended discussion of the two metaphors, see T. D. Weldon, *States and Morals: A Study in Political Conflicts* (New York: Whittlesey House, 1947).

9. Friedrich Nietzsche, *On the Genealogy of Morals*, trans. Walter Kaufmann and R. J. Hollingdale (New York: Vintage, 1969), Third Essay, section 12, p. 119.

10. Peckham, pp. 66–67.

11. Julian Jaynes, *The Origins of Consciousness in the Breakdown of the Bicameral Brain* (Boston: Houghton Mifflin, 1976), pp. 62–63.

12. Noted in Peckham, p. 242.

13. Ibid.

Chapter 2: The Politics of Scientific Inquiry

1. Paul Kress, "Against Epistemology: Apostate Musings," *Journal of Politics* 41 (May 1979): 526–42.

2. Thomas Kuhn, *The Structure of Scientific Revolutions*, rev. ed. (Chicago: University of Chicago Press, 1970); Jon P. Gunnemann, *The Moral Meaning of Revolution* (New Haven: Yale University Press, 1979).

3. Paul K. Feyerabend, *Against Method: Outline of An Anarchist Theory of Knowledge* (London: N.L.B., 1975).

4. Morse Peckham, *Explanation and Power* (New York: Seabury, 1979), pp. 146–53.

5. Ibid., p. 157.

6. Kuhn, pp. 143–48.

7. Examples of defenders of the "Faith" are Carl Sagen and Martin Gardner.

8. Stephen Toulmin, "The Construal of Reality: Criticism in Modern and Postmodern Science," *Critical Inquiry* 9 (September 1982): 95.

9. Michael Polanyi, *Personal Knowledge* (Chicago: University of Chicago Press, 1958), p. 170.

10. Ibid., p. 67.

11. Friedrich Nietzsche, *On the Genealogy of Morals*, trans. Walter Kaufmann and R. J. Hollingdale (New York: Vintage, 1969), Third Essay, section 28, p. 162.

12. Peckham, p. 56.

13. R. W. Ashby, "Basic Statements," *Encyclopedia of Philosophy*, vol. 1 (New York: Macmillan and the Free Press, 1967), p. 253.

14. Morse Peckham, "Order and Disorder in Fiction," collected in Peckham, *The Triumph of Romanticism* (Columbia, S. C.: University of South Carolina Press, 1970), p. 294.

15. Roberto M. Unger, *Knowledge and Politics* (New York: Free Press, 1976), p. 137.

16. Norman T. Uphoff and Warren F. Ilchman, "The New Political Economy," in Uphoff and Ilchman, eds., *The Political Economy of Development* (Berkeley: University of California Press, 1972), p. 9.

17. Polanyi, p. 163.

18. Ibid., pp. 212–13.

19. Ibid., p. 164.

20. Ibid., p. 165; Kuhn, p. 158.

21. Polanyi, p. 167. See also Gerald Doppelt, "Kuhn's Epistemological Relativism: An Interpretation and a Defense," reprinted in Michael Krausz and Jack W. Meiland, eds., *Relativism: Cognitive and Moral* (Notre Dame, Ind.: University of Notre Dame Press, 1982), pp. 113–46.

22. Cf. Charles Taylor, "Interpretation and the Sciences of Man," in Paul Rabinow and William M. Sullivan, eds., *Interpretive Social Science* (Berkeley: University of California Press, 1979), pp. 25–71.

23. Polanyi, pp. 135–36.

24. Jürgen Habermas, *Knowledge and Human Interests*, trans. Jeremy J. Shapiro (Boston: Beacon, 1971), p. 309.

25. This, of course, is the argument of Alfred Schutz, among others. See Schutz, *The Phenomenology of the Social World*, trans. George Walsh and Frederick Lehnert (Chicago: University of Chicago Press, 1967).

26. Taylor, pp. 50–53.

27. This is a major problem raised by the "critical" theorists. For a useful introduction, see Richard J. Bernstein, *The Restructuring of Social and Political Theory* (Philadelphia: University of Pennsylvania Press, 1978), pp. 171–236. Bernstein also examines the phenomenological approach, pp. 115–69.

28. W. E. Connolly, *Appearance and Reality in Politics* (New York: Cambridge University Press, 1981), p. 18.

29. Schutz, p. 181.

30. Donald Moon argues, however, that when discussing certain collective outcomes (e.g., the "savings effect"), social scientists can ignore individual motivation. See J. Donald Moon, "The Logic of Political Inquiry," in F. Greenstein and N. Polsby, eds., *Handbook of Political Science*, vol. 1 (Reading, Mass.: Addison-Wesley, 1975), pp. 131–228, especially pp. 182–206.

31. Peter C. Sederberg, "Subjectivity and Typification: A Note on Method in the Social Sciences," *Philosophy of the Social Sciences* 2 (June 1972): 167–76.

32. Alfred Schutz, "Common-Sense and Scientific Interpretation of Human Action," in Maurice Natanson, ed., *Philosophy of the Social Sciences* (New York: Random House, 1963), p. 342.

33. Morse Peckham, "The Intentional? Fallacy?" collected in Peckham, *The Triumph of Romanticism*, p. 441.

34. Connolly, p. 38.

35. Eugene J. Meehan, *The Theory and Method of Political Analysis* (Homewood, Ill.: Dorsey, 1965), p. 34.

36. Peckham, *Explanation and Power*, pp. 77–78.

37. See Hubert L. Dreyfus, *What Computers Can't Do; The Limits of Artificial Intelligence*, rev. ed. (New York: Harper Colophon, 1979), pp. 159–62; also Erich Harth, *Windows on the Mind: Reflections on the Physical Basis of Consciousness* (New York: William Morrow, 1982).

38. Allan Chase, *The Legacy of Malthus* (New York: Knopf, 1977), chapters 10, 11, 12.

39. Peckham refers to the spreading of behavior due to weakening controls as the "delta effect." See *Explanation and Power*, pp. 164–66.

40. Richard Rorty, "Introduction: Pragmatism and Philosophy," in *The Consequences of Pragmatism* (Minneapolis: University of Minnesota Press, 1982), p. xliii.

Counterpoint to Chapter 2: Art as Antimethod

1. Morse Peckham, *Explanation and Power* (New York: Seabury Press, 1979), p. 252.

2. Ibid.

3. Ted Robert Gurr, *Why Men Rebel* (Princeton: Princeton University Press, 1971), p. 234.

4. Thomas C. Pollack, *The Nature of Literature: Its Relation to Science, Language, and Human Experience* (Princeton: Princeton University Press, 1942), p. 94.

5. Walter Kaufmann, *Life at the Limits* (New York: Readers Digest, 1978), p. 78.

6. For a more extended discussion of this point, see Peter C. Sederberg, "Transmitting the Non-Transmissible: The Function of Literature in the Pursuit of Social Knowledge," *Philosophy and Phenomenological Research* 36 (December 1975): 173-96.

7. Edward O. Wilson, "Biology and the Social Sciences," *Daedalus* 104 (Fall 1977): 127-40.

8. Ibid., p. 128.

9. Edmund Burke, *The Sublime and the Beautiful*, vol. 24 (New York: P. F. Collier and Son, 1909), *passim*.

10. Morse Peckham, *Man's Rage for Chaos: Biology, Behavior, and the Arts* (New York: Schocken, 1967), p. 41.

11. Ibid., p. 128.

12. Michael Polanyi and Harry Prosch, *Meaning* (Chicago: University of Chicago Press, 1975), p. 109.

13. Morton Kroll, "Politics in Literature," *PROD* 3 (January 1960): 3.

14. Peckham, *Man's Rage*, p. 71.

15. Ibid., pp. 217-22.

16. See Morse Peckham, "Order and Disorder in Fiction" in Peckham, *The Triumph of Romanticism* (Columbia, South Carolina: University of South Carolina Press, 1970), pp. 290-317. See also, Peter C. Sederberg "Faulkner, Naipaul, and Zola: Violence and the Novel," in Benjamin Barber and Michael J. McGrath, *The Artist and Political Vision* (New Brunswick, N.J.: Transaction Books, 1981), pp. 245-65.

17. Peckham, *Man's Rage*, p. 220.

18. Roberto M. Unger, *Knowledge and Politics* (New York: Free Press, 1976), p. 144.

19. John Hospers, "Problems of Aesthetics," *The Encyclopedia of Philosophy*, Vol. 1 (New York: Macmillan, 1967), p. 50.

20. Morse Peckham, "Hawthorne and Melville as European Authors," in Peckham, *The Triumph of Romanticism*, p. 156.

21. Peckham, *Man's Rage*, pp. 65, 81-82. See also Norman H. Holland, *The Dynamics of Literary Response* (New York: Oxford University Press, 1968), pp. 72, 75.

22. Peckham, "Hawthorne and Melville," p. 156.

23. Morse Peckham, *Beyond the Tragic Vision: The Quest for Identity in the Nineteenth Century* (New York: George Braziller, 1962), p. 369.

Chapter 3: The Struggle to Control Shared Meaning

1. Plato, *The Republic*, trans. Francis M. Cornford (New York: Oxford University Press, 1945), p. 18.

2. Compare Ralph Dahrendorf, *Class and Class Conflict in Industrial Society* (Stanford, California: Stanford University Press, 1959), pp. 161–62.

3. See, for example, Jürgen Habermas, "What is Universal Pragmatics?" reprinted in Habermas, *Communication and the Evolution of Society*, trans. Thomas McCarthy (Boston: Beacon Press, 1979), pp. 1–68.

4. Stephen K. White, "Rationality and the Foundations of Political Philosophy: An Introduction to the Recent Work of Jürgen Habermas," *Journal of Politics* 41 (November 1979): 1169.

5. Friedrich Nietzsche, *Twilight of the Idols*, reprinted in *The Portable Nietzsche*, ed. and trans. Walter Kaufmann (New York: Penguin Books, 1976), p. 481.

6. Morse Peckham, "The Arts and the Centers of Power," reprinted in Peckham, *Romanticism and Behavior* (Columbia, S.C.: University of South Carolina Press, 1976), p. 335.

7. René Girard, *Violence and the Sacred*, trans. Patrick Gregory (Baltimore: Johns Hopkins University Press, 1977), pp. 143–49.

8. The discussion in the next two subsections is partly based upon Peter C. Sederberg, "The Betrayed Ascent: The Crisis and Transubstantiation of the Modern World," *Journal of the Developing Areas* 13 (January 1979): 128–29.

9. Morse Peckham, *Explanation and Power: The Control of Human Behavior* (New York: Seabury Press, 1979), pp. 245–56.

10. For a comprehensive development of an exchange perspective, see Warren F. Illchman and Norman Thomas Uphoff, *The Political Economy of Change* (Berkeley: University of California Press, 1969).

11. I have developed a more elaborate discussion of these resources in Peter C. Sederberg, *Interpreting Politics* (San Francisco: Chandler and Sharp Publishers, 1977), pp. 34–45.

12. Compare Illchman and Uphoff, p. 81.

13. Compare Carl J. Friedrich, *Man and His Government: An Empirical Theory of Politics* (New York: McGraw-Hill, 1963), especially chapter 12.

14. This observation is based upon Norman T. Uphoff and Warren F. Illchman, "Development in the Perspective of Political Economy," eds., *The Political Economy of Development* (Berkeley: University of California Press, 1972), pp. 96–98.

15. The discussion of relative and absolute scarcity is developed further in Peter C. Sederberg and Marcia Whicker Taylor, "The Political Economy of No-Growth," *Policy Studies Journal* 9 (Spring 1981): 735–55.

16. The distinction between relative and absolute scarcity reflects that made between "material" and "positional" goods in Fred Hirsch, *The Social Limits to Growth* (Cambridge: Harvard University Press, 1976), p. 27.

17. Ibid., pp. 1, 26.

18. Ibid., pp. 152–58.

19. Ibid., pp. 1, 7.

20. Harry Eckstein and Ted Robert Gurr, *Patterns of Authority: A Structural Basis for Political Inquiry* (New York: John Wiley and Sons, 1976), p. 134.

21. Ibid., pp. 134–35.

22. Ibid., p. 137.

23. Peckham, *Explanation and Power*, p. 272. See also Lester C. Thurow, *The Zero-Sum Society* (New York: Penguin, 1981), especially chapter 1.

24. Ibid.

25. Ibid., p. 121.

26. Friedrich Nietzsche, Selections from *The Dawn*, in *The Portable Nietzsche*, section 557, p. 91.

27. Norbert Elias, *The Civilizing Process: The History of Manners*, trans. Edmund Jephcott (New York: Urizen Books, 1978).

28. Friedrich Nietzsche, *On the Genealogy of Morals*, trans. Walter Kaufmann and R. J. Hollingdale (New York: Vintage, 1969), Second Essay, section 16, p. 84.

29. Peckham, *Explanation and Power*, p. 130.

30. Ibid., pp. 199–200.

31. Developed in David Riesman et al., *The Lonely Crowd* (Garden City, N.Y.: Doubleday Anchor, 1956), pp. 26–34.

32. Arnold Brecht, *Political Theory: The Foundations of Twentieth Century Political Thought* (Princeton: Princeton University Press, 1967), p. 117.

33. Ibid., p. 118.

34. Carl G. Hempel, *Aspects of Scientific Explanation* (New York: The Free Press, 1965), p. 101.

35. Paul W. Taylor, *Normative Discourse* (Englewood Cliffs, N.J.: Prentice-Hall, 1961), p. 77.

36. Carl Wellman, *Challenge and Response: Justification in Ethics* (Carbondale: Southern Illinois University Press, 1971), p. 27.

37. Ibid., p. 47.

38. Ibid., pp. 52–53.

39. Henry W. Johnstone, "The Nature of Philosophical Controversy," *The Journal of Philosophy* 51 (1954): 298.

40. Richard Rorty, "Introduction: Pragmatism and Philosophy," in *Consequences of Pragmatism* (Minneapolis: University of Minnesota Press, 1982), pp. xli–xlii.

41. Friedrich Nietzsche, *The Will To Power*, trans. Walter Kaufmann and R. J. Hollingdale (New York: Vintage, 1968), section 430, pp. 234–35.

42. Tracy B. Strong, *Friedrich Nietzsche and the Politics of Transfiguration* (Berkeley: University of California Press, 1975), pp. 25–26.

43. Arthur Kalleberg, "The Logic of Normative Political Theory: Exploratory Reflections on How to Develop Normative Political Argument," p. 30 (paper presented at the 1981 Annual Meeting of the American Political Science Association, New York, September 3–6, 1981). I am indebted to Kalleberg's paper for introducing me to the work of Taylor, Wellman, Johnstone, and others in this area.

44. J. Donald Moon, "Political Ethics and Critical Theory: On the Logic of Legitimation Problems" (unpublished paper presented at the University of South Carolina, April 1980), p. 27.

45. John Rawls, A *Theory of Justice* (Cambridge: Harvard University Press, 1971), pp. 17–22.

Counterpoint to Chapter 3: On Revolution and Nihilism

1. Jon P. Gunnemann, *The Moral Meaning of Revolution* (New Haven: Yale University Press, 1979).

2. Ibid., p. 30.

3. Ibid., p. 32.

4. Ibid., p. 29.

5. Ibid., p. 40.

6. Ibid.

7. Richard L. Rubenstein, *The Cunning of History; The Holocaust and the American Future* (New York: Harper Colophon, 1978), p. 89.

Chapter 4: The Politics of Definition

1. This notion of definition approximates the "pragmatic-contextual" approach elaborated by Raziel Abelson in "Definition," *The Encyclopedia of Philosophy*, vol. 2 (New York: Macmillan, 1967), pp. 314–24.

2. Samuel DuBois Cook, "Coercion and Social Change," in J. Roland Pennock and John W. Chapman, eds., *Coercion* (Nomos XIV, Chicago: Aldine, Atherton, 1972), p. 115.

3. Ibid., p. 116.

4. Christian Bay, *The Structure of Freedom* (Stanford, California: Stanford University Press, 1958), p. 93.

5. Ibid., p. 92.

6. Cook, p. 126.

7. Mulford Q. Sibley, for example, uses coercion in this broad fashion when he writes of "the coercions by Nature." See Mulford Q. Sibley, *Nature and Civilization; Some Implications for Politics* (Itasca, Ill.: F. E. Peacock, 1977), p. 141.

8. Again, I think Sibley uses the term too broadly even when he moves from "Natural" to human coercions. See Sibley, p. 150.

9. See, for example, Virginia Held, "Coercion and Coercive Offers," in Pennock and Chapman, eds., pp. 49–62.

10. For an elaboration of this point, see Bernard Gert, "Coercion and Freedom," in Pennock and Chapman, eds., pp. 30–48.

11. Michael D. Bayles, "A Concept of Coercion," in Pennock and Chapman, eds., p. 19.

12. John Locke, *Two Treatises of Government*, Thomas I. Cook, ed. (New York: Hafner, 1966), Second Treatise, section 6, p. 123.

13. This interesting notion is developed by Michael A. Weinstein, "Coercion, Space, and the Modes of Human Domination," in Pennock and Chapman, eds., pp. 63–80.

14. For more extensive discussions of the hermeneutical approach, see the essays in Paul Rabinow and William M. Sullivan, eds., *Interpretive Social Science* (Berkeley: University of California Press, 1979). See also Morse Peckham, "The Problem of Interpretation," *College Literature* 6 (1979–80): 1–17.

15. For a good study of the limits of methodological individualism, see Alan Garfinkel, *Forms of Explanation: Rethinking Questions in Social Theory* (New Haven, Conn.: Yale University Press, 1981).

16. I think this constitutes a reasonable clarification of Max Weber's well-known definition involving the state's "monopoly"of the use of force. Actually, at one point Weber states that "the use of force is regarded as legitimate only so far as it is either permitted by the state or prescribed by it." Max Weber, *Economy and Society*, G. Roth and C. Wittich, eds. (Berkeley: University of California Press, 1978), p. 56.

17. Cook, p. 113.

18. Sibley, pp. 143–49.

19. Robert Paul Wolff, "Is Coercion Ethically Neutral?" in Pennock and Chapman, eds., pp. 144–47.

20. Richard L. Rubenstein, *The Cunning of History: The Holocaust and the American Future* (New York: Harper Colophon, 1978), especially chapter 6.

21. Ibid., *passim*.

22. B. F. Skinner, *Beyond Freedom and Dignity* (New York: Bantam, 1971). See also B. F. Skinner, *Walden Two* (New York: Macmillan, 1970).

23. Morse Peckham, *Art and Pornography* (New York: Harper and Row, 1971), p. 141.

24. Peckham refers to this as the "delta effect"; see *Explanation and Power*, pp. 164–66.

25. Sibley, pp. 148–49.

26. Walter Kaufmann, *Without Guilt and Justice* (New York: Peter H. Wyden, 1973), especially chapters 2 and 3.

27. Gene Sharp, *The Politics of Nonviolent Action* (Boston: Porter Sargent, 1973), pp. 72–73. Sharp's impressive study does much to dispel the "myth of inefficacy" surrounding nonviolent action.

28. Friedrich Nietzsche, *The Twilight of the Idols*, collected in *The Portable Nietzsche*, trans. and ed. Walter Kaufmann (Baltimore, Md.: Penguin/Viking 1976), p. 479.

29. Richard Rorty, "Philosophy in America Today," in Richard Rorty, *The Consequences of Pragmatism* (Minneapolis: University of Minnesota Press, 1982), p. 222.

30. Noble lies, however, may have their uses. See, for example, H. Vaihinger, *The Philosophy of "As If,"* trans. C. K. Ogden (New York: Barnes and Noble, 1924).

Counterpoint to Chapter 4: Complexity, Shared Meaning, and Violence

1. Fred W. Riggs, "Prismatic Society Revisited" (Morristown, New Jersey: General Learning Press, 1973), p. 5.

2. Based on Riggs, p. 7.

Chapter 5: Organization and Explanation

1. Colin M. Turbayne, *The Myth of Metaphor* (Columbia: University of South Carolina Press, 1970), p. 17.

2. Gilbert Ryle, *The Concept of Mind* (London: Hutchinson's University Library, 1949), p. 16.

3. Martin Landau, "On the Use of Metaphor in Political Analysis," *Social Research* 28 (Autumn 1961): 334.

4. Eugene F. Miller, "Metaphor and Political Knowledge," *American Political Science Review* 73 (March 1979): 163.

5. Turbayne, p. 21. See also George Lakhoff and Mark Johnson, *Metaphors We Live By* (Chicago: University of Chicago Press, 1980).

6. Turbayne, p. 26.

7. Ibid., p. 69.

8. Ibid., pp. 46–50.

9. Gareth Morgan, "Paradigms, Metaphors, and Puzzle-Solving in Administrative Theory," *Administrative Science Quarterly* 25 (December 1980): 605–22.

10. Turbayne, p. 214.

11. Compare Max Weber, *Economy and Society*, ed. G. Roth and C. Wittich (Berkeley: University of California Press, 1978), p. 48.

12. Peter Berger, *The Sacred Canopy* (Garden City, N.J.: Doubleday, 1967), pp. 3–4.

13. Abraham Kaplan, *The Conduct of Inquiry* (San Francisco: Chandler, 1964), p. 330.

14. Morse Peckham, *Explanation and Power* (New York: Seabury, 1979), pp. 189–91.

15. Kaplan, p. 332.

16. Robert Michels, *Political Parties*, trans. E. & C. Paul (New York: Free Press, 1966), p. 365.

17. Charles Perrow, *Complex Organizations* (Glenview, Ill.: Scott, Foresman, 1979), pp. 53–55.

18. Robert Presthus, *The Organizational Society* (New York: St. Martin's, 1978), pp. 23–24. See also Victor A. Thompson, *Modern Organizations* (New York: Alfred A. Knopf, 1961), pp. 493–97.

19. Peckham, p. 191.

20. Martin Landau, "On the Concept of a Self-Correcting Organization," *Public Administration Review* 33 (November–December 1973):539–42.

21. Sheldon Wolin, *Politics and Vision* (Boston: Little-Brown, 1960), p. 382.

22. Richard Rubenstein, *The Cunning of History* (New York: Harper-Colophon, 1978), pp. 27–28.

23. Max Weber, *From Max Weber*, trans. and ed. H. H. Gerth and C. W. Mills (New York: Oxford, 1958), pp. 215–16.

24. Ralph Hummel, *The Bureaucratic Experience* (New York: St. Martin's, 1977), p. 14.

25. Alasdair MacIntyre, *After Virtue* (Notre Dame, Ind.: University of Notre Dame Press, 1981), pp. 82–83.

26. Michael Foucault, *Discipline and Punish* (New York: Pantheon, 1977), p. 228.

27. Hummel, pp. 57–58.

28. Herbert Bernstein, "Idols of Modern Science and the Reconstruction of Knowledge," *Journal of Social Reconstruction* 1 (January–March 1980):27–56.

29. Garrett Hardin, *Promethean Ethics* (Seattle: University of Washington Press, 1980), p. 7.

30. Ibid., p. 16.

31. Morse Peckham, "The Current Crisis in the Arts: Pop, Op, and Mini," in Peckham, *The Triumph of Romanticism* (Columbia: University of South Carolina Press, 1970), p. 248.

32. For a consideration of these issues, see Richard J. Bernstein, *The Restructuring of Social and Political Theory* (Philadelphia: University of Pennsylvania Press, 1978), *passim*.

33. This paragraph encapsulates Hummel's argument. See Hummel, pp. 92–142.

34. Wolin, p. 410.

35. Morse Peckham, "The Intentional? Fallacy?" in Peckham, *The Triumph of Romanticism*, p. 441.

36. F. E. Emery and E. L. Trist, "The Causal Texture of Organizational Environments," *Human Relations* 18 (February 1965): 21–32.

37. Perrow, pp. 150–51.

38. Abraham Kaplan suggests eight reasons why explanations must remain open to innovation: (1) All explanations are partial, accounting for only some of the factors affecting the phenomenon. (2) Explanations are conditional, depending on the presence of certain factors. (3) Explanations are approximate, yielding more or less inexact results. (4) Explanations are indeterminate in application, if not in form. (5) Explanations are inconclusive, establishing what is probably so, not what must be so. (6) Explanations are uncertain; they can never be definitively and finally established. (7) Explanations are intermediate; it is always possible to push the problem back another stage. (8) Explanations are limited in the sense that they are relevant in some situations and not others. (See Kaplan, *The Conduct of Inquiry*, pp. 351–55.) Similarly, all organizational responses, from overt directives to covert premises, may be thought of as incomplete and open to revision for analogous reasons.

39. Ibid., p. 152.

40. Landau, "On the Concept of a Self-Correcting Organization": 538–39.

41. Thomas Kuhn, *The Structure of Scientific Revolutions* (Chicago: University of Chicago Press, 1970).

42. Lakoff and Johnson, p. 6.

43. Turbayne, p. 21.

44. Ibid., p. 213.

Counterpoint to Chapter 5: Science, Bureaucracy, and Violence

1. Richard L. Rubenstein, *The Cunning of History* (New York: Harper-Colophon, 1978), p. 27.

2. René Girard, *Violence and the Sacred*, trans. Patrick Gregory (Baltimore, Md.: Johns Hopkins University Press, 1977).

3. Ibid., p. 15.

4. Ibid., pp. 20–21.

5. Ibid., p. 134.

6. Ibid., p. 28.

7. Ibid., p. 238.

8. Lewis Thomas, "The Hazards of Science," in *The Medusa and the Snail* (New York: Viking, 1979), p. 69.

9. Girard, p. 189.

Chapter 6: Leadership and the Innovation of Meaning

1. Joseph Campbell, *The Hero With a Thousand Faces* (Princeton, N.J.: Princeton University Press, 1968.).

2. Friedrich Nietzsche, *Beyond Good and Evil*, trans. Walter Kaufmann (New York: Vintage, 1966), section 212, p. 139.

3. James MacGregor Burns, *Leadership* (New York: Harper and Row, 1978), p. 17.

4. Ibid., p. 19.

5. James V. Downton, *Rebel Leadership: Commitment and Charisma in the Revolutionary Process* (New York: Free Press, 1973), pp. 25–52.

6. Proponents of the "decline of ideology" thesis take the former view. For a summary, see Mostafa Rejai, ed., *Decline of Ideology?* (Chicago: Aldine-Atherton, 1971). For an example of the latter position, see William T. Bluhm, *Ideologies and Attitudes: Modern Political Culture* (Englewood Cliffs, N.J.: Prentice-Hall, 1974).

7. Jon P. Gunnemann, *The Moral Meaning of Revolution* (New Haven: Yale University Press, 1979), pp. 30–31.

8. The distinction is made by Mark N. Hagopian in *The Phenomenon of Revolution* (New York: Dodd, Mead, 1974), pp. 269–71.

9. Burns, pp. 19–20.

10. Downton, pp. 77–80.

11. Burns, p. 20.

12. Max Weber, *Economy and Society*, vol. I (Berkeley: University of California Press, 1979), pp. 241–45.

13. Ann Ruth Wilner, *Charismatic Political Leadership: A Theory* (Princeton, N.J.: Center for International Studies, 1968), p. 7.

14. Morse Peckham, "The Deplorable Consequences of the Idea of Creativity," in Morse Peckham, *Romanticism and Behavior* (Columbia, S.C.: University of South Carolina Press), p. 218.

15. Ibid., pp. 218–19.

16. Ibid., p. 214.

17. See, for example, Hubert Dreyfus, *What Computers Can't Do*, rev. ed. (New York: Harper Colophon, 1979), pp. 159–62.

18. Daniel Dennett, "Why the Law of Effect Will Not Go Away," in Daniel Dennett, *Brainstorms* (Montgomery, Vt.: Bradford Books, 1978).

19. Ibid., p. 77.

20. Ibid.

21. Ibid.

22. Ibid., p. 85.

23. Ibid.

24. Morse Peckham, "Arts for the Cultivation of Radical Sensitivity," in *Romanticism and Behavior*, p. 298.

25. Ibid., p. 303.

26. I have based this discussion largely on the argument of Morse Peckham contained in "Romanticism and Behavior," in *Romanticism and Behavior,* pp. 16–31. I have altered his order somewhat, placing "vandalism" at the end.

27. Ibid., p. 25.

28. Peckham, "Arts for the Cultivation of Radical Sensitivity," p. 308.

29. Based on Robert Merton, *Social Theory and Social Structure* (New York: Free Press, 1957), pp. 139 ff.

30. In developing this argument, I have drawn upon the work of David Schwartz, *Political Alienation and Political Behavior* (Chicago: Aldine-Atherton, 1973).

31. John McMurtry, *The Structure of Marx's World View* (Princeton: N.J.: Princeton University Press, 1978), p. 153.

32. Gunnemann, pp. 15–20.

Counterpoint to Chapter 6: Pornography and Innovation

1. Morse Peckham, *Art and Pornography: An Experiment in Explanation* (New York: Harper and Row, 1969, 1970), p. 36.

2. Ibid., pp. 11–12.

3. Ibid., p. 11.

4. Ibid., p. 47.

5. Ibid., p. 66.

6. Ibid., p. 76.

7. Ibid., p. 77.

8. Ibid., p. 78.

9. Ibid., p. 59.

10. Ibid., p. 124.

11. Ibid., p. 169.

12. Ibid., p. 186.

13. Ibid., pp. 173–74.

14. Ibid., pp. 214–22.

15. Ibid., pp. 251–56.

16. Ibid., p. 14.

17. Ibid., p. 253.

18. Ibid., p. 256.

19. Ibid., p. 285.

20. Ibid., p. 298.

Chapter 7: Freedom and Order in the Construction of Self and Society

1. Reinhold Niebuhr, *Moral Man and Immoral Society: A Study in Ethics and Politics* (New York: Charles Scribner's Sons, 1932).

2. Plato, *The Republic*, trans. Francis Cornford (New York: Oxford, 1945), especially chapters XXIX–XXXII.

3. Friedrich Nietzsche, *Beyond Good and Evil*, trans. Walter Kaufmann (New York: Vintage, 1966), section 108, p. 85.

4. Friedrich Nietzsche, "On Truth and Lie," excerpted in *The Portable Nietzsche*, trans. and ed. Walter Kaufmann (New York: Penguin, 1976), p. 46.

5. Friedrich Nietzsche, *Thus Spoke Zarathustra*, reprinted in *The Portable Nietzsche*, p. 171.

6. Friedrich Nietzsche, *The Dawn*. excerpted in *The Portable Nietzsche*, p. 76.

7. Norbert Elias, *The Civilizing Process: The History of Manners*, trans. Edmund Jephcott (New York: Urizen Books, 1978), p. 261.

8. Ibid.

9. Morse Peckham, *Explanation and Power* (New York: Seabury, 1979), p. 246.

10. Nietzsche, "On Truth and Lie," p. 46.

11. Friedrich Nietzsche, *The Twilight of the Idols*, reprinted in *The Portable Nietzsche*, p. 480.

12. Peckham, p. 247.

13. Peter L. Berger and Thomas Luckmann, *The Social Construction of Reality* (Garden City, N.Y.: Doubleday, Anchor, 1967), p. 172.

14. Steven Lukes, *Power: A Radical View* (London: Macmillan Press, 1974), pp. 46–50.

15. Berger and Luckmann, p. 172.

16. Nietzsche, *Zarathustra*, p. 171.

17. Elias, p. 258.

18. Ibid., p. 260.

19. Ibid., p. 261.

20. The song was written by Kris Kristofferson.

21. Attributed to Diogenes.

22. B. F. Skinner, *Beyond Freedom and Dignity* (New York: Knopf, 1971).

23. See, for example, Daniel Dennett, "Skinner Skinned" and "Why the Law of Effect Will Not Go Away," both in *Brainstorms* (Montgomery, VT: Bradford Books, 1978), pp. 53–70 and 71–89.

24. Morse Peckham, *Art and Pornography: An Experiment in Explanation* (New York: Harper and Row, 1971), p. 181.

25. Nietzsche, *Zarathustra*, p.139.

26. Ibid.

27. Frithjof Bergmann, *On Being Free* (Notre Dame, Ind.: University of Notre Dame Press, 1977), p. 52.

28. Ibid., p. 48.

29. Ibid., pp. 90–92.

30. Ibid., p. 237.

31. Peckham, *Explanation and Power*, pp. 264–65.

32. Nietzsche, *Zarathustra*, p. 139.

33. Peckham, *Explanation and Power*, pp. 263–64.

34. See Peckham, *Art and Pornography*, p. 186.

35. Berger and Luckmann, p. 174.

36. Peckham, *Explanation and Power*, p. 273.

37. Morse Peckham, "Literature and Behavior," unpublished ms., pp. 19–20.

38. Erving Goffman, "Normal Appearances," in *Relations in Public* (New York: Harper Colophon, 1971), pp. 238–333.

Counterpoint to Chapter 7: Explanatory Instability in the Evaluation of Social Arrangements

1. Aristotle, *Nicomachean Ethics*, trans. Martin Ostwald (Indianapolis, Ind.: Bobbs-Merrill, 1962), pp. 118–19.

2. James Fishkin, *Tyranny and Legitimacy* (Baltimore: Johns Hopkins University Press, 1979), p. 3.

3. Ibid., pp. 122, 123.

4. Ralf Dahrendorf, *Life Chances: Approaches to Social and Political Theory* (Chicago: University of Chicago Press, 1979), p. 123.

5. Ibid., p. 133.

6. Carl Friedrich, *Man and His Government* (New York: McGraw-Hill, 1963), p. 251.

7. Compare Arnold Brecht, *Political Theory: The Foundations of Twentieth Century Political Thought* (Princeton, N.J.: Princeton University Press, 1967), p. 396.

8. Friedrich, pp. 260–61.

9. Peckham, *Explanation and Power* (New York: Seabury, 1979), p. 283.

10. Ibid.

Chapter 8: The Entropy of Meaning and the Future of Politics

1. Melvin Lasky, *Utopia and Revolution* (Chicago: University of Chicago Press, 1976), p. 5.

2. Matthew Arnold, "Dover Beach."

3. Nietzsche, *On the Genealogy of Morals*, trans. Walter Kaufmann and R. J. Hollingdale (New York: Vintage, 1969), p. 159.

4. This critique is forcefully stated by Jeremy Rifkin and Ron Howard in *Entropy: A New World View* (New York: Viking, 1980).

5. Marion J. Levy, Jr., *Modernization: Latecomers and Survivors* (New York: Basic Books, 1972), p. ix.

6. More extensive analyses may be found in numerous volumes on modernization. See, for example, Peter Berger, Brigitte Berger, and Hansfried Kellner, *The Homeless Mind: Modernization and Consciousness* (New York: Vintage, 1973); C. E. Black, *The Dynamics of Modernization: A Study in Comparative History* (New York: Harper Torchbooks, 1967); Marion J. Levy, Jr., *Modernization and the Structure of Societies* (Princeton: Princeton University Press, 1966); and the various essays in parts I, II, and III of Jason L. Finkle and Richard W. Gable, eds. *Political Development and Social Change*, sec. ed. (New York: John Wiley and Sons, 1971).

7. Donella H. Meadows et al., *The Limits to Growth* (New York: Universe Books, 1972).

8. For a critique see H. S. Cole et al., eds., *Models of Doom: A Critique of the Limits to Growth* (New York: Universe Books, 1973); for a revision see Mihajlo Megarouic and Edward Pestel, *Mankind at the Turning Point* (New York: E. P. Dutton, 1974). See also Julian L. Simon, *The Ultimate Resource* (Princeton, N.J.: Princeton University Press, 1981).

9. William Ophuls, *Ecology and the Politics of Scarcity* (San Francisco: W. H. Freeman, 1979), p. 112.

10. William I. Thompson, *At the Edge of History* (New York: Harper, Colophon, 1972), p. 72.

11. *New York Times*, 11 December 1977, p. 83.

12. Rifkin, p. 139.

13. Quoted in Ophuls, p. 157.

14. Ibid., p. 120.

15. Garrett Hardin, *Exploring New Ethics for Survival* (Baltimore: Penguin, 1974), p. 151; see also Ophuls pp. 121-22.

16. Kenneth Boulding, "The Diminishing Returns of Science," *New Scientist* 49 (March 25, 1971): 682-84.

17. Fred Hirsch, *The Social Limits to Growth* (Cambridge: Harvard University Press, 1976), p. 27.

18. Ibid., pp. 117-36.

19. Hardin, pp. 113-18.

20. Michael Polanyi makes a similar argument with respect to the value basis of scientific inquiry. See his *Personal Knowledge* (Chicago: University of Chicago Press, 1958), especially chapters 9 and 10.

21. Berger et al., p. 185.

22. Ibid., p. 82.

23. Pitirim Sorokin, *Social and Cultural Dynamics* (Boston: Porter Sargent, 1957).

24. Ibid., pp. 487-89.

25. Kenneth Boulding, "The Economics of the Coming Spaceship Earth," reprinted in Kenneth Boulding, *Collected Papers*, 2 vols., ed., Fred R. Glahe (Boulder: Colorado Associated University Press, 1971), 2: 491.

26. For a stimulating examination of the relationship between inequality and overpopulation, see William W. Murdock, *The Poverty of Nations: The Political Economy of Hunger and Population* (Baltimore, Md.: Johns Hopkins University Press, 1980.).

27. William I. Thompson, *Passages About Earth* (New York: Harper and Row, Perennial Library, 1974), p. 123.

28. Sorokin, p. 700.

29. Rifkin, p. 237.

30. Ibid., pp. 238–39.

31. Jeremy Rifkin, with Ted Howard, *The Emerging Order: God in the Age of Scarcity* (New York: G. P. Putnam Sons, 1979), p. 232.

32. Rifkin, *Entropy*, p. 239.

33. Friedrich Nietzsche, *On the Genealogy of Morals*, p. 162.

Counterpoint to Chapter 8: Ethical Action in the Absence of Absolutes

1. Morse Peckham, *Beyond the Tragic Vision* (New York: Braziller, 1962), p. 369.

2. Ibid.

3. Ibid.

4. Alasdair MacIntyre, *After Virtue* (Notre Dame, Ind.: University of Notre Dame Press, 1981), especially chapters 9 and 18.

5. Ibid., p. 206.

INDEX